THE STRAIGHT DOPE

THE STRAIGHT DOPE

THE INSIDE STORY OF SPORT'S BIGGEST DRUG SCANDAL

CHIP LE GRAND

MELBOURNE UNIVERSITY PRESS

MELBOURNE UNIVERSITY PRESS
An imprint of Melbourne University Publishing Limited
11–15 Argyle Place South, Carlton, Victoria 3053, Australia
mup-info@unimelb.edu.au
www.mup.com.au

First published 2015
Reprinted 2015
Text © Chip Le Grand, 2015
Design and typography © Melbourne University Publishing Limited, 2015

This book is copyright. Apart from any use permitted under the *Copyright Act 1968* and subsequent amendments, no part may be reproduced, stored in a retrieval system or transmitted by any means or process whatsoever without the prior written permission of the publishers.

Every attempt has been made to locate the copyright holders for material quoted in this book. Any person or organisation that may have been overlooked or misattributed may contact the publisher.

Text design and typesetting by Cannon Typesetting
Cover design by Philip Campbell Design
Printed in Australia by McPherson's Printing Group

National Library of Australia Cataloguing-in-Publication entry

Le Grand, Chip, author.

The straight dope/Chip Le Grand.

9780522868500 (paperback)
9780522868517 (ebook)

Includes index.

Australian Sports Anti-Doping Authority.
Essendon Football Club.
Doping in sports—Australia.
Australian football players—Drug use.

362.29088796

CONTENTS

Author's note   vii

1. Is it Essendon? Say no more   1
2. Grey cardigans, blackest day   19
3. There's plenty of Danksy juice getting around   49
4. What's in that bloody drug?   76
5. Peptide Alley   109
6. Get the biggest stick you can   139
7. If this is all they've got, you will win   167
8. A very unfortunate matter   187
9. A Faustian compact   218
10. Enthusiastic amateurs   244

Acknowledgements   271
Notes   273
Index   295

AUTHOR'S NOTE

THE WORST THING you can do in sport is cheat. It is a lesson we learn from the time we are old enough to kick a ball, dive into a pool, answer a starter's gun. Given the national obsession with sport, some might think it is the worst thing anyone can ever do in life. We reserve a particular loathing for sporting villains: Lance Armstrong and his boosted blood, Hansie Cronje and his bookmaker buddies, Maradona and his hand of God.

That said, there is cheating and cheating. Grabbing a handful of jumper when the umpire isn't looking, refusing to walk when you've feathered one through to the keeper, taking a dive in the penalty box—these are lesser forms, tolerated if not entirely accepted. Doping and match fixing—these are the capital crimes, the sins against sport from which no coach or athlete recovers.

The great drugs scandal was pitched as a diabolical double. 'If you want to dope and cheat we will catch you,' declared the Minister for Sport. 'If you want to fix a match we will catch you.' In the end, it was about neither of these things but something else; a tale of power, betrayal and ineptitude unmatched in Australian sport.

This story has taken me inside the basement office where Essendon sports scientist Stephen Dank worked throughout the club's ill-fated 2012 season, to the plush boardroom at AFL House, to the visitors rooms at Shark Park, to the aptly named bunker room within the Australian Sports Anti-Doping Authority's (ASADA) Canberra headquarters and to Melbourne's Peptide Alley, a cluster of South Yarra shops where you can buy youth, virility and a great tan for a few hundred dollars.

What I discovered over two years of exhaustive reporting, hundreds of hours conducting interviews and countless more in the company of lawyers, football figures and scoundrels, is no one has a mortgage on the answer—not James Hird nor anyone at Essendon, not Andrew Demetriou nor anyone at the AFL, not the Australian Crime Commission, not ASADA. Not the colourful crew of Peptide Alley. Not Stephen Dank.

After more than twenty years writing about sport, crime and politics for *The Australian* newspaper, this was a career story— one with the lot. What happened at Essendon, what happened at Cronulla, did not start and finish with the prick of a syringe. Whether banned substances were taken by footballers at either club, the scandal that followed destroyed friendships, threatened reputations and careers and exposed the failings of government, anti-doping authorities and powerful sporting bodies.

In the final days of 2014, with ASADA's case against thirty-four current and former Essendon players lurching towards inevitable collapse, I was convinced that this epic mess required a complete, unvarnished telling. After so much misadventure and, at times, misinformation, a sharply divided public deserved to be given the straight dope.

The foundations of this book are sourced from the documented history of the anti-doping investigation—transcripts of interviews given by footballers and club officials to ASADA, transcripts of Federal Court and Supreme Court proceedings, lawyer letters, text messages and emails exchanged between protagonists, the summaries of ASADA investigators and the findings of an AFL tribunal.

Essential context, texture and depth are provided by the recollections and reflections of those at the centre of this saga. Most were willing to be interviewed, some for the first time since the scandal broke. Others chose to remain off the record. A relative few refused to co-operate in any way.

The World Anti-Doping Agency (WADA) announced in May 2015 that it is appealing the findings of the AFL tribunal. For thirty-four footballers accused of taking a banned peptide, the scandal and uncertainty continues. The WADA appeal is a re-hearing of the case before the Court of Arbitration for Sport. The same evidence, subject to the same standard and onus of proof, will be presented to a new panel, with anti-doping authorities hoping for a different result. Whatever the finding is, it won't change what happened.

1
IS IT ESSENDON? SAY NO MORE

THE GREATEST DRUGS SCANDAL in Australian sport breaks in the middle of dinner. It is James Hird's fortieth birthday and the Essendon coach is sitting down to celebrate with his wife and four children when the telephone rings. Tania Hird feels a flash of annoyance as her husband leaves the table to take the call. She soon realises this is no ordinary interruption. David Evans, president of the football club, is on the other end of the line.

'We're in a lot of trouble,' Evans tells his friend. 'The AFL believes that we've taken performance-enhancing drugs. Get over here straight away.'[1]

Throughout his 253 games for Essendon, James Hird always had time. In the maelstrom of an Australian Rules football match, his were the safe hands, the clear thoughts, the sure steps. Whether for Essendon or another AFL club, few footballers have played the game with such elegant purpose. Yet, as Hird fumbles for the car keys inside his Toorak house, he feels harried, flustered. The sun has just set on a warm, late summer's day. A two-year ordeal that will plunge Essendon, the AFL and the Australian Sports Anti-Doping

Authority (ASADA) into crisis, embarrass a federal government and expose the vanities of Melbourne's ruling boys' club is about to begin.

Evans' home, a stately Victorian mansion in the neighbouring suburb of Hawthorn, is a short drive away through some of Melbourne's most exclusive streets. For Hird, it is a well-travelled path. Even after the scandal has ravaged and torn their friendship, Evans will say he loves Hird like a brother. He was Hird's professional mentor when the pair worked together at stockbroking firm JB Were and, before that, an unabashed fan. Like all Bombers supporters, Evans lost count of the times Hird was the difference between leaving a football ground in victory chorus or hearing the other team's song rasp in his ears.

The Essendon Football Club, the first club to win a premiership in the Victorian Football League when it was formed before the turn of the previous century, is family to both men. Evans' father Ron played for Essendon, served on its committee and chaired its board. The grandstand at Windy Hill, Essendon's old training ground, is named after Allan T Hird, Hird's grandfather. When David Evans joined the Essendon board, it was with Hird's support. At the end of 2010, Evans' first year as club president, he had convinced Hird to return as coach. Their wives were friends. Their children played together. Neither could imagine these bonds ever being severed.

Essendon chief executive Ian Robson is already at Evans' house when Hird arrives. Within minutes they are joined by Danny Corcoran, an experienced sports administrator and friend and confidant to Hird. The last to arrive is Bruce Reid, Essendon's long-serving club doctor and private physician to the Evans and Hird families. It is nearly 9 p.m. on a Monday night. They all know why they are here. The club is suspected of using banned drugs. Evans says his information has come straight from Andrew Demetriou, chief executive of the AFL. The club chairman tells them that a major report accusing Essendon of doping is about to be made public.

Evans needs information. He turns to Reid and Hird, the two people he trusts most at the club. Hird is incredulous at the suggestion of doping, Reid horrified. The doctor thinks back to a little known substance called AOD-9604 that was injected into players under his care the previous season. But he is sure—isn't he?—that the World Anti-Doping Agency (WADA) approved its use. Hird is adamant AOD-9604 was approved and can't think of any other substances that would arouse the interest of anti-doping authorities. The allegations are rubbish, he tells Evans. He demands to know Demetriou's source. Hird doesn't wait long for an answer. Evans' mobile phone rings. It is Demetriou returning an earlier call. Evans excuses himself from his company and takes the call in a bedroom. When he returns, his face has darkened.

'He's definitely saying we've taken them.'[2]

Drug rumours about Essendon have been building like a summer storm. Danny Corcoran, the club's football manager, hears the first rumble before Christmas at the opening of Athletics Australia's new Albert Park headquarters. Corcoran's other sporting love is athletics. His career in football administration was split by six years spent as chief executive of Athletics Australia. At the Albert Park function, a senior track and field administrator well connected in anti-doping circles mentions to Corcoran he's heard of trouble to do with Stephen Dank, a sports scientist who worked with Essendon the previous football season. A few days later, a journalist calls Corcoran to relay a curious story from a taxi driver: the word on the rank is Dank had been dropped off at the Australian Federal Police headquarters in La Trobe Street.

'Why would a sports scientist be talking to the feds?' the journalist asks. Corcoran hopes he'll never know. The story sleeps uneasily over the Christmas break then stirs in the hot weeks of January 2013, as footballers get back to training and football journalists back to work. Rival club officials, always more forthcoming with gossip about clubs other than their own, start wording up reporters: 'Off the record, mate, you need to check out Essendon.'

'The tom toms were beating,' says Corcoran.[3]

Evans hears the drums as well. The Essendon president has just returned from a business trip to the United States. No sooner than he clears customs, he starts getting worrying calls about the football club. One of Essendon's players let go by the club at the end of last season, Kyle Reimers, has apparently given a television interview to journalist Damian Barrett, yet to be broadcast, in which he raises questions about Dank's work at Windy Hill. A reporter from *The Age* newspaper, Michael Gleeson, has been in touch with club officials, asking questions about drugs at Essendon. As an honorary chairman of the Essendon board, Evans tries not to spend too much time on football club business during the summer. He knows that come the winter months footy will consume his weekends. He also knows he can't ignore what he is hearing. He calls Andrew Demetriou, the AFL chief executive who has overseen the national competition for more than a decade. He calls Gillon McLachlan, Demetriou's deputy and the man widely expected to be running the game before too long. He calls them both many times. From each conversation he learns a little more. With each new piece of information he fears for his football club.

Three days before the meeting at Evans' house, the Essendon president arrives unannounced on the doorstep of Dr Bruce Reid. Evans is a frequent visitor to Bruce and Judy Reid's place, usually with a fine bottle of red tucked under his arm. This is no social call. When the Essendon club doctor opens the door he immediately sees the stress on his friend's face. There are none of the usual pleasantries, the questions about the kids or grandkids, the latest chatter from the club. Evans asks his friend outright, 'Do you reckon we have taken prohibited substances?' Reid is taken aback. He doesn't know where this has come from.

'No, I don't,' he tells his chairman.

'Are you sure?' The doctor doesn't know how to respond.

'I'd be horrified,' Reid says. Evans presses further.

'Can you guarantee it?' The doctor pauses to think, too long for Evans' comfort.

'No, I can't guarantee it.' Evans' face falls. It is not the answer he wants.[4]

Evans trusts Reid implicitly. He trusted him with the lives of his children and the death of his father. When his father Ron was terminally ill, Evans turned to Reid to ensure his dad's remaining weeks and days held as much dignity and little pain as possible. He trusts him, as his father did, with the health of Essendon's players. Two things trouble him about what Reid tells him next. The first is Reid's discomfort with what went on at Windy Hill the previous season. Reid is the club's senior medical officer. The treatment of players is his responsibility. Yet he is telling Evans about practices he didn't condone, injections he didn't authorise. It is the first time Evans is hearing any of this. The second is Reid's description of a letter he wrote the previous summer, setting out his concerns about substances that Stephen Dank was giving players—a letter Evans has neither seen nor previously been told about. While the friends talk, Reid searches for the letter but cannot find a copy.

As Evans is driving back home, Reid calls, the relief plain in his voice. He has found the letter and reads it over the phone: 'I have some fundamental problems being club doctor at present. This particularly applies to our administration of supplements.' As Reid continues reading, Evans does well to keep his car on the road.

'It is my belief in the AFL that we should be winning flags by keeping a drug-free culture … I think we are playing at the edge.' Reid is pleased he has found the letter. Once it is read to him, Evans knows it is far from good news.

As soon as he returns home from Reid's house, Evans calls his chief executive Ian Robson and asks him to come over. Robson is an experienced and competent administrator. He was lured to Essendon after overseeing the rebuilding of bitter rival Hawthorn into a football and financial powerhouse. Prior to that he worked with the Auckland Warriors in the National Rugby League (NRL). Like Danny Corcoran, Robson has fielded speculative questions from journalists, heard suggestions that something sinister took place inside the Essendon football department. When Evans asks Robson what he knows of Bruce Reid's letter, Robson replies he has never read it or even heard of it. There is now a low, rising panic within the club president. It is Friday night. They agree to be patient, to talk again first thing Monday morning. A long, fretful weekend beckons.

Football clubs in February are normally calm, industrious places. No team has lost a game. No one is calling for the coach's head. The players have completed the worst of their pre-season training program—the leg-burning, lung-busting runs, the torturous gym sessions. Their training has tapered, their legs feel light, they are prepared. Never been fitter, they all say. Looking forward to Round 1. The older players laugh as they offer last season clichés. No one expects them to depart from the summer script. Nothing serious is at stake. Not yet. This time of year, even AFL coaches are relaxed.

For anyone who wandered down to Windy Hill on Monday, 4 February 2013, the Essendon Football Club would have felt much the same way. The players are spread across the grass oval, an intra-club practice match underway. Some coaches are out in the middle, encouraging, exhorting. Others stand on the sidelines, taking mental notes. The shouts of the players can be heard above the slap of bodies, the kick-drum sound of boot meeting ball. The scene laid out before the weathered timber bleachers of the Allan T Hird grandstand is business as usual. When James Hird returns to his first floor office at the end of the training session, it is anything but.

Evans is waiting in the coach's office. He looks like a man who has not slept for three days. His face is haggard, his eyes red-rimmed.

'Do we have a problem with drugs?' he asks. Hird thinks Evans is talking about illicit drugs; party drugs. Footballers are guaranteed an eight-week break at the end of the season. For players and clubs alike it is a fraught time of year. Professional footballers are young, cashed-up men who, come October, crave release from the discipline required to succeed in the AFL. Many travel overseas to seek anonymity. They know that drug testers won't follow. Inevitably, some stuff up closer to home. Club managers dread the call from police, or worse, a journalist, when an off-duty player has gotten into strife. When the Essendon president asks about drugs, Hird assumes Evans means cocaine or ecstasy. Worst-case scenario: ice. Is Evans saying that someone at Essendon has returned a positive test under the AFL's three-strikes illicit drug policy? Under the policy, the clubs aren't supposed to know. Hird tells Evans he can't be sure but he doesn't think any of their players has a strike.

'No', says Evans. 'Have our players been given performance-enhancing drugs?' Hird is emphatic: 'Mate, I don't know what you are talking about. David, I believe that's complete rubbish. I've never seen performance-enhancing drugs at the football club. They wouldn't be taken by our players.'[5] Evans is not convinced. This is not what he is being led to believe from his phone calls with the AFL's two most senior executives. It is not what the AFL has been told by the Australian Crime Commission (ACC).

'I hope you're right,' the club president tells his friend.

That night in his Hawthorn house, the night of Hird's half-eaten birthday dinner, Evans again asks the club doctor and the senior coach what they know. About AOD-9604. About other injections. Reid reads his letter out loud:

> I have some fundamental problems being club doctor at present ... players were given subcutaneous injections, not by myself, and I had no idea that this was happening and also what drug was involved ... I am still not sure whether AOD-9604 is approved by the drug authorities in Australia at this stage ... I am very frustrated by this and now feel I am letting the club down by not automatically approving of these things.

Hird listens quietly as the plainly spoken frustration and exasperation of a club doctor on the brink of quitting fills the room. Although Hird knows of the letter he has never read it.[6] He remembers the doctor coming to him a year ago, furious that players were being injected with stuff without his approval. They hadn't ignored it. They had addressed it. In Evans' house, they talk about the players signing consent forms to be injected with certain substances, about the guarantees provided by Dank, the sports scientist, that it was all above board, all WADA compliant. Evans remains sceptical.

'Why are we giving injections?' the club president wants to know.[7] He is assured injections are common at football clubs, that vitamins and other supplements can be more effective delivered that way.[8] Injections aren't a problem; it depends what's in the needle. Reid says he hasn't seen anything to suggest that performance-enhancing drugs were used. Evans wants to believe him but he is still not convinced. Not after his phone call with Demetriou. Whatever Essendon is caught up in, it is too big for the football club to deal with alone. He has already decided. He will go to the AFL.

Early the next morning, Hird is back at Windy Hill, searching the club for documents showing what went on the previous year. He rises at dawn, drops his older kids at their swimming squad and is at the club before 7 a.m., unaware of the fateful events that within a few hours will place him at the centre of the Essendon scandal. The Essendon football department is split across three levels. On the first floor, a narrow corridor connects the cramped offices belonging to the coaches and senior staff. On the ground floor, an indoor training area leads straight to the medical rooms. Hird begins his search in the basement, where high-performance manager Dean Robinson and sports scientist Stephen Dank worked throughout the 2012 season.

They call Robinson 'The Weapon'. An intense man with a big reputation, he oversaw the strength and conditioning programs at Manly in the NRL and Geelong in the AFL, and helped build them into gang-tackling, uncompromising football machines. He was hired by Essendon in August 2011 and given a fat salary, broad licence and a clear mandate to make the players bigger and stronger. He was put in charge of all fitness and conditioning, sports science and medical staff. He assumed responsibility for a substantial budget and was given authority to hire the people he deemed necessary to take Essendon from finals aspirants to premiership contenders. One of the first he hired was Stephen Dank.

An enigmatic figure, Dank has worked in elite sport, largely beyond public view, for twenty years. At Essendon, he presents himself as a biochemist and a pharmacologist, a peer-reviewed researcher and an expert in athletic recovery. Where Robinson's task is to build the bodies of premiership footballers, Dank's speciality is helping them repair and recuperate between training sessions and matches. His methods are unorthodox and idiosyncratic. While working with Robinson at Manly, he briefly came to prominence for his use of exotic-sounding substances such as Actovegin, a derivative of calf's blood, and Lact-Away, a herbal remedy extracted from the bark of a French species of pine tree. The pair reunited at the AFL's new franchise club, the Gold Coast Suns, at the start of the 2011 pre-season before joining Essendon's staff the following year. Mark Thompson, a premiership captain at Essendon and premiership coach at Geelong who has returned to Windy Hill to mentor Hird in his first coaching job, says Dank was engaging and passionate about his work. He is easy to talk to, impossible to control.

'He basically did what he wanted,' Thompson says. 'He is probably a lot smarter than all of us. I don't think he went out to give any illegal substances. I thought, what he was doing, he genuinely wanted to help athletes in the club.'[9]

Other views of Stephen Dank are less charitable. On a Saturday at Shark Park, the home ground of NRL club Cronulla, two experienced sports doctors confer. It is early in the 2011 NRL season and Cronulla is hosting Manly-Warringah. The match is billed as the battle of the beaches, a throwback to the epic contests between the two clubs in the 1970s. For Cronulla doctor David Givney and his Manly counterpart Paul Bloomfield, it is also a chance to compare notes about Dank, who, after five seasons with the Sea Eagles, is now swimming with the Sharks. Givney first learned of Dank's loosely managed involvement at Cronulla a month earlier and is troubled by some of the things he is hearing. Bloomfield delivers a blunt prognosis: 'Get rid of him as soon as possible. He is poison.'[10] Due largely to the interventions of Givney, Dank is booted out of Cronulla five weeks later. For Cronulla, it is not soon enough. Dank's brief involvement at Shark Park ensures that a national drug scandal will burn savagely on two fronts.

By the morning of 5 February 2013, Dank is long gone from Essendon and so it seems are any reliable records, if they ever existed, about substances given to Essendon players throughout 2012. What Hird principally wants is written confirmation from WADA that AOD-9604 is permitted for use by athletes. AOD-9604 is a fragment of growth hormone being developed as a therapeutic drug. Some researchers believe it is a treatment for obesity and diabetes, others hope it can restore the worn knee cartilage that forces so many footballers into early retirement. Essendon is convinced AOD-9604 is its problem.

Hird believes, as does Reid, that Dank received written approval from anti-doping authorities to use the substance a year earlier. They remember him coming to training one night waving a document on WADA letterhead, telling them that AOD-9604 is all cleared, that they are good to go. Approval for every substance taken at Essendon is supposed to be attached to the back of consent forms signed by the players. Hird finds the forms on a bookshelf in the office of club psychologist Jonah Oliver. There is no WADA approval attached, nor approval of any kind. The consent forms were intended to give the players comfort. In the doping case that engulfs a football club and competition, they provide none.

―――――――――

It is a little after 10 a.m. on Tuesday, 5 February, when Essendon's president, chief executive and coach walk into the boardroom at

AFL House. With wood panelling and oil-painted portraits of past commissioners and administrators lining the walls, it is a shrine to old Melbourne power and influence, housed in a modern corporate headquarters. The Essendon trio, Evans, Robson and Hird, are accompanied by club media minder Justin Rodski and Liz Lukin, a crisis management specialist brought in by Evans. They are greeted warmly by the tall, well-tailored figure of Gillon McLachlan, a politically connected, commercially savvy sports administrator and scion of one of South Australia's richest landowners. A year earlier, McLachlan turned down an offer to take over as chief executive of the NRL. It is now accepted that the top AFL job is his whenever Demetriou takes his leave. A little while into the meeting they are joined by Brett Clothier, a media lawyer who manages integrity issues for the AFL.

What is said at this meeting, like so much of the drugs scandal, is heavily disputed. It is also crucial to understanding what emerges as a central dynamic: James Hird's mistrust of the AFL and his fear that David Evans, his friend and club chairman, is under the thumb of the game's governing body. Hird says Essendon is told at this meeting that the ACC is about to publish a report implicating the club in the use of performance-enhancing drugs.[11] According to Hird, McLachlan urges Essendon to invite ASADA to investigate the club because it 'would look better for us.' When Hird seeks to convince them that the club had secured WADA approval to administer AOD-9604 to its players, the integrity manager cuts him short: 'They're not worried about AOD-9604.' They are not told what substances ASADA suspects Essendon players of using but McLachlan is adamant that banned drugs were taken at Windy Hill.

Immediately after the boardroom meeting, Evans, Robson and Hird are to face a media conference where they will publicly reveal that Essendon is under investigation for the use of performance-enhancing drugs. Hird's instinct is to do nothing of the sort. He wants to declare Essendon clean, that he is certain his players haven't taken any banned substances, that although he is happy for anti-doping authorities to investigate, he doesn't believe Essendon has a case to answer. McLachlan tells him he can't say these things.

'I was certain we hadn't given performance-enhancing drugs and I wanted to say it at a press conference and I was advised if I said that I'd look stupid,' Hird says. '[McLachlan] was very strong in saying to me, "You can't say that because it won't be right".' Liz Lukin, the crisis manager brought in by Evans, urges Hird to take ultimate responsibility.[12] Hird pushes back.

'I expressed to David Evans, to Ian Robson and to Liz Lukin and to Gill McLachlan that I didn't agree with what they were asserting had happened at our club—or what Gill McLachlan was asserting was happening at our club.'[13] It is made clear to Hird, however, that for the sake of the Essendon Football Club, he needs to take his seat at the press conference, to say what he has been asked to, to play his part.

Hird's insistence that the ACC and its pending report are openly discussed in the AFL boardroom is not supported by other witnesses in the room. Nor is it contradicted. Evans says he cannot remember the ACC being mentioned during the meeting but he is not certain.[14] Lukin, Robson and Clothier similarly say they cannot recall the ACC being mentioned, although Clothier concedes he was not in the boardroom for the entire meeting. Hird's version of events is given further weight by Essendon football manager Danny Corcoran, who recalls a conversation he had with Robson when the Essendon chief was still inside AFL House. Robson telephoned Corcoran, who was back at the club, to instruct him to immediately stand down Dean Robinson.

'Robson said a huge report was coming down midweek. They got this information purely from the AFL. Robson said, "Don't even worry about it, stand him down immediately",' Corcoran says.[15] Shortly after this phone call, Corcoran walks Robinson onto the red-brick footpath outside Windy Hill, a blank stare on the fitness coach's face and a box of personal belongings in his arms. It is a decision taken in haste and panic, for which Essendon will later pay dearly.

How could the AFL know that Essendon was about to be named in an ACC report? The answer is carefully written in the neat longhand of career public servant Aurora Andruska in a spiral notebook she took to a meeting between the AFL and ACC on 31 January 2013 in Canberra, less than a week before the exchange in the AFL boardroom that Hird describes. Andruska is the chief executive of ASADA, the organisation responsible for investigating any suspected use of performance-enhancing drugs by an Australian athlete. She is asked by the chief executive of the ACC, John Lawler, to sit in on a briefing he plans to give to senior AFL officials about Project Aperio, a year-long examination of the links between organised crime, performance-enhancing drugs and sport. As she has throughout her 37-year career in the federal public service, Andruska takes diligent notes of what is said at the meeting. Also in the room are Lawler, his deputy Paul Jevtovic, the AFL's two most senior executives, Andrew Demetriou and Gillon McLachlan, and the league's manager of integrity services, Brett Clothier.

The ACC lawyers have vetted the information to be given to the AFL. For much of the meeting, Lawler reads from a prepared script, outlining the risks posed by the trade of new generation performance-enhancing drugs known as peptides, criminal elements involved in the black market supply of peptides and unscrupulous sports scientists working within professional football clubs. The ACC's principal concern is not the use of performance-enhancing drugs but the potential this has to compromise athletes and allow organised crime to dig its hooks into professional sport and manipulate the burgeoning sports betting market. Demetriou, who has been concerned for a while about the rising influence of sports scientists within AFL clubs, remarks he is not surprised by what he is being told. Lawler says an AFL club features heavily in Project Aperio but will not say which one. When McLachlan presses the question, Andruska notes the following exchange: 'McLachlan: "Is it Essendon?" Jevtovic: "Say no more."'[16] It is a brief departure from the script but enough for the AFL. As Federal Court Justice John Middleton later remarks, 'It was a wink and a nod.'[17] The ACC makes clear to everyone in the room which club is in the gun.

As the AFL delegation boarded its flight back to Melbourne, it faced a dilemma. The ACC is one of Australia's most powerful and secretive organisations. Created by the Howard Government in 2002 to tackle serious and organised crime, it is armed with broad, coercive powers to intercept phone and other electronic communications and compel witnesses to attend interviews and answer questions. Witnesses summoned to an interrogation by an ACC examiner have no choice but to attend, answer all questions and produce any documents that are requested. Witnesses can be charged, prosecuted and jailed for refusing to answer questions or giving misleading answers. Once a witness is summoned, they are forbidden from telling anyone about it. Under the strict secrecy provisions of the ACC Act, a witness can be jailed for telling their husband, wife or mother that they are attending an examination, much less the detail of any questions asked. What Demetriou, McLachlan and Clothier learned about Essendon was protected by the ACC's secrecy provisions and the threat of criminal prosecution. Yet nothing they tell Essendon will compromise the ACC report, which is already back from the printers. Do the representatives of the AFL say nothing to Essendon and let events take their course, or do they seek to get in front of the coming scandal, to limit the damage, to control the outcome?

Demetriou's response to suggestions he forewarned Evans has been consistent. He confirms the briefing with the ACC but says Essendon was not named. He confirms a conversation with Evans on 4 February but denies telling Evans about the ACC report. He insists he did not tell Evans that Essendon was under scrutiny. On 25 July 2013, the morning the 'tip-off' allegation is first reported in Melbourne's *Herald Sun* newspaper, Demetriou offers a steadfast denial. This is to become Demetriou's refrain until his final days as AFL chief, whenever the tip-off story re-emerges:

I did not know who the club in question was. The AFL wasn't aware who the club in question was because the ACC, who briefed us a few days earlier on the Thursday, wouldn't disclose to us who the clubs involved were. There absolutely was a discussion I had with David because I had spoken to him throughout the day and I did speak to him that night because I was returning his phone call. But it wasn't tipping off David Evans about Essendon was the club because we didn't know who the club was.[18]

The apparent discrepancy between Andruska's notes and Demetriou's explanation has never been resolved. Evans has not publicly revealed what Demetriou told him during that telephone conversation on the night of Hird's birthday. Despite what Evans said to the other Essendon officials immediately after the call—'He's definitely saying that we've taken them'—he supports Demetriou's position that Essendon representatives weren't tipped off. Corcoran and Reid back Hird's account. Club chief executive Ian Robson has never spoken publicly about it. The ACC, understandably, was not inclined to investigate a possible breach of secrecy provisions that began with a wink and a nod from its second most senior official. Within hours of Demetriou's denial on radio, the ACC issues a short statement suggesting everyone should move on: 'The ACC has no information to support the assertion that any information about Project Aperio and the links between drugs in sport and organised crime was unlawfully disclosed,' the statement read. 'Further, the ACC does not have any information to support the assertion that representatives of the Australian Football League failed to honour their written undertakings given to the ACC in accordance with the *Australian Crime Commission Act 2002*, to protect the content of the confidential briefing they received.'[19]

Whether the secrecy provisions of the ACC were breached or not, the impact on the Essendon drugs scandal is profound. What Demetriou tells Evans that night at his Toorak house and what McLachlan and Clothier tell Essendon's senior officials at AFL headquarters the following day cleaves a fault line between Evans and Hird and between Hird and the AFL. Under the pressure of a rolling, uncontrollable crisis, this opens into a chasm, swallowing Evans and destroying his friendship with Hird. It causes Evans to ask Hird to withhold information from ASADA and Hird to publicly expose his friend and club chairman. It fuels a brutal AFL campaign to discredit and sanction Hird; a campaign that leaves the Essendon coach wounded but determined to expose the cant and deceit of the AFL. It clouds the judgement of Andrew Demetriou, who leaves the AFL midway through the drugs scandal with his legacy diminished.

Essendon is family to David Evans but so is the AFL. If Ron Evans was admired at Essendon he was revered inside AFL House, where he served for nine years as commission chairman. He mentored Andrew Demetriou in Demetriou's early years with the AFL and chaired the board that promoted him to chief executive. Where Demetriou was the AFL's guiding force, indeed a 'force of nature' as Western Bulldogs president Peter Gordon describes him,[20] Ron Evans was its ethical compass. Like his father, David Evans is successful in business, astute and well liked. It seemed a natural progression that he would one day follow his dad onto the AFL board. On Ron Evans' deathbed, long-serving commissioner and former Australian Council of Trade Unions secretary Bill Kelty vowed to look out for David, a pledge not given lightly. Once David Evans receives the phone call from Demetriou the Essendon chairman is hopelessly torn between two fundamental loyalties.

'They played him,' says Mark Thompson. 'They put him in a situation that I wouldn't like to be in; to choose between his love of Essendon, his love of the AFL, his reputation, everything. He was put in a situation where it was inevitable that he was going to lose something in his life.'[21]

As for Hird, it is clear to everyone inside the AFL boardroom on 5 February that he is the greatest point of resistance between Essendon, the AFL and the AFL's primary objective: a managed, controlled resolution to the doping saga. As the senior coach and dominant figure within the Essendon football department, Hird's influence on the events of 2012 requires close scrutiny. He shares responsibility for Dean Robinson and Stephen Dank joining the club, he encouraged them to bring a harder-edged, high-performance culture to Windy Hill. He knew early in the 2012 season that there were problems with Dank and his overuse of injections, that Robinson was clashing with the medical staff, that Bruce Reid didn't like what was going on. As with everyone else in a position of authority at Essendon, he could have done more to prevent what happened in 2012, as he has admitted since. It wasn't in his job description to hire or manage the fitness and conditioning staff but it was within his power to call them out. In February 2013 Hird believes this was done, that safeguards were put in place, that there is no reason to think that any Essendon footballer was given a banned substance. He wants the club to stay in control of its own affairs, to find out what happened, rather than blindly putting its trust in the AFL and ASADA.

At the end of the AFL boardroom meeting, Robson calls ASADA chief executive Aurora Andruska and invites the anti-doping body to investigate Essendon. Robson tells Andruska that the Essendon board, coach and players support this action. He tells her the club has always adhered to anti-doping rules and if doping has gone on behind his back, he wants to see 'swift justice'.[22] Andruska does not tell Robson that ASADA has already decided to launch an investigation into his club with the knowledge and active involvement of the AFL. Evans is also unaware of this. The Essendon chairman believes inviting ASADA into the club is the right thing to do. To this day, he believes that Essendon 'self-reported' to ASADA. It is a myth that perpetuates well into the scandal.

As Robson telephones Andruska, AFL media minders escort football journalists and camera crews into the league's Docklands headquarters for a press conference. Three microphones are placed on the table; there won't be anyone from the AFL in front of the cameras to share Essendon's pain. When Evans, Robson and Hird take their seats, they are shoulder to shoulder yet miles apart.

At the first question directed to Hird, he duly states what he has been asked to say: 'As a leader of the football department, as the coach, I take full responsibility for what happens in our football department.' With one sentence, against his better judgement, Hird takes ownership of whatever is to come. It is a dangerous place for anyone to be.

2
GREY CARDIGANS, BLACKEST DAY

IT IS KNOWN as the blackest day in Australian sport. Aurora Andruska remembers it as the day she nearly blacked out. The executives who run Australia's major professional sports have been called, some cajoled, to Canberra on 7 February 2013 for a media spectacular. They are greeted by John Lawler, chief executive of the ACC. He is armed with a stack of glossy, unclassified reports of Project Aperio, a year-long examination of the links between organised crime, performance-enhancing drugs and sport. At his side are two ministers of the Crown: Jason Clare, Minister for Justice and a rising star within the Australian Labor Party, and Kate Lundy, an ACT Senator who after nearly twenty years in parliament is living her dream job as Minister for Sport. Andruska, the chief executive of ASADA, should be home on the couch. Her left knee, freshly scarred from surgery two weeks earlier, is throbbing as she walks with shuffling steps down the polished parquetry floors of Parliament House. What she wouldn't give for the rented Zimmer frame parked next to her desk back in her Fyshwick office. As the cameras roll her teeth are clenched in pain.

'Quite frankly, I couldn't have lasted much longer on that stage,' she says. 'I was close to passing out.'[1] From these inauspicious beginnings, the most important investigation in ASADA's history is announced to a national audience.

It is not unusual for the ACC to call a press conference when it publishes a report, or for a handful of journalists to turn up, stifle a collective yawn and file a few paragraphs. The strict secrecy provisions that govern the ACC ensure that most reports it publishes are so bereft of details they are hardly worth the printer's ink. This isn't one of those reports. For starters, it is about football. Big league football. Throw in a roll call of exotic, performance-enhancing drugs, dire warnings of nefarious links to organised crime and the startling claim that an entire team has doped its way to premiership points and Project Aperio is a ball-tearing yarn. The ACC knows it. The executives who run the sports know it. Jason Clare and Kate Lundy absolutely know it. Andruska knows something else: the information gathered by the ACC is only that. It can't be used as evidence in a criminal case. It can't be used as evidence in a doping case. It will be someone's job—her job—to turn this information into evidence. That job only gets harder once the ACC and the Gillard Government go so brazenly public with what they know.

Aurora Andruska hasn't spent her working life chasing drug cheats. Her formal training is in organic chemistry and her expertise is in social policy. She joined the Australian Public Service in the first year of the Fraser Government. Her two proudest professional achievements were developing the socio-economic status model for non-government school funding, a reform that began under the Keating Government and was realised during John Howard's first term as prime minister, and the work she did to establish a national training agreement with the states and territories. When she was headhunted for the ASADA job in 2010, she was deputy chief executive of the government's peak welfare agency, Centrelink.

'I was worried about whether indigenous people are spending all their money on pornography and alcohol and if they actually had some food for their kids, making sure that stores in the outback had food that was in date,' she says.² Now it is her task to oversee a doping investigation of a complexity and scale that had never been attempted in Australia; an investigation that few people in federal government, the AFL or the NRL truly want to succeed.

The investigation is into peptides in professional football. In particular, the suspected use of secretagogues, a class of peptide that stimulates the natural production of growth hormone, a biological agent that builds muscle, strengthens bones, repairs frayed tendons and restores vital health to an athlete's body. Growth hormone-boosting peptides are banned in sport and are virtually undetectable by drug testers. Cheaply manufactured by biochemical companies in China, Thailand and Canada and readily available in Australia through online suppliers, secretagogues are everything that makes anti-doping so difficult to enforce—a potent, portable substance seemingly two steps ahead of the people trying to catch drug cheats.

ASADA first started hearing about peptides at NRL clubs in 2011. Drug testers visiting clubs overheard players talking about new, undetectable substances. Anonymous callers phoned in with a tip-off about this or that club being on the gear. Customs seizures showed a dramatic increase in the volume of peptides being intercepted. The jilted ex-girlfriend of an NRL player called the ASADA hotline and offered something more specific: she recalled her former beau and some of his mates talking about a clinic in Castle Hill, in Sydney's northwest, where they could get the good stuff. There is only so much ASADA can do with low-level tip-offs, hearsay and gossip. In 2011 they had no coercive powers and they still can't tap phones. But within the agency's Fyshwick office in Canberra, a file of information begins to grow.

On 26 July 2011 another titbit is added. While a doping control officer is at Windy Hill testing players, he is approached by Essendon senior coach James Hird. Hird wants to know about peptides and which AFL clubs were using them. The drug tester couldn't answer the question but made a note of the conversation.

'We were getting phone calls, tip-offs, saying that something is going on,' Andruska recalls. 'Then, out of the blue, we get this information that James Hird is asking this question.'³ Two weeks later, ASADA follows up Hird's query with a few questions of its own. Through Brett Clothier, the AFL's integrity services manager who has a good rapport with ASADA, the anti-doping authority arranges for a meeting with Hird. It takes place at AFL House on 5 August 2011, following an Essendon training session at the Docklands ground.

Hird walks into the meeting accompanied by Danny Corcoran and Paul Hamilton, the two senior managers within Essendon's football department. They are greeted by Clothier and ASADA investigator Paul Roland, who asks Hird a series of questions about his knowledge and interest in peptides. Hird explains he was asked about peptides by one of his cycling friends while they were pedalling in a group one morning along Melbourne's Beach Road, a collar of bitumen around Port Phillip Bay that is home to dozens of amateur pelotons. Hird's cycling buddy said he'd heard rumours of peptides being used by cyclists and wanted to know if they were permitted in sport. Hird told his friend he'd never heard of peptides. When he saw the drug tester at the club, he asked about them.⁴ According to Roland, the Essendon coach's response prompts a general discussion about peptides, including ASADA's belief that more were being imported into the country and that they were banned in sport. Nearly two years after the exchange, Clothier adds something to this account, a contentious postscript that casts ASADA's meeting with Hird in a harsher light. This episode, emblematic of the mistrust and antipathy that develops between Hird and the AFL, is detailed in chapter 6. Andruska says she accepts Hird's explanation.

'I believe what he said. I accepted it and didn't think any more about it. It was minor. It happened and, maybe, what then emerged made it look more important.'⁵

At the time ASADA speaks to Hird about peptides, it assumes the drugs are a far bigger problem in the NRL than the AFL. An off-chance discovery of a pamphlet distributed in a Sydney gym by a peptide supplier takes the investigation in a new, unexpected direction. Suddenly, investigators find themselves exploring the unfamiliar and largely unregulated world of anti-ageing medicine and compounding pharmacies and barely concealed links to criminal figures.

'I'm being told people in outlaw motorcycle gangs are involved, people with criminal histories,' Andruska says. 'I'm blown away with this and thinking, I don't know how we are going to get there but we have got an obligation to get this out there. We have got to nail this somehow.'[6] In September 2011, ASADA formally launches Operation Cobia, an investigation into the suspected use of banned peptides and growth hormones in the NRL.

Andruska doesn't need to have spent her working life chasing drug cheats to realise that ASADA, an organisation with a tiny investigations budget, no coercive powers and no experience in cracking this kind of a case, needs help. When ASADA was established by the Howard Government, it was intended to take Australia's anti-doping effort into a new, investigative age. Anti-doping cases are a doddle when athletes return a positive test to a banned substance. In these circumstances, the burden of proof is reversed; it is up to the athlete to show why a mandatory two-year ban—since doubled to four years—should not apply. In a case where there is no positive test, the burden of proof falls on anti-doping investigators. Previous cases exposed the limitations of ASADA's forerunner, the Australian Sports Drug Agency, in dealing with suspected doping in the absence of a positive test. A report into doping allegations against Australian track cyclists by prominent jurist Robert Anderson QC recommended an overhaul of anti-doping in Australia and the establishment of an independent, investigative anti-doping body.[7]

When Howard Government Minister Kevin Andrews rose in federal parliament on 7 December 2005 to second read the ASADA Bill, he declared the establishment of ASADA would mean 'sports, athletes and the public can have complete confidence that doping allegations will be investigated and pursued in an independent, robust and transparent way.'[8] They were fine words but the only investigative tool that came with them was an information-sharing arrangement with customs, the Australian Federal Police and other law enforcement agencies. When former AFP commissioner Mick Palmer's consultancy reviews ASADA's work early in the Essendon investigation, it describes these arrangements as the powers of begging and pleading.[9]

Even if it had power, ASADA is not resourced for a big game hunt. Its 2011/12 budget is under $15 million. Of that, only $637,000 is set aside for intelligence and investigations.[10] Much of ASADA's investigative work consists of running down names and addresses connected to packages of performance-enhancing drugs intercepted by customs in the hope the drugs authority will happen across an athlete or a coach. Long hours are spent following up tips, many of which are provided by jealous competitors. ASADA exposes the occasional drug taker, including some using peptides, but they are athletes performing well off-Broadway.

'We were picking up people who were playing in the 4th division in the Kiama competition,' Andruska says. It is a long way from the sleepy Illawarra coast to big city stadiums. The one thing ASADA does have is broad licence to drug test professional footballers. A reliable test for peptides isn't available but ASADA starts to collect, freeze and store blood and urine samples in the hope there soon will be. Eventually, samples are sent to a specialist lab in Cologne, Germany. The results don't yield a positive test but they suggest ASADA could be on the right track. Of greater importance is the work being done by Andruska and senior ASADA officials to strengthen their relationship with bigger, more powerful investigative bodies. For several months in 2011, ASADA courted a reluctant ACC with the aim of establishing a formal information-sharing arrangement between the organisations. This relationship is about to be consummated.

In November 2011, the ACC reveals to ASADA its plans for Project Aperio, an examination of the nexus between crime, drugs and sport. The project is in its infancy. For ASADA, the timing is perfect. The ACC, having previously examined match fixing, wants to have a closer look at whether criminal networks are using drugs to get their hooks into athletes and, potentially, compromise the integrity of sporting competitions. ASADA has something of its own to show the ACC. It opens the book on Operation Cobia. The ACC can't believe its luck. It will happily take things from here.

Staring down the barrel of a television camera from within the Blue Room of Parliament House, Justice Minister Jason Clare warns that the findings of the ACC report will shock and disgust Australian sports fans. Sounding like Eliot Ness hot on the heels of Al Capone, he has a message for any athletes dabbling in doping: 'Don't underestimate how much we know and, if you are involved in this, come forward before you get a knock at the door.' Senator Lundy is even more direct: 'If you dope we will catch you. If you want to fix a match we will catch you.'[11]

The published version of the ACC report, leached of vital detail and only forty-three pages long, contains a series of sweeping assertions. The use of peptides and growth hormones by Australian athletes is widespread, facilitated by unscrupulous sports scientists, high-performance coaches and support staff. The market for performance-enhancing drugs is highly profitable and organised, and the range of substances are large and diverse. Loopholes in regulations are being exploited by unethical anti-ageing clinics and compounding pharmacists. What the unclassified version of the report doesn't reveal, and indeed can't reveal due to the ACC secrecy provisions, is that the doping allegations raised by Project Aperio revolve almost entirely around one person: Stephen Dank.

Nearly every club, every coach, every athlete implicated by the report has a connection to Dank. He was at the Gold Coast Suns at the end of 2010, at Cronulla for about three months in 2011, and throughout most of the time that Project Aperio is running he is on the Essendon payroll. The emerging scandal follows him like a spotlight on a darkened stage. ASADA knows this before the ACC releases its report. Twice throughout 2012, in May and again in

November, Dank is called to the ACC and interrogated about his work. Both times, transcripts from his interrogation are provided to ASADA. The anti-doping authority is stunned by what is going on at Essendon but because of its arrangement with the ACC it can do nothing to warn either the club or the AFL.

'We are in new territory,' Andruska says. 'We need to behave appropriately and show we can be trusted. We aren't going to start rushing around doing stuff. We didn't want to raise any alerts. We just let the ACC get on and do their thing.'[12] ASADA's time to act comes soon enough.

Within ASADA there are concerns that once the ACC reveals Project Aperio its own investigative task will be compromised. At the time of the 7 February press conference, ASADA's intelligence and investigations section is run by Michael O'Leary. A former intelligence analyst with the Australian Federal Police and Department of Immigration, he warns his boss that, if the ACC goes public, ASADA's investigation will become a media circus. Aurora Andruska tells O'Leary she has no say, no control and no prospect of stopping what is about to happen. Andruska says that, in an ideal world, ASADA wouldn't have embarked on a major investigation with so much background noise. In reality, she doesn't see any circumstance in which a major probe into AFL and NRL clubs by anti-doping investigators can be kept quiet for long.[13] The ACC decided to release its report months earlier. From early January, the provisional date of 7 February was pencilled in. Andruska did not oppose this course. Nor did she anticipate what would unfold.

'Up until late in the piece it was going to be John Lawler doing what he'd normally do, where he calls in the press, releases his report and talks to it. It was going to be absolutely normal. He had asked if I could be in the shadows in case any journalist had any questions about the next steps. That was the plan. And then the plan changed.'[14]

Kate Lundy accepts responsibility for changing the plan. Lundy was an unusual minister for sport. Whereas most government front-benchers accept the sport portfolio as a welcome add-on to more weighty ministerial responsibilities—a series of box-seat tickets and photo-ops with athletes to brighten the tedium of parliamentary life—Lundy is serious about sport. She spent eleven years in opposition as Labor's spokeswoman for sport. She is intimately familiar with the ASADA Act and the National Anti-Doping Code, having scrutinised them closely, along with all other sport legislation introduced throughout the Howard years. When Labor was elected she was well qualified and prepared to take over as sports minister save for one glitch on her CV: she could not abide Kevin Rudd. As things turned out, she was merely a step ahead of many of her Labor colleagues, but her prescience cost her. Rudd snubbed Lundy and gave the sport portfolio to South Australian MP Kate Ellis. It was not until Julia Gillard took over in June 2010 that Lundy got a crack at the job she had long coveted. Shortly after Rudd returned as prime minister in June 2013 to lead Labor to its September election train wreck, the portfolio was stripped from Lundy again.

When Kate Lundy is briefed on the contents of the Project Aperio report, she decides that if the ACC is going to make it public, government and the major professional sports need to show they understand the gravity of the allegations and a willingness to confront them. She believes the ACC is right to make the report public and alert athletes and sports administrators to the potential health risks proposed by substances that, in some cases, haven't been approved for human consumption. The political atmosphere within Canberra is raw with the Gillard prime ministership in its death throes. Eight days before the 7 February press conference, Gillard announces a September election date, ensuring everything that happens over the next seven and a half months will be set against the backdrop of the rancorous campaigning. Lundy is dismayed though not surprised that the press conference is derided as a political stunt.

'It wasn't a stunt. It was my genuine and honest effort to have a response at hand to say we are going to do something about this, we are not going to run and hide, we are not going to step away from it. There was absolutely no other path for me as sports minister but to stand up and ask Australian sport to work with me to clean up the problem in anticipation of an investigation.'[15] As for asking the ACC not to release its report, Lundy says this would have been unconscionable.

'There was no way that I would have made a political decision to suppress a document in the face of the crime commission wanting to table it. Can you image the result of that? No way. That is why I can say confidently that I had no choice but to stand up in some capacity. I can second-guess all I like about how that press conference unfolded and maybe something low-key would have been better but I don't think it would have changed much and I still would have been there.'[16]

Whether the ACC should have publicly released its report, whether its findings were over-egged in the manner of its release and the commentary that followed—including former ASADA chief executive Richard Ings' enduring pronouncement of 7 February 2013 as 'the blackest day in Australian sport'[17]—the events of that day ensure ASADA begins its investigation in a climate of political and public scepticism. Part of this stems from the ACC's mischaracterisation of its own work. It describes Project Aperio as an investigation but, in truth, it is an information-gathering exercise. Its exploration of the links between sport, drugs and crime figures tells a troubling tale but did not lead to any criminal investigations. A classified, highly confidential version of the ACC report is distributed among state and federal police agencies. The reflections of Graham Ashton, Victoria's newly appointed police chief commissioner, are indicative of how police agencies view the uncut edition.

At the time, Ashton was a deputy commissioner with Victoria Police overseeing the establishment of a specialist integrity in sport investigations unit. He would have loved to have launched the new unit with a red-hot criminal case involving sport, drugs and match fixing. Project Aperio didn't unearth any such thing.

'A lot of stuff in there were things that ASADA needed to pick up,' Ashton says. 'We didn't see it as being in the criminal space.

We added it to our intel holdings around some of the broader drug stuff we knew about but the actual integrity in sport aspects of it were squarely in ASADA's ballpark. We just took a step back from it and let them play with it.'[18] ASADA soon realises it has been tossed a hospital pass.

Two days after the 7 February press conference, the AFL returns to Canberra. This time, Essendon comes with them. It is a Saturday. The weekend papers are laden, front pages and back, with news, conjecture, and keyboard-thumping opinion about the drugs scandal. Julia Gillard is in Queenstown, New Zealand, holding an important bilateral meeting with New Zealand Prime Minister John Keys, but you'd be hard-pressed to read anything about it. There is only one story and ASADA is in the thick of it.

Early on 9 February, Aurora Andruska meets with her team at ASADA's headquarters in Fyshwick, a drab building in a semi-industrial suburb dotted with legal brothels and strip clubs. Andruska's two most senior team members, general manager of anti-doping programs and legal services Elen Perdikogiannis and chief operating officer Trevor Burgess, worked with Andruska at Centrelink and followed her to the anti-doping authority. Paul Simonsson, a straight-talking former All-Black and rugby league player and NSW detective, has only been at the organisation for two weeks. When he applied for the job he thought he'd be working on anti-doping issues in cycling. Instead, as ASADA's new director of intelligence and investigations, he will oversee the investigation into the suspected use of peptides at AFL and NRL clubs. They have all come in on a weekend to meet Gillon McLachlan and Brett Clothier from the AFL, and David Evans and Ian Robson from Essendon. The other person in the room is Richard Eccles. The federal government's most senior bureaucrat responsible for sport, Eccles will have a 'persisting involvement' in the drugs scandal.[19]

The discussion that follows is long, rambling and revealing. Essendon chairman David Evans fears the impact the scandal is already having on his players, particularly young footballers, some from remote areas and small towns, some indigenous, who don't understand what is happening to them. Players don't want to leave their houses, he says. Some have been spat on and abused. He says his players need some kind of assurance, an explanation from ASADA about what they are facing. The AFL already has an idea how this mess should be sorted out. Before the investigation has started, it volunteers an outcome: punish the club and any staff responsible but declare the players innocent. After all, if they did take banned drugs they didn't know it. Eccles smiles to himself. He has dealt with the AFL before.

'What is it you are after?' he asks the league heavies. Andruska's spiral notebook records McLachlan's response: 'Come to arrangement. Players found to be innocent. This is the outcome. Sanctions against Essendon. Held responsible. Hold individuals accountable.'[20]

The meeting continues. The AFL wants ASADA to consider a no fault or negligence case against the players, a provision rarely used in any doping case, anywhere in the world. That way, the AFL reasons, even if Essendon players are found guilty of taking a banned substance they won't be punished. Andruska tells them it can't happen, won't happen. Still they press on. Towards the end of the meeting, in exasperation, Andruska makes a note: 'This debate is getting stupid.' A few lines down, her note is followed by something more telling: 'PM wants it to end.' This is Eccles' contribution. The government is getting hammered because of the press conference, the blackest day in sport hype. Every sport has been tarnished. What can ASADA do about it?

'They wanted it off the page but the genie was out of the bottle,' says Andruska. 'Now that it was out there how are we going to stop it?'[21]

ASADA offers this much. It will draft an explanatory statement for the players. Its intent is to explain in plain English what the process will be, to soothe jangling nerves. Paul Simonsson is the perfect man to deliver it. He played rugby and rugby league at the top level. He can relate to professional footballers. He'll arrange to talk to the players at Essendon. As for the AFL's idea of a no fault or negligence defence for Essendon players, Andruska thinks they are dreaming. The only case she knows of is a hockey player given a banned substance while unconscious on an operating table, undergoing emergency surgery.

'I said to them the bar for no fault is so high you are not going to jump it.'[22]

Neither ASADA nor the AFL make the rules that govern how athletes are dealt with in doping cases. The AFL ceded that right to the World Anti-Doping Agency (WADA) in 2005, though it did not do so readily. It was the last major professional sport in Australia to throw its lot in with WADA, an international body headquartered in Montreal, Canada, and only after a long, bruising campaign by the Australian Sports Commission and threats of funding withdrawals by the Howard Government. WADA, through its World Anti-Doping Code, assumes strict liability for athletes. This means athletes are considered responsible for any banned substances that enter their bodies in all but the most exceptional circumstances. ASADA's primary function is to implement the World Anti-Doping Code in Australia. The AFL's anti-doping policy must be compliant with the World Anti-Doping Code.

Within the World Anti-Doping Code, an athlete who takes a banned substance and establishes no fault or negligence receives zero penalty. The version of the World Anti-Doping Code in force during the 2012 AFL season provides a fine-print explanation of no fault or negligence and examples of when it would and wouldn't apply. It would apply, for instance, if an athlete proved sabotage by a competitor. It wouldn't apply if an athlete ingested a mislabelled supplement or if an athlete's doctor or trainer administered a banned substance without telling them. It wouldn't even apply in cases of deliberate sabotage by a coach or spouse, because athletes are considered responsible for the actions of those they trust with their food and drink. To an athlete confronting the hot, dry sands of a two-year, mandatory doping ban, no fault or negligence is a mirage on the horizon.[23]

Andruska is emphatic on this point: a no fault or negligence defence was never open to the Essendon players. Yet this was not accepted by the AFL, the government's Richard Eccles or ASADA's newly hired director of investigations Paul Simonsson. In one of the more perplexing episodes of the entire doping saga, senior figures within the AFL, the federal government and ASADA spent the next two weeks after the 9 February meeting discussing precisely how no fault or negligence might apply to the Essendon case.

In a sequence of emails, Clothier of the AFL first writes to Simonsson of ASADA raising the notion of Essendon players having no culpability for banned substances they are found to have taken. This is followed by an email from Simonsson to Clothier containing a paragraph that will later raise accusations of a secret deal, enrage the NRL and prompt ASADA's senior counsel to quit the case. On 13 February Simonsson writes: 'ASADA and the AFL will fully explore all avenues in an attempt to provide substantial assistance to a no fault or no negligence defence.'[24] On the same day, ASADA's senior legal adviser Elen Perdikogiannis is drawn into the exchange along with Eccles. According to Eccles, McLachlan is also involved. Eccles wrote to Perdikogiannis:

> Spoke with Gillon—not sure he was fully in the loop. Anyway, I took him through the fact that the para, where ASADA forms the view that the defence of no fault or no negligence is available in relation to a particular player, ASADA and the AFL agree that they will support the application of that defence to that player in proceedings before relevant sports tribunals was as far as possible and a really good thing—and all he then needed was an assurance that the AFL Tribunal would view things in a certain light, and it is as locked in as it can be.[25]

As locked in as it can be. This is what the AFL and Essendon want to hear. This is what McLachlan and Clothier from the AFL and Evans and Robson from Essendon spent a long, tedious Saturday in Fyshwick trying to establish—that the Essendon players, if they do the right thing, can get off scot-free. No fault. No negligence. No penalties. More discussions follow between Perdikogiannis, Eccles and McLachlan. By 18 February, an agreement has been reached, although Perdikiogiannis is unhappy with the 'crappy words' that everyone has settled on.[26]

Paul Simonsson is forwarded a letter to give the Essendon players, which he does at a meeting of all players, staff and coaches at Windy Hill on 20 February. It becomes known as the comfort letter and reads in part:

> To provide an immediate level of comfort for the Essendon players, ASADA has determined the following assistance be given to the Essendon players.
>
> ... ASADA will explain to the players that these are exceptional circumstances and the defence of no fault or negligence may be available. It will be explained to players that under a no fault or negligence defence a player can receive a complete elimination of sanction. (Ultimately whether a player receives a no fault or negligence defence or substantial assistance will depend on the individual's circumstances.) Where a player does come forward and provides a sworn statement regarding his involvement and the involvement of any other person, ASADA will fully explore all avenues in an attempt to provide a no fault or negligence defence or substantial assistance.[27]

The words were certainly crappy and the tone conditional but to footballers panicked at the prospect of being rubbed out of the game for two years for taking banned drugs, the message is clear enough: come clean and you'll be sweet.

Aurora Andruska says the 20 February letter has been misconstrued. She says there was no deal done with the AFL to offer the Essendon players a no fault or negligence defence and that no deal so flagrantly in breach of the World Anti-Doping Code could ever be contemplated.

'Do you think that I, as head of ASADA, would want to do a deal with the AFL that is then reviewed by WADA and WADA says we think ASADA went too soft? Can you imagine what that would look like? We would look like Russia to the rest of the world.'[28] Never mind what the rest of the world makes of it. Within two weeks of Simonsson visiting Windy Hill, word of the letter reaches Sydney, where the NRL's newly appointed chief executive Dave Smith is trying to navigate his own sport's doping scandal. Rugby League smells something rotten south of the Murray. Whatever deal the AFL has stitched up for the Essendon boys, it wants for Cronulla. Stephen Dank's association with Cronulla was not long but its impact was devastating. Unlike Essendon, Cronulla has no inkling the blackest day in Australian sport is coming. It is only after the 7 February press conference that the Sharks realise they are a club of interest in the ACC report and ASADA's unfolding investigation. On 14 February, Cronulla football manager Darren Mooney rings Melbourne lawyer Richard Redman. Mooney explains he's been given Redman's name as someone who knows their way around anti-doping.

'Could you come up and talk to our players?'[29]

For football clubs and athletes at the centre of a growing drugs scandal, Redman is an obvious lawyer to call. He spent three and a half years as ASADA's director of legal services and three years working with ASADA's British equivalent, UK Anti-Doping. He understands how anti-doping works, inside and out. He knows every clause of the World Anti-Doping Code. At the time Mooney calls, Redman has already offered preliminary advice to the AFL Players Association (AFLPA), which is organising representation for the Essendon players. When Redman arrives at Shark Park, the coaches and players are gathered under a grandstand.

'We really don't know what is going on,' Mooney tells him. 'We only know what has happened on the TV and we think it involves us because the name they keep mentioning, well that bloke was here for a while.'[30]

The meeting begins and the Cronulla players start talking, each recalling similar tales of what happened at the club in 2011. Redman begins piecing together Dank's involvement and explains in broad terms how the ASADA investigation might unfold. After fifteen minutes he abruptly stops the meeting and beckons Mooney and the coaches into a corner.

'Have you brought me up here to be the players' lawyer or the club lawyer?' he asks them.

'We are all in this together,' say the men who run Cronulla.

'No, you are going to need two sets of lawyers.'

For the next eighteen months, Redman advises the Cronulla players through an extraordinary saga. Not long after he returns from Sydney, the lawyer reads a curious document. It is a draft copy of the letter that Simonsson is planning to give to the Essendon players, attached to a lengthy email train. Redman has been cc'd in along with the AFLPA's legal team. The email makes clear the wording is still being tinkered with but Redman is intrigued, particularly by the references to Essendon players being offered a no fault or negligence defence. Knowing the World Anti-Doping Code as he does, Redman thinks it will never fly. He replies to all, saying the letter would be very helpful to the players but he can't imagine ASADA agreeing to its terms. It is the last he hears of it until 4 March, when he is called as the lawyer for the Cronulla players to a high-level meeting involving ASADA, the NRL and Cronulla in the Sydney offices of Russell Kennedy, a prominent law firm advising the NRL.

ASADA has already begun interviewing Essendon officials as part of its investigation. It also believes it has a fair idea of what went on at Cronulla in 2011. Tricia Kavanagh, a former justice of the Industrial Court of NSW and an arbitrator for the Court of Arbitration for Sport, is one of the lawyers in the room. She has nearly finished a report, commissioned by Cronulla, that outlines a disturbing chronology of events at Shark Park. John Marshall QC, one of the most experienced sports law barristers in Australia, has been ASADA's senior counsel for twenty years. It is said he has never lost a doping case. He tells the meeting that ASADA has evidence of what went on at Shark Park and is sympathetic to the players. He urges the club and players to work with ASADA rather than against it.

'Work with us and, using the code, we will get the lowest possible sanction,' he says.[31]

Damian Irvine, the chairman of Cronulla, wants something more. He wants the same deal for his players that ASADA is offering Essendon. Marshall looks at him blankly.

'There is no deal.' Irvine and Alan Sullivan QC, Cronulla's lawyer, are adamant. They want the same deal ASADA is offering the AFL. Marshall says he doesn't know of any deal. The meeting ends uneasily, with Cronulla suspicious they are being taken for mugs. The next morning, Marshall sends an email to Redman and Sullivan. Attached is a document negotiated between ASADA, the federal government and Essendon; the document Paul Simonsson presented to Essendon players two weeks earlier. Marshall is apologetic. The previous day, when he told them there was no deal between ASADA and the AFL, that was absolutely his belief. He has since been shown the document. It had been sitting in Marshall's inbox since February but he hadn't read it.

Redman does not hesitate. He writes an email to ASADA saying John Marshall has shown him its deal with the AFL. He wants the same for his clients.

'I hit send and the shit hit the fan. ASADA tried to pull out of the deal they had done because they didn't want to give it to the AFL. The AFL thought who is this effing Richard Redman that has caused this to come undone?'[32]

The repercussions are swift. Marshall tells ASADA that what the letter promises is in breach of the World Anti-Doping Code and ASADA must renege. ASADA refuses, Marshall quits. He has no further involvement in the case. Dave Smith calls Prime Minister Julia Gillard to express his concerns that the AFL is getting preferential treatment.[33] Two days later, ASADA's Elen Perdikogiannis writes to the AFL withdrawing the 20 February letter and offering a new statement in its place. There is no negotiation this time. The new letter no longer accepts what happened at Essendon involved exceptional circumstances or that a defence of no fault or negligence may be available. Instead of a promise to 'fully explore all avenues' to establish no fault or negligence, it commits only to give favourable consideration to not opposing an application to rely on this defence.[34]

The AFL is furious. The investigation has begun. It is too late to change the ground rules now. McLachlan won't accept the new statement. On the same day, he writes back to Perdikogiannis: 'It is the AFL's, Essendon Football Club's (and its players and officials), and the AFL Players Association's clear understanding that the investigation and any subsequent actions will be conducted in accordance with your Original Statement.' McLachlan's response is cc'd to ASADA chief executive Aurora Andruska and Richard Eccles, the senior bureaucrat within Kate Lundy's department who is emerging as a key figure in the developing saga. ASADA ignores the AFL's protest. The revised letter is sent to the Essendon players, in a bundle of other ASADA documents, when they are called to their interviews with anti-doping investigators. If they read it, they do not quibble with the altered wording from what Simonsson previously told them. They are unaware of the political machinations shaping the drugs scandal and, possibly, their own futures.

Kate Lundy says she didn't interfere with ASADA's work. She didn't exert political pressure to bring its investigation into Essendon to a close; she played no part in trying to manufacture an outcome. As she reflects on the role she did play within the doping scandal, she can speak freely about what went on. Labor is no longer in power in Canberra. After twenty years as a federal parliamentarian, she has announced her intention to quit the Senate when it heads into its 2015 winter recess. She insists any accusations of political skulduggery are far removed from actual events.

'It is too easy to use this issue of political involvement to create a spectre of impropriety around an investigation that was unprecedented, highly emotive for everybody and obviously going to end up in the courts.' To illustrate this, she points out that, throughout the scandal, she never met once with Aurora Andruska on her own—a fact confirmed by Andruska.

'I never had any direct interaction, gave them any instruction through the course of the inquiry,' Lundy says. 'I was quite meticulous about staying away from ASADA.'[35]

It is clear however, that ASADA feels intense pressure, from the government and the AFL, to rein in its investigation. Andruska does not meet alone with Lundy and nor does she speak regularly with the AFL's Gillon McLachlan. Eccles does. Eccles has the full confidence of Lundy and the ear of McLachlan. It is Eccles who makes sure that Andruska knows what the government needs and the AFL wants.

Eccles is an ambitious and talented career public servant. His brother Chris Eccles is one of Australia's best-known public servants, having served as secretary of premier and cabinet in state governments in NSW, Victoria and South Australia. Chris Eccles jokingly refers to himself as 'Mr Wolf', the name of Harvey Keitel's uber-efficient Mr Fixit character in the Quentin Tarantino film *Pulp Fiction*.[36] Richard Eccles hasn't risen to the same prominence in national affairs as his brother but he is well known to the senior executives who run professional sport, including the AFL. He previously worked closely with McLachlan during Australia's unsuccessful bid for the 2022 FIFA World Cup. If Australia had won the bid, venues normally used by the AFL would have been required for international football matches. AFL backing was an essential prerequisite to a viable bid. Eccles secured the AFL's support.

Eccles' first confirmed involvement in the doping scandal reaches back to 11 January 2013, when he attends a meeting called by ACC chief executive John Lawler to inform Andruska and other senior ASADA officials that Project Aperio is essentially complete.[37] It continues well into August that year. It is Eccles who announces at the 9 February meeting between the AFL, Essendon and ASADA that the prime minister wants it to end. It is Eccles who advises Andruska, further into the scandal, that Kate Lundy is getting hammered by Cabinet colleagues worried about the electoral blowback from the blackest day in sport.[38] Kate Lundy says the drugs scandal was never a frontline issue for Labor in the lead-up to that year's September federal election. This is not Aurora Andruska's recollection.

On a cold, June morning in Canberra, Eccles' boss Glenys Beauchamp, secretary for the Department of Regional Australia, Local Government, Arts and Sport, spells it out clearly to ASADA. During a 9 a.m. meeting, she tells Andruska she has clear instructions from Senator Lundy: her Labor colleagues are accusing her of hampering their re-election chances; Andruska needs an outcome.[39] The previous day, Andruska is told much the same thing by David Lording, an experienced government and corporate crisis manager brought in by ASADA to help navigate the drugs scandal. Andruska's notes of his advice, recorded in one of her spiral notebooks, are distilled to a single, urgent phrase: 'Lundy needs something.'

'They realised this is not stopping, this is not going to go away,' Andruska says.[40]

The AFL needs something as well. The 2013 football season is like no other. Instead of the game gripping the nation, scandal grips the game. Every weekend matches are played, remarkable sporting deeds performed, teams are triumphant, others vanquished. Yet every Monday the conversation is about Essendon, about drugs, about the epic battle of wills between the AFL executives and commissioners and James Hird, the coach who is stubbornly, defiantly, refusing to give up his job. Just as ASADA has never undertaken an investigation of this complexity, the AFL has never confronted crisis on this scale. AFL officials are inside the investigation. They know the most damaging allegations against Essendon and Hird. They know the worst of what went on at Windy Hill. What they don't anticipate is Essendon, a team ravaged by scandal, keeps winning football games. Against all sporting orthodoxy and logic, the Bombers win their first six. Midway through the season, they are considered a genuine premiership chance. It is a prospect that triggers alarm within AFL House. Cripes, what if they win the bloody thing?

By the start of winter, the AFL decides this cannot happen. Essendon cannot play finals. The club officials responsible for the 2012 disgrace will be held to account. The AFL Commission is briefed to this effect. Richard Eccles is told as much by the AFL. On 13 June, he passes on this information to Trevor Burgess, ASADA's chief operating officer. The AFL is preparing to take on the Essendon support staff. James Hird is looking at a ban of six months or longer. Ducks all lined up notes Burgess.[41] Who is Eccles' deep throat inside AFL House? Burgess' notes refer only to a mysterious 'G'.[42]

In the lead-up to the blackest day in Australian sport, ASADA decides its best chance of uncovering doping at Essendon is to work alongside the AFL. It is a vexed decision, one that fiercely divides legal opinion and, eventually, is challenged in a Supreme Court writ, a Federal Court trial and an appeal to the Full Bench of the Federal Court. In practice, the AFL and ASADA's joint investigation is a simple enough arrangement. ASADA, having no coercive powers at the start of its investigation, uses the AFL's contractual arrangements with players and club staff to compel Essendon footballers, coaches and other club staff to attend interviews, produce documents and answer questions. To enable this, an AFL investigator sits in on the ASADA interviews. In most cases, the AFL investigator is Abraham Haddad, an intelligence co-ordinator who worked alongside Brett Clothier in the league's integrity services unit. The AFL and ASADA are each provided transcripts of the interviews. At the same time, the AFL contracts Deloitte, an external audit company, to analyse data obtained from telephones and computers of players and staff. All evidence gathered by the investigation is stored in a secure, electronic data room. As the investigation unfolds, Haddad reports to Clothier who, in turn, briefs McLachlan and the AFL's general counsel Andrew Dillon on any significant developments. In this way, the AFL is able to track in real time the evidence being gathered.

The idea of ASADA co-opting the AFL's coercive powers into its investigative arsenal is first proposed by Clothier to Aurora Andruska on 1 February, the day after the ACC briefs the AFL about Project Aperio. ASADA has never done this before and despite the initial reservations of its director of legal services, Darren Mullaly, it sees no major obstacle to doing it. From the AFL's point of view, it is a clever move on two counts. Firstly, as ASADA's investigative partner, the AFL is unlikely to become a target of the anti-doping probe. Secondly, once the AFL is inside the investigation, it is ideally placed to shape future events towards its own ends. It does not take long for these ends to become clear to ASADA.

On 18 April, two days after James Hird is formally interviewed by ASADA and AFL investigators, Brett Clothier writes to Darren Mullaly requesting ASADA to provide an interim investigation report to the AFL. The stated purpose of the report is to inform any disciplinary actions the AFL takes against Essendon.[43] When he writes to Mullaly, Clothier already knows that ASADA's investigators are working on a report documenting what they have unearthed at Essendon. The idea that this information can be shared with the AFL is supported by John Nolan, the ASADA investigator leading the probe into the Bombers. The final call, however, rests with ASADA's lawyers. It takes another four months of hectoring from the league for it to get its hands on ASADA's interim report, a highly confidential, immensely damaging 433-page document. It is only after ASADA gives it to the AFL that it realises the potentially catastrophic mistake it has made.

The AFL is the most influential sporting competition in Australia. During the 2013 season, 6.37 million people go to the football and, every week, an average of 4.7 million people watch games on television. Its eighteen clubs are spread across the five mainland states. Three quarters of a million people are club members. With this vast reach comes enormous commercial and political clout. The AFL's governing board, the AFL Commission, includes heavy hitters in sport, business, unions and media. When the doping scandal breaks, AFL chief executive Andrew Demetriou has been running the game for ten years. Demetriou was a good footballer. In private business, he was a middling success. As an AFL chief executive, he is a once in a generation talent.

Demetriou was a schoolteacher during his playing days and after his retirement from football he established a business selling acrylic teeth. He entered the AFL's orbit when he became chief executive of the AFLPA. Such was his hard-headed negotiation of a collective bargaining agreement on behalf of players in 1998, the AFL moved quickly to bring him to their side of the industrial divide. After three years running the AFL's football operations, a job that regularly involved butting heads with intransigent club officials, Demetriou was appointed chief executive in September 2003. That year he inherited total AFL revenue of $170.9 million. When he left the job in 2014, AFL revenue was nearly half a billion dollars. The primary driver of this growth was television. During his tenure Demetriou oversaw the negotiation of two monster broadcast rights agreements: the five-year $780 million deal between 2007 and 2011, and the $1.25 billion deal between 2012 and 2016. He oversaw the expansion of the AFL from sixteen to eighteen teams. His final year's salary, padded by performance and parting bonuses, was close to $4 million. The AFL has not had a more commercially successful chief executive.

By midway through the 2013 season, the AFL is increasingly worried that the doping scandal is undermining its commercial foundation: the AFL brand. Although the AFL doesn't put a dollar figure on what this means, Gillon McLachlan tells Andruska that, for the first time, fan surveys are showing people are losing faith in the game.[44] In a rare meeting between the sports minister, the AFL boss and the ASADA chief executive, Demetriou expresses his dissatisfaction at the pace of the investigation. He declares the timeline for completion completely unacceptable. What can ASADA provide the AFL by the end of July?[45] On 4 June, Andruska travels to Melbourne for another meeting at AFL House. This time, there are no lawyers in the room; just McLachlan from the AFL, Evans from Essendon, Andruska from ASADA and Eccles from Senator Lundy's department. McLachlan speaks about the integrity of the 2013 season, the AFL brand and the national competition. He needs to sell one million tickets by the first two weeks of the finals series. This is the moment Andruska says she fully grasps the AFL's motives. If so, her epiphany comes staggeringly late.

'Their objectives and ASADA's objectives are almost at odds with each other,' she says. 'They are about protecting their business, protecting their brand. We are about making sure that Australia complies with its legal obligations.'[46]

Andruska offers a further, salient reflection. In cases where an athlete returns a positive test to a banned substance, the AFL is a dependable partner in anti-doping. Drug tests are incontrovertible, the penalties set. In such circumstances, the AFL is only too happy to join the fight against performance-enhancing drugs. She remarks that in the case of Essendon, where there are no positive tests and the circumstances are far from clear, the AFL proves to be a less reliable deputy.

Two weeks pass and another meeting follows. Again in the AFL boardroom. Again with ASADA under pressure to make a report of its investigation to the AFL. Gillon McLachlan declares that if Essendon plays in the 2013 finals series, it will undermine the competition for ten years. The AFL will not let this happen. It wants a detailed, written report from ASADA and wants it by 1 August. The report will form the basis of whatever actions the AFL Commission takes against Essendon, James Hird and other Essendon staff. It needs 'the fullest report possible'.[47] ASADA's response is telling. It is willing to provide the AFL with a report but not the report it wants. Its legal team will produce a high-level summary. The AFL can use this for its disciplinary purposes against Essendon. The more detailed and damaging investigator's report will stay under wraps. This is what ASADA says. It is not what it does.

For three weeks in July, Aurora Andruska takes leave for family reasons. In her absence, Trevor Burgess is acting chief of ASADA. Burgess is a chartered accountant by trade and meticulous by nature. He spent years working in risk assessment in the National Audit Office and Health Insurance Commission. When Andruska left Centrelink to run ASADA, Burgess took a substantial pay cut to follow her across. As she prepares to travel overseas, she leaves him with clear instructions about how to deal with the AFL: ASADA will provide a summary report, Elen Perdikogiannis and Darren Mullaly from the legal team are writing it, it will be completed by the AFL's due date of 1 August.

On his second day in charge of the anti-doping authority, Burgess has McLachlan and Clothier on the line, pressing him about the type of information that will be in ASADA's report. In response, Burgess writes a detailed letter. ASADA will provide a confidential report to the AFL but not its investigator's report. ASADA has considered its legal position; it cannot budge. The Burgess letter warns: 'ASADA's position ... is that providing this report would disclose information which ASADA is not able to lawfully disclose to the AFL, such as Australian Crime Commission information. Further, the level of detail needed in the internal ASADA report is such that, if disclosed, is likely to prejudice future anti-doping investigations and support personnel and potentially, players.'[48] The message from ASADA cannot be clearer: if we give you what you want it might screw our case. The AFL is not deterred. A week later Clothier is back on the line, this time with AFL general counsel Andrew Dillon. They want to know if the report will make clear whether ASADA intends to prosecute the players for taking AOD-9604 or any other substance. This telephone conference prompts Burgess to fly to Melbourne to meet Brett Clothier.

The AFL integrity services manager is not satisfied with the level of detail ASADA is offering the AFL. He tells Burgess that the AFL already has access to transcripts of interviews with Essendon players and staff and the material secured by Deloitte from mobile phones and computers.

'If you don't give us something, we're just going to have to sit down one weekend and do it ourselves,' Clothier says.[49] Burgess returns to Canberra deeply concerned. The AFL doesn't have confidence that ASADA will deliver. Burgess is not sure they will either. The summary being prepared by the lawyers runs to only thirty pages. Meanwhile, the investigations team led by John Nolan has substantially completed their hefty draft report. To bridge the gap between what the AFL wants and what ASADA is prepared to give, Burgess proposes a compromise: Clothier can be shown a redacted version of the investigators' work.

It is a decision that reshapes the doping scandal and reflects the skewed power relationship that has developed between the anti-doping body and the AFL. Says Burgess, 'I was conscious of the need to maintain a good working relationship with the AFL. It is very important for a body like ASADA to have cooperative relationships with the peak bodies of sports. Cooperation is vital for ASADA's purpose of upholding integrity in sport and achieving the task, which it shares with sports of addressing anti-doping issues … I was concerned that the AFL not lose confidence in ASADA over this issue of the summary report that already had been promised to the AFL.'[50] Burgess' remarks underscore ASADA's acute dilemma in dealing with the AFL. It has become the junior partner in its own investigation.

Clothier does not need to be asked twice. He flies to Canberra and spends two days reading the investigator's report. It is just what the AFL needs. Clothier describes the contents as extraordinary and outstanding. He has just two questions: 'Why are you spending all this time writing a separate report? Why don't you just give us that?'[51] Against its own legal advice taken a few weeks earlier, this is what ASADA does. On 2 August, an interim investigation report into Operation Cobia is delivered to the AFL.

Aurora Andruska says ASADA was right to provide an interim report to the AFL. Yet the explanation she gives betrays the broken trust and bitterness that lingers between the one-time investigative partners. The AFL could have written its own report. On this,

Clothier was absolutely right. This is the action the NRL takes several months later when it needs material by which to assess the governance failings at Cronulla. Andruska says she didn't trust the AFL to write its own report. She was concerned that if the AFL had it would have intimated, if not outright stated, that the doping investigation against Essendon was at an end.

'I decided we need control,' Andruska says. 'There was a level of, can I totally trust them? What I didn't want was that report to be seen as "this is the end; there is no case to answer". I wanted to be really clear that it was interim and the investigation was ongoing. It is the power of the person who holds the pen. I thought it was better that we write it.'[52]

Not for the first time, ASADA misunderstands the nature of the AFL. If ASADA feels it has scant power over the AFL before it provides its interim report, it has none once copies of the report are in the hands of AFL executives and commissioners.

Within days of ASADA providing the AFL with the interim report, the anti-doping agency becomes concerned by what the AFL plans to do with it. Some information in the report is critical to an ongoing doping investigation and protected by the ASADA Act. Other information is subject to the Privacy Act. ACC information and sensitive medical information is redacted from the version provided to the AFL but the unredacted contents are highly embarrassing to Essendon staff who aren't accused of doping, and damaging to players who are but haven't been charged. All this is spelled out to the AFL in a carefully worded covering letter signed by Aurora Andruska that accompanies the interim report. Yet within a week of receiving it, Demetriou publicly floats the idea of publishing it.[53]

Demetriou's comments, combined with threatening legal letters that ASADA has already received from James Hird's lawyers, prompt a torrent of legal correspondence from ASADA and Australian Government Solicitor Craig Rawson to the AFL. The AFL replies it does not intend to make the report public and will abide by ASADA's conditions about how it could be used.

However, a fundamental dispute emerges between the AFL and ASADA about what these conditions are. The AFL, through its general counsel Andrew Dillon, makes clear its intention to rely on the report to take disciplinary action against Essendon. ASADA makes clear its objection to this. On 20 August, Rawson writes to Dillon stating there is no reason for the AFL Commission to use the interim report or any part of it at its meeting scheduled in six days' time to hear charges against Essendon, Hird, assistant coach Mark Thompson, football manager Danny Corcoran and club doctor Bruce Reid.[54] The AFL refuses to back down. The following day, it publishes a 34-page 'Statement of Grounds', which includes some of the most damaging allegations against Essendon and its officials contained in the report.

Amid the fierce exchange of lawyer emails, Andruska receives a phone call from Eccles, the departmental deputy secretary. He tells the ASADA chief that he has just gotten off the phone from the AFL's Gillon McLachlan.

'What do you think you are doing?' the bureaucrat demands to know. 'I have just had a call from the AFL and it is going to cost them $20,000 in legal fees to respond to your letter that you have just sent. It is taking time away from James Hird.'[55] Not for the first time, Andruska feels like a small player in a much bigger game. 'I couldn't believe what I'm hearing. I'm thinking, what do you think your role in this is?' Lundy insists that at all times, Eccles represented the interests of the government.

Within ASADA, the crisis peaks during an hour-long conference with Andruska and ASADA's lawyers on one end of a phone line and government officials, including Eccles, on the other. Andruska reveals that ASADA came close to taking legal action against the AFL.

'I had a letter drafted that was to be sent, where I was going to threaten, if I didn't get the response I wanted, to seek an injunction,' Andruska says. 'The lawyers were very clear. I just said to them, "I'm the CEO and I'm signing it. If this organisation can't protect information provided to it then I may as well walk out of this office right now and suggest everybody pack up their desk and walk out." Maybe the AFL are used to getting their own way. In this case they did not get their own way. They didn't get their own way because the investigation wasn't closed down, there weren't any deals done. Maybe they thought we were just a pack of grey cardigan wearing people sitting in an office in Fyshwick. We weren't going to just lie down and take it.'[56]

Andruska is adamant that, throughout the doping scandal, ASADA stuck to its principles. In this instance, her belief is difficult to reconcile with the timing of the settlement reached between ASADA and the AFL. On 29 August, the AFL and ASADA sign a formal protocol setting out how the interim report can be used by the AFL.[57] It amounts to detailed instructions on how to shut a barn door after the horse has bolted. Two nights earlier, the interim report was put to the main use the AFL intended. On 27 August Essendon is booted out of the 2013 finals series. Danny Corcoran is suspended for four months, Mark Thompson is fined $30,000 and James Hird is banned from coaching for a year. As far as the AFL is concerned, the doping scandal is over.

3

THERE'S PLENTY OF DANKSY JUICE GETTING AROUND

IT IS THREE days before Christmas in 2014 and the Essendon drug scandal has been raging for nearly two years. The fate of thirty-four players accused of taking a banned substance is before an AFL tribunal. Essendon has abandoned Windy Hill and shifted its operation into a new, $30 million purpose-built facility next to Melbourne's Tullamarine Airport. Rather than sheltering beneath a disused grandstand, the Essendon Football Club is housed in a modern, three-level, high-performance centre. The gym is three times the size of the old one. There is a cavernous indoor training centre. The site sprawls over 100,000 square metres and has been designed to the finest detail. There are two football ovals; one the precise dimensions of the MCG playing surface, the other a mirror of the Docklands ground where Essendon plays most of its home matches. The administration, coaching and high-performance staff have open, airy offices under the one roof. There are no longer any dark corners. There are also many new faces. Essendon president David Evans, chief executive Ian Robson, football managers Paul Hamilton and Danny Corcoran, high-performance manager Dean Robinson and sports scientist Stephen Dank are long gone from the club. Mark Thompson is recently departed. Having coached the senior team during Hird's season of exile, he discovered there was no longer a job for him when Hird returned. Hird is back coaching, but for how long no one is game to say.

On a cool, damp night in Melbourne I approach the front door of a white, Victorian-era cottage in a quiet Hawthorn street. The door swings open and Dr Bruce Reid beckons me inside. He has decided to talk publicly for the first time about what went on at Windy Hill. The Essendon club doctor is a small, genial man with grey hair and a deep crinkle of laugh lines etched around his eyes. He is a partner in a successful sports medicine practice and, until the drugs scandal, had an unimpeachable reputation as the longest-serving club doctor in the AFL. He has worked in football since 1976, when he was part of the medical team at Richmond. When Kevin Sheedy finished his playing career at Richmond and started his coaching career at Essendon, he urged Reid to follow him. Reid agreed and has been a part of Essendon ever since. Reid has seen the best of football: finals matches won, premierships clinched. He has also shared its worst moments: the sharp pain then awful nothing when an anterior cruciate ligament snaps inside a knee, the desperate realisation on a player's face when they feel the grab of a torn hamstring in grand final week. None of this prepared him for football's drug scandal. Bruce Reid sits at the family dining table where, for countless nights and hours over the past two years, he has searched the decisions he made, the actions he took and those he didn't. He pours two glasses of a full-bodied red wine, pauses, and then begins.

'What happened at our club is a disgrace,' he says with a bluntness that takes me by surprise. 'What happened to the players and their parents is even worse. You have to start with that.'

At the end of the 2011 season, Essendon is a football club going places. James Hird, one of its most revered players, has returned to Windy Hill and, in his first year as coach, taken the team into a finals series. That the club's finals campaign ended after one match in bruising defeat by arch-rival Carlton has served only to motivate.

'I personally cannot wait for the football season to start again,' declares club president David Evans in the first line of his chairman's report to members. Due in no small part to the return of Hird and his senior assistant Mark 'Bomber' Thompson, another celebrated figure at Essendon, the supporter base is swollen to beyond 50,000 paid-up members. Essendon is profitable, asset-rich and eyeing off what it considers its rightful place atop the AFL ladder. Yet inside the football department of the Essendon Football Club a cultural revolution is taking place.

Essendon believes its players are not strong enough to compete against the best teams in the AFL. It is a view held by the coaches and shared by the senior management of the club. Essendon players are too readily pushed off the ball, too easily out-muscled in one-on-one contests. Where football at the elite level is merciless, Essendon has become indulgent. When the Bombers have the ball, they charge forward with tearaway speed and thrilling purpose. When the other team has it, they are not so eager to push back. They are offensively good but defensively poor; good players but too easy to play against. Hird and Thompson know this has to change if Essendon is to become a contender.

Thompson is Hird's assistant coach. Years before that he was Hird's premiership captain. When Essendon first approached Hird in 2010 about returning to Windy Hill as senior coach it knew the risks. Hird had never coached. He hadn't even worked as an assistant. The clincher to the deal was Thompson's preparedness to quit Geelong and join Hird as assistant coach and, more importantly, a mentor. It was Thompson's job to teach Hird on the job. Thompson coached Geelong to two premierships. He knows what it takes. After his season back with the Bombers, he can see that even in matches that Essendon wins, the other team dictates play.

'That determined our form, rather than us being in control of our destiny,' Thompson explains. 'We didn't think they were that physically strong.'[1] The players are warned that things are about to change. As they prepare to take leave of the club for their eight-week, post-season break, Thompson advises them to go shopping and buy some bigger jeans. He laughs when he says it but he is only half joking.

The Essendon coach responsible for physically preparing Essendon's players in 2011 is Stuart Cormack. Cormack is an experienced fitness expert. He learned his craft at the Australian Institute of Sport and, prior to working for Essendon, spent eight years in charge of conditioning at the West Coast Eagles. By midway through the football season, Cormack's working relationship with the club is strained. He came to Windy Hill under the previous senior coach Matthew Knights and seems resistant to the new broom. There are arguments about control; the coaches second-guess his work. He is considered too soft on the players and too conservative in his approach.

'The coaching group decided they knew more about the way a training program should be designed than me, and therefore I wasn't the person for the role,' Cormack says.[2] He quits in June 2011.

Enter The Weapon. Dean Robinson, a barrel-chested fitness and conditioning expert, isn't the club's first choice to become its new high-performance manager. Essendon advertises nationally for the position and more than a hundred people apply. From this cattle call, a shortlist of a dozen possibilities is drawn up and three preferred candidates selected for interview by the club's two football managers, Danny Corcoran and Paul Hamilton. Robinson, employed at the time with the Gold Coast Suns, is neither an applicant nor on the shortlist. He soon emerges as the only candidate in the running. Paul Hamilton says Robinson's name 'came up sort of out of the blue'[3] when he and Corcoran were interviewing the three preferred candidates. Had the football managers been allowed to complete the recruitment process they'd started, the job would have gone to Peter Mulkearns, a qualified and respected figure in the football industry. Mulkearns is instead hired by the AFL to train and condition its umpires. For Essendon, it is one of many sliding door moments.

The Weapon has come to Essendon's attention through his old Geelong network. Robinson initially expresses an interest to

Brendan McCartney, a former Geelong assistant coach then working at Essendon, and McCartney passes this on to Thompson. Thompson has no hesitation in recommending Robinson for the job. Thompson worked with Robinson at Geelong and believes he is exactly what Essendon needs. Thompson tells this to Hird in no uncertain terms.

'I knew that he could build bodies,' Thompson says. 'He was good at rehab and was good at getting people strong and fit. He was always looking for new ways to do things. He always had his eyes open, looking for a better way.'[4] Thompson convinces Hird that Robinson has a proven record of developing the physical strength and size in footballers required to win premierships. According to Corcoran, Thompson's sales pitch to the senior coach is simple and seductive: 'He will get 'em big and strong for you. Nothing more than that. He will get 'em big and strong for you.'[5] It is what Hird wants to hear. Thompson knows Robinson's shortcomings. He knows he is a poor organiser and, at times, an over-bearing manager. He knows he is prone to wandering beyond his own area of responsibility. He needs to be carefully, diligently managed. Yet Thompson believes Robinson's upside justifies the risks. Despite all that happens, he still does. Once Thompson sells Hird on the idea, Hamilton and Corcoran have little choice but to approve the appointment.

ASADA's investigators are damning of Essendon for its failure to adhere to normal human resources practices in hiring Robinson; a charge that later forms part of the AFL's disciplinary action against Essendon. Putting aside the question of whether an anti-doping body is qualified to offer management appraisals, ASADA's criticism is devoid of essential context. Robinson is hired as most people are by football clubs—on the personal recommendation of someone already at the club. Robinson was Thompson's fitness adviser for four years at Geelong, a period that included two premierships. Brendan McCartney, having also worked with Robinson, was a trusted, in-house referee. Football is an intensely competitive business. If a club is looking to poach a coach or staff member from a rival club it doesn't ask for a reference. Nor would it trust any it received.

Geelong's 2007 premiership, Thompson's first as a senior coach, ended a barren, forty-four years without a flag. The revived fortunes of the Geelong team mirrored those of the Victorian regional town. Having endured a deep recession, the collapse of financial institutions and the erosion of the industrial and manufacturing base that previously supported its local economy Geelong was pronounced a city reborn. One of the celebrated stories behind the premiership was Geelong's preparedness to trial a radical treatment advocated by a mysterious German doctor so that one of its players could run out on grand final day.

Midway through the 2007 season Geelong defender Max Rooke ripped his hamstring. Rooke wasn't Geelong's best player but he was a talismanic figure within the team. Amid fears the injury could be season ending, Geelong sent Rooke to Munich for treatment by Dr Hans-Wilhelm Müller Wohlfahrt. 'Healing Hans' as he is known, was the club doctor at football giant Bayern Munich for nearly forty years. He gained global prominence and notoriety for treating celebrity sportspeople including Usain Bolt, Cristiano Ronaldo, Michael Jordan and Boris Becker, and less sporting stars such as Bono, Madonna and Luciano Pavarotti. Rooke's treatment involved a series of injections of Actovegin, a derivative of calf's blood, which is claimed to stimulate healing. Rooke returned to football in time for Geelong's qualifying final and was part of the team that thrashed Port Adelaide on grand final day. Rooke's successful return from injury left an impression on Robinson, who was part of the medical and high-performance team that authorised and planned the Munich treatment. One of his first ideas after starting work at Essendon is to inject muscle-sore players with Actovegin. Bruce Reid shakes his head as he recalls the episode.

Essendon is preparing for the last game of the season. It is a game it needs to win to qualify for finals. The team is tired and depleted. Players are fatigued. Many are carrying injuries. At Windy Hill, the coaches, high-performance staff and medical staff are discussing who is fit to play. Robinson suggests a radical intervention: that all the players be injected with Actovegin to help their muscles recover in time for the match. Reid is dismissive of the idea, his disdain obvious.

'This is bullshit,' the doctor says.

'No, we did it at Geelong,' replies Robinson. The doctor is not convinced.

'Three millilitres of Actovegin, which is spun down calf's blood, into a muscle—the actual factors that help healing are going to be so diluted it is going to do absolutely nothing for recovery. How do you know it works?'

'We won a premiership,' Robinson says.

Hird asks the doctor to make a decision. Reid's judgement is blunt and prescient: 'That is absolute bullshit. And how would it look if the press write that forty Essendon players have had calf's blood intramuscularly as a recovery agent?' Reid wins the argument, this time. Sitting at his dining table, the doctor takes another sip of wine.

'That is where we started.'[6]

The impact of Robinson's arrival at Windy Hill is immediate. Respected physiotherapist Bruce Connor is one of the first to leave. Benita Lalor, Essendon's nutritionist, also quits. In their places Robinson introduces two new physios, poaches Suki Hobson from Geelong to run the weights program, hires Paul Turk as conditioning coach, brings in Jarrod Wade, another ex-Geelong staffer, to help analyse performance, and arranges for Stephen Dank to interview for the newly created position of Essendon sports scientist.

Dank has long worked in the shadows of elite sport. One of his earliest involvements with professional football is with Sydney Rugby League club St George. It was in the mid 1990s. Brian Smith was the coach, Illawarra was still a rival club and the Superleague war was yet to split the game. Dank was a thirty-something, post-graduate exercise physiology student working part-time with sleep apnoea patients at a local clinic. As part of his master's course at the University of New South Wales, Dank was encouraged by his lecturers to get involved in high performance sport. Midway through the football season he wrote a letter to St George, asking if he could work at the club on a voluntary basis. He spent the rest of the season filling water bottles at training and doing other menial tasks. When the Dragons came back from their end-of-season break, Dank was offered a part-time job managing the rehab running program. It didn't pay much and the work was basic. Whenever a St George player tore a hamstring or a quad, it was Dank's job to make sure they stuck to the running regime designed by the physiotherapist. Dank took to the task with enthusiasm—perhaps too much. Before long, he was questioning the physio's instructions. Then he started offering a second opinion on the doctor's diagnoses. St George feared that if Dank stayed for much longer he'd be trying to coach the team. They decided he wasn't the right fit for the job. Dank, however, was hooked. He liked working with athletes. He could see that rugby league clubs were professional in name only and AFL clubs weren't much better, that their approach to training and recovery was amateurish. He could see opportunity abounds in both codes for someone who really knows his stuff, someone like him.

Kevin Norton taught Dank at the University of NSW and remembers him as one of his brightest students. While Dank was studying, the pair co-authored a paper on Barbie dolls. Their research question—comparing the proportions of life-sized Barbie and Ken dolls to average Australians—hardly suggests Dank was destined to become the nation's most notorious sports scientist. The next time Norton saw Dank was in Adelaide, many years later, when Dank was selling genetic testing to football clubs. The testing was crude. For $400 a pop, the tests claimed to determine whether a footballer was endowed with a greater spread of fast-twitch or slow-twitch muscle fibres and, therefore, more suited to sprinting or endurance running. Norton, a professor of exercise science at the University of South Australia, was called in by the Adelaide Crows to assess what Dank was selling. Dank didn't make a sale but he left a further impression on Norton.

'He was the sort of bloke where you'd enjoy his company and enjoy a beer with but you'd never invest any money with him,' Norton offers. 'I'd imagine he would be a great salesman. He is believable; he is knowledgeable. He probably embellishes the truth a little bit and doesn't have all the research necessary but he would convince you that he did.'[7]

ASADA boss Ben McDevitt's opinion is less forgiving. He draws a sinister caricature of unethical sports scientists preying on vulnerable athletes, 'plying their trade and their snake oil'.[8] Dank is a snake oil salesman, although perhaps not in the way that McDevitt implies. Selling snake oil carries the modern connotation of peddling worthless remedies, of being a charlatan. The original snake oil salesmen, the Chinese immigrants who worked on America's expanding railways in the nineteenth century, were nothing of the sort. Snake oil, the proper stuff extracted from Chinese water snakes, is rich in omega-3 fatty acids.[9] When rubbed on as a lotion, it can ease the pain of arthritis and other aches and pains. At the time of the railway boom, the Chinese had known this for three hundred-odd years. It was only when home-grown quacks started boiling up rattlesnake juice and selling the greasy residue as medicine that snake oil sellers got a bad name. Dank isn't a charlatan. He is a qualified biochemist, he knows pharmacology and he firmly believes the substances he peddles to professional athletes are good for them and helps them do their jobs. His essential flaw is to assume he is the smartest man in every room he enters. Listening to Dank, you'd think he knows more about medicine than doctors, more about litigation than lawyers and more about the World Anti-Doping Code than WADA. While working with Cronulla Sharks players in 2011, Dank oversees a program of injections that includes two banned peptides. Dank has privately admitted he gave Cronulla players these substances. His argument is that neither was banned at the time, that WADA didn't understand its own anti-doping code. They were, and WADA did. The Cronulla players pay a heavy price. On 22 August 2014, a dozen plead guilty to doping offences.

I first meet Stephen Dank about two months before the Cronulla plea deal. He walks into a Port Melbourne cafe well dressed and well tanned, with an air of permanent impatience, as if there are half a dozen places he needs to be. He calls me son, as he does nearly everyone. Most of his sentences are prefaced 'with all due respect', including those in which he intends none. He is charismatic, confident, fiercely intelligent, yet appears evasive. Throughout our hour-long discussion, his mobile phone intermittently intrudes. He takes the calls. He doesn't feel it necessary to apologise. He says he has documentation accounting for every substance taken at Essendon and can prove none of it was banned by WADA. He has been saying this for many months, to me and other journalists, to lawyers representing Essendon and Cronulla players suspected of doping. He promises that all will be revealed when he takes ASADA and the AFL to the Federal Court. He promises a lot.

The first time Danny Corcoran meets Dank he is unimpressed. It is 2010 and Corcoran is general manager of the Melbourne Rebels, a newly established Rugby Super 15 franchise. He has flown to Sydney to interview Dank for a job running the high-performance program at the Rebels. Corcoran has a list of about six candidates to talk to, including Dank, whom he has heard about through Dank's work at Manly. Corcoran doesn't know much about Dank but his record at the Sea Eagles is impressive—five consecutive finals series, two grand finals and a premiership. His punctuality is not. An hour after the time they've arranged to meet, Dank turns up wearing shorts. The interview lasts twenty minutes and both men deem it a waste of time. Corcoran needs someone to manage his high-performance staff; Dank is more interested in pursuing his own work.

'I didn't think he was suitable for that role at that time,' Corcoran says. 'He wasn't suitable to head up a high-performance operation. He said that himself; he wanted to be a consultant.'[10]

On 28 September 2011 Corcoran meets Dank for the second time. It is three days before the grand final, an event remembered as much for Meat Loaf murdering his greatest hits in the pre-match entertainment than Geelong beating Collingwood. Dank has flown to Melbourne to be interviewed by Essendon for a sports science job. Alongside Corcoran are Mark Thompson, James Hird, chief executive Ian Robson and football manager Paul Hamilton. They have mixed views about Dank. Thompson is impressed by his resume and passion for sport but not convinced a full-time job exists for him at Essendon. Corcoran is sceptical. He has read reports of Dank's use of exotic substances at Manly and has heard that Dank has fallen out with the former Manly coach, Des Hasler. When Corcoran asks Dank whether there is anything in his background relating to doping issues that could embarrass Essendon, Dank becomes defensive. Corcoran later urges Hamilton to 'check this bloke out'. To Hird, Corcoran offers his opinion and a quiet word of caution in the coach's ear: 'He's no good, this bloke.'[11]

Hird doesn't take Corcoran's advice. Hird is interested in Dank and his ideas. The sports scientist seems knowledgeable and experienced. As a footballer, Hird was fastidious in his approach to physical preparation, training and recovery. Such was his attention to detail that in the final years of his playing career he managed his own pre-season training away from the club, working to a tailored program devised by Corcoran and Essendon's long-serving conditioning coach John Quinn. Hird believes in the value of protein powders and other dietary supplements in a way that club doctor Bruce Reid does not. Dank's professed speciality, one vouched strongly for by Robinson, is recovery and, particularly, the use of supplements to help repair an athlete's body from the damage inflicted by matches and in training. According to the resume that Dank presents to Essendon, he has a Bachelor of Applied Sciences, majoring in biochemistry and microbiology, from the Queensland University of Technology and a master's qualification in pharmacology from the University of Sydney. He has worked in professional football, across the two rugby codes and the AFL, for a long time. He also talks a very good game, good enough to convince Hird. Reid does not sit in on the interview but, later, his many long conversations with Dank give him no cause to doubt his bona fides.

'I thought he was legit,' the doctor recalls. 'I had no reason not to think he was legit. I thought he was an expert in all sorts of things.'[12]

Hird isn't the only one on the interview panel impressed with Dank. Dean Robinson worked with Dank at Manly. They worked together, albeit briefly, at the Gold Coast Suns, another AFL club. Robinson knows what Dank can offer. He wants him on his high-performance staff. Hird says Robinson is insistent that he needs Dank to do his job.

'Dean was, "We must get him, I need the help. I don't have enough people to run the department, he's my friend, I've worked with him for a number of years and trust him to do a very good job."'[13] Robinson does not deny he wanted Dank to work with him at Essendon. Where his recollections differ from Hird is the enthusiasm shown by the senior coach for Dank's appointment. According to Robinson, Hird was 'jumping out of his skin' to get Dank.[14] Hird disputes this. This much, however, is clear: Robinson does not tell Essendon everything he knows about Dank. He does not tell them that Dank is his family peptide supplier.

When Robinson worked for the Gold Coast Suns, an AFL-owned expansion franchise in its first season in the national competition, he convinced the club to hire Dank as a sports science assistant. Although Dank's tenure at the Suns was short-lived—he was hired in November 2010 and sacked in February 2011—his involvement there informed several aspects of the Essendon and Cronulla doping scandals. The summer that Dank worked with the Suns, he commuted from Sydney. When he was required at the club's Carrara training base, he stayed with Dean and Tori Robinson at their Gold Coast home, sleeping on the couch. The Robinsons had been married for eight years. They had two young children and another two on the way. They were generous hosts, allowing Dank to come and go as he pleased. Robinson considered Dank a close friend. He respected his knowledge and trusted his judgement. During this time, Dank supplied both Dean and Tori Robinson with a peptide called CJC-1295.

CJC-1295 is named after a Canadian biochemical company, ConjuChem, which developed the substance in the mid 2000s for the treatment of obese AIDs patients. It was never approved as an AIDS drug but gained a cult black market following among body builders who believe it has anabolic properties. It has also been adopted by anti-ageing doctors as an elixir of youth. There is dispute over how CJC-1295 works but WADA believes it is a growth hormone-releasing peptide. As men reach mid life, they produce less and less growth hormone. Anti-ageing doctors believe peptides like CJC-1295 help to arrest this decline. When injected, the peptide is said to stimulate the pituitary, a gland the size of a pea at the base of the brain. In response, the anterior lobe of the pituitary releases growth hormone into the blood stream. As the hormones circulate, they help strengthen bones and muscle, repair skin and provide a younger man's deep, uninterrupted sleep. They also trigger a chemical reaction in the liver, which responds by secreting insulin-like GF-1, an anabolic agent. For this reason, WADA does not allow athletes to use CJC-1295.

Robinson is not an athlete. Under the WADA rules in force at the time, he can take any peptide he likes. He takes the vials of CJC-1295 supplied by Dank and injects the contents into the skin of his abdomen. He believes the peptide will make him feel young and strong. But under WADA rules, under the AFL anti-doping code, Dank cannot supply CJC-1295 to Robinson. Not if it is banned. Once Dank is on staff at any football club he is considered an athlete support person. A support person who provides another person with a banned substance can be found guilty of trafficking, a serious anti-doping offence.[15] Corcoran says that if anyone at Essendon knew about Robinson's use of banned peptides, he wouldn't have been employed.

'You can't have in that environment a person who is prepared even in their personal life to go to those. Particularly when they are around young men. I think Hirdy, in his naivety, his rush for success, led him to believe we need to do something quick. I don't think he knew what he was dealing with in Robinson and he definitely didn't know what he was dealing with in Dank.'[16]

When Robinson is promoting Dank for the Essendon job, he also knows the sports scientist has supplied CJC-1295 to Nathan Bock, a star recruit for the Gold Coast Suns. An All Australian defender, Bock was lured to the Suns after a long career with Adelaide. He arrived in late 2010 ahead of the club's first season in the AFL but, before Christmas, his preparations are cruelled by injury. Dank suggested he try a series of amino acid injections. On 14 December, Dank allegedly arrived at the Robinsons' house carrying a styrofoam box packed with vials, dry ice and syringes. Dank told Robinson that the vials contained CJC-1295. He assured him that the substance is permitted by WADA. Two days later, Bock came to the house. Robinson prepared a needle for himself, showing Bock how to inject the peptide into a fold of skin. Bock was told to inject himself twice a week. He later paid Robinson $800 for the peptides. When ASADA investigated the case, Bock confirmed that he injected himself with whatever was in the vials. ASADA has since made clear its view CJC-1295 was banned at the time but, inexplicably, it has taken no action against Bock or Robinson. An AFL tribunal eventually found that Dank attempted to traffick CJC-1295 to Robinson. However, due to the unknown provenance of this and other substances supplied by Dank throughout the doping scandal, the tribunal was not convinced that whatever Bock injected was in fact CJC-1295.

Questions asked of Essendon's lack of due diligence in hiring Dank can similarly be asked of the Suns. When the Gold Coast terminated Dank's contract, the reason given had nothing to do with the substances he was administering Bock or any other Suns player. They dumped him because they suspected Dank was offering his services to their cross-town rivals, the Brisbane Lions, when he was on the Gold Coast payroll, an allegation Dank denies. Had Robinson told Essendon about all this, about the peptides and the personal use and the treatment of Bock, the Essendon doping scandal may well have been averted. Instead, Dank is hired on a handshake and $100,000 salary. Among his job responsibilities is WADA compliance.[17] The irony is not apparent at the time.

In early November 2011, Dank begins work at Essendon. Although there is disagreement over his precise job description he is hired principally to do three things: manage the recovery of players, manage the nutrition of players, and analyse Global Positioning System (GPS) data collected from monitors strapped to players during training and matches. It soon becomes clear that Dank has a different view of what his job is.

'He was supposed to do the GPS and he kept turning up to the ground forgetting equipment and results,' Thompson says. 'We didn't use any of his stuff for the first three months because he was so disorganised. We had to employ someone else to do the GPS, which we employed him to do. He was supposed to do the food, all the food the players were supposed to be eating pre- and post-training and on interstate trips. We had to employ someone else to do that. What we thought we were getting, we weren't getting.'[18] Jarrod Wade is given responsibility for GPS analysis. Dank becomes the club's full-time recovery guru.

The peptides at the centre of the doping scandal at Essendon and Cronulla are referred to as supplements. What happened at Essendon became known as the supplement scandal and Dank's ill-fated regime of injections as a supplements program. These are misnomers. Dietary supplements have been used at professional football clubs since the 1970s. For many seasons, Essendon was sponsored by Musashi, a global manufacturer and supplier of protein-rich supplements designed to assist weight training. Throughout these years, Reid was sceptical of the benefits. He considers supplements an extension of nutrition. 'Hirdy knows I'm a doubter. I believe in iron when you're iron deficient, I believe in

B12 when you are deficient.'[19] What happens at Essendon in 2012 has nothing to do with nutrition.

Reid's concerns about the direction Essendon is taking begin on the first day of pre-season training. In keeping with time-honoured ritual, the players are welcomed back from holidays with a gut-busting running session. The venue is the home of Collingwood Harriers, an athletics club in Melbourne's inner north. The synthetic running track is nestled in a loop of Merri Creek, surrounded by gum trees. It is a picturesque setting but there is nothing pleasant about the training session that Robinson has planned. To help the players through it, he asks one of his staff, Paul Turk, to give each a dose of Tribulus Forte.

Tribulus is a herbal supplement made from *Tribulus terrestris*, a plant commonly known as Bindy. In Australia, the plant is considered a noxious weed and grows like one, even in drought conditions. Tribulus was first used as a sports supplement by Bulgarian weightlifters who believed the plant had metabolic properties that increased testosterone, strength and lean muscle mass. Some manufacturers also claim it enhances sexual performance. It is not banned by WADA because there is no accepted scientific evidence that it actually works. It has been used by AFL clubs for at least fifteen years.

When Reid sees Turk handing out pills, he intervenes.

'Why are you doing that?' he asks the newly hired conditioning coach. Turk replies that Robinson has asked him to give two each to the players. The doctor is incredulous.

'What the shit are they? No one has passed it by me.'[20] Reid doesn't believe Tribulus is harmful. He remembers John Quinn, Essendon's fitness coach during the Kevin Sheedy era, advocating it years earlier. But he is sufficiently concerned about its WADA status to call Peter Harcourt, the AFL's chief medical officer, and explain what has happened. Harcourt assures him it is not banned, although he doesn't encourage its use. Not for the last time, Reid tells Robinson that he must get approval from medical staff before giving any new substances to players.

The Tribulus episode tells us three things. The first is that Reid, Essendon's club doctor for more than thirty years, knows from the outset of Essendon's 2012 campaign that Robinson is willing to give the players a therapeutic substance he had not approved. The second is Robinson knows Reid is an impediment to the cultural shift at Essendon he has been hired to implement. The third is the AFL, through Harcourt, has information in November 2011 that Essendon's newly assembled high-performance department is marginalising the club's medical staff.

Reid and Harcourt have differing recollections about the timing of the conversation and precisely what was said. Nonetheless, as an experienced sports physician, Harcourt should be alarmed that AFL players are being given a substance without the knowledge of their club doctor. The growing influence of sports scientists at clubs is already a hot button issue within AFL medical circles. In April 2012, the AFL distributes to the clubs a survey of fourteen club doctors in which half the respondents say non-qualified personnel have exerted undue influence on medical decisions. Two years after the Tribulus episode, Peter Harcourt delivers a presentation about the Essendon scandal to a FIFA anti-doping conference in Zurich. Looking over the top of his glasses and clicking through the overhead slides, Harcourt notes the passive acceptance of the Essendon players towards Dank's supplement regime.

'This shocked us—the players did not jack up and say what the hell is going on?' The same might be said of Harcourt after he received the call from Reid. In the same presentation, Harcourt indicates he knows that ASADA has sent urine samples from AFL players to Germany to test for banned peptides. Could the AFL have done more to prevent what happened at Essendon? Reid thinks so.

'They owe a duty of care to the players and the parents,' he says. 'They are the governing body. I feel they have let the players down and their parents down and, personally, they have let me down. I felt the AFL gave me nothing.'[21]

Reid soon has further cause to question how Robinson is running the show. A few weeks later, he discovers that the new high-performance manager, without consulting anyone on Essendon's medical staff, has taken nine players who had torn muscles the previous season to an off-site osteopath. Reid is furious.

'There is no communication with the physio or doctor,' he recalls. 'There is no referral letter. There are no MRI results. There is no knowledge by us that the players are going there. I hit the roof.' Reid calls a meeting with Robinson and senior football department officials in the Windy Hill match committee room. 'I said he can be my boss but from now on, anything medical I'm in charge. Well, he stormed out. He said that is against my contract.'[22]

Reid is incensed that players are being sent to have their backs cracked without any consultation with him or discussion of their medical histories. As Reid explains, this is fundamental to practising medicine.

'You do not refer people off without notes and knowledge and investigation history. You know, it is history, examination, special investigations, opinion. That's drilled into us. It's drilled into us when we're junior residents—history, examinations, special investigations, refer if you don't know.'[23] Osteopathy involves spinal and muscular manipulations. Scott Gumbleton, one of the Essendon players sent by Robinson to see the osteopath without a medical referral, has a history of back injuries. Shortly after Gumbleton's visit to the osteopath he undergoes back surgery and does not play a senior game for eight months. He is traded to Fremantle at the end of 2013 and is now retired from league football.

Bruce Reid remembers clearly the day James Hird comes to him with a serious health concern and the most outrageous suntan he has ever seen. It is late 2011, Reid has just returned from an overseas trip and Hird from a family holiday in Queensland. For many years, James and Tania Hird have taken their kids to stay at the Hyatt resort in Coolum, a once idyllic, family retreat endangered by nickel magnate Clive Palmer's decision to buy the hotel and populate its grounds with enormous, model dinosaurs. Usually, Hird comes back from these trips relaxed and ready for another football season. This time, he is glowing an unnatural shade of orange and deeply worried.

'He looks like a Fijian,' Reid says. 'He said I have had this stuff for sleep.'[24]

Hird regularly took sleeping pills throughout his playing career. In his 2007 autobiography Hird explains he never slept well during the football season. The night before games, it was not unusual for him to be lying awake at 3 a.m., stressing about the next day's match.[25] It is a common affliction among footballers, many of whom become addicted to the pills readily prescribed by club doctors. It is more than anxiety, however, that keeps Hird from sleeping. On a hot Perth afternoon on 4 May 2002, Hird collided with teammate Mark McVeigh with a force that changed him forever. In a desperate lunge to prevent his opponent, Fremantle's Matthew Pavlich, from beating him to the ball, Hird lost his footing and pitched face-first into McVeigh's knee. The impact fractured Hird's face in seven places and dented his skull. The scars from Hird's extensive reconstructive surgery are barely visible today but, beneath the skin, his face is scaffolded by a series of titanium plates. Those plates give him neuralgia, a stabbing, burning pain. It is this pain that keeps him awake at night.

Bruce Reid usually prescribes Temazepan to help Hird sleep. On occasion, the club doctor has had to administer Hird pethidine and morphine injections to numb the pain. In the countdown to Christmas 2011, Reid is away and Hird's script for Temazepan runs out. One day at the club, the coach mentions his sleeping difficulties to Robinson. Robinson says he has something that Hird can take that will help him sleep and lose weight.

'Well, I don't need to strip weight obviously but if you can help me sleep I'll think about it,' Hird says.[26] According to Hird, Robinson says the substance is Melatonin, a hormone used to treat insomnia. He gives Essendon's coach a small vial, some needles and shows him how to inject it into a fold of stomach skin.

Hird injects himself with the drug for five or six days. He sleeps as well as he ever has. He stops taking it when he flies to Queensland for his family holiday. After a few days in the sun he notices his skin has turned a bizarre hue and moles on his back are darkening. When Hird gets back to the club he explains to Reid what has happened. According to Reid, Hird withholds a crucial detail: that he injected the substance Robinson gave him rather than merely ingested it. This is not Hird's recollection. Regardless, Reid doesn't understand why Hird would take anything supplied by Robinson.

'I think Hirdy is mad, of course I think that,' the doctor says. 'What the fuck are they doing?'[27]

ASADA's investigators, after interviewing Robinson and Hird and other officials at Essendon, suspect Hird was given Melanotan II, a peptide used by body builders as a tanning agent, and not Melatonin. The insinuation is that Hird took the substance not to sleep but to look better on the beach, and he lied about it. Neither substance is banned by ASADA for use by athletes or support staff and, normally, neither would be of any interest to anti-doping investigators. In the case of Essendon, ASADA sees Dank and Robinson's administration of Melanotan II and other peptides to coaches and support staff as indicative of a disturbing culture at Windy Hill. This culture, 'the injection mentality' as Essendon football manager Paul Hamilton describes it, becomes central to ASADA's investigations. In the case of Hird, the revelation that Essendon's senior coach injected himself with an exotic substance is personally damaging and embarrassing.

To this day, Hird cannot say for sure what he took but insists it was given to him as Melatonin. The evidence about what it was is mixed. Melatonin was used at Essendon in 2012. Vials of Melatonin prescribed to Dank by Robin Willcourt, a Melbourne-based anti-ageing doctor, were recovered by ASADA at Windy Hill. No physical trace of Melanotan II was found at the club but other Essendon staff, including Robinson, testified to being injected with it. The substance taken by Hird helped him sleep, consistent with the primary use of Melatonin. The side effect he experienced is consistent with Melanotan II. Reid is circumspect about the episode and what Hird told him.

'I believed him at the time,' he says. 'I had no reason not to. But he didn't mention injections.'[28]

Throughout the 2012 season, Dank's office serves as a one-shot stop for club officials looking for a deeper tan, a little extra pep, to lose a few kilos or lift a few more in the gym. Some of the substances administered by Dank are permitted by WADA. Two of them are banned. There is nothing under the World Anti-Doping Code at the time preventing Essendon staff from taking performance-enhancing drugs but it is naive and foolish for anyone working at a professional football club to dabble in a banned substance. That Essendon staff are willing to sample Dank's wares shows the trust they have in him and the intoxicating promise of what he is offering: improved health, looks and vitality with the prick of a syringe. Dank says he openly treated Essendon coaches as part of his program,[29] but what went on inside his office at Windy Hill was secretive. Corcoran says he is 'blown away'[30] when, after Dank leaves, he discovers what has gone on. Thompson says it was stupid. It also sent a disastrously mixed message to Dank. Later in the 2012 season, when Essendon officials including Thompson are ordering Dank to stop injecting players, staff members are still lining up for a jab.

'It was just careless,' Thompson says. 'That sort of stuff, people just didn't have their eyes open. I didn't have my eyes open, obviously. It was poor. Having that many staff treated by him was just a dumb and stupid thing to do. By all parties.'[31] As for the Essendon players, they didn't know Essendon staff were being treated by Dank but they did notice something odd going on. As club officials show up to work with luminescent tans, the players start joking about Oompa Loompas at Windy Hill, in reference to Roald Dahl's tangerine-coloured factory workers in *Charlie and the Chocolate Factory*. There is no evidence that Dank sought to profit from this. The peptides injected into Essendon staff appear to have been mostly freebies. For the club and individual staff involved, the visits to Dank's basement office come at a later cost.

Robinson, in addition to being Dank's boss, is a return peptide customer. Having already administered himself with the growth hormone-boosting CJC-1295 while at the Gold Coast Suns, the high-performance manager injects himself with two peptides supplied by Dank; AOD-9604 and Melanotan II, the tanning agent Robinson says he gave to Hird. Suki Hobson, a UK-born strength and conditioning expert, trained aspiring Olympians at the Australian Institute of Sport before working with Geelong and Essendon. At Dank's suggestion she injects herself with Hexarelin, a growth hormone releasing peptide. Hobson says it comes about by chance. It was in early February 2012, when the pre-season training program was nearly complete. The summer months are Hobson's busiest time of the year and she found herself joking with Dank about the irony of being a conditioning coach; when the players are at their fittest, you feel exhausted.

'I might be able to help you with that,' Dank replied. He suggested she try Hexarelin.

Hobson is no mug footballer. She is a qualified sports scientist from her university days at Leeds in the United Kingdom. She understands physiology. She hadn't heard of Hexarelin but listened as Dank explained the properties of the peptide, how it stimulated the natural production of growth hormone, how this helped to repair and regenerate the body. It didn't occur to her that the substance was banned by WADA. She agreed to try it. Dank gave her a small, clear glass vial marked only with a handwritten label: Hexarelin. She took it home and stored it in her kitchen fridge. For the next twenty days she administered the peptide to herself, taking a fold of stomach skin between her finger and thumb on one hand and injecting it with the other. The peptide didn't seem to do much but her science training kicked in. She kept a diary, carefully noting the days on which she injected herself, recording any changes in mood or health. After three weeks, she could discern no difference. It was only weeks later, when she was talking to Robinson's wife Tori, that she learned Hexarelin is supposed to be dispensed with a doctor's prescription. Concerned, she turned to the internet. Within a few clicks she realised she'd been taking a banned substance.

'I never even thought about whether it was banned' she says. 'Looking back now, how stupid can you be?'[32]

Dank offered Hexarelin to another of Robinson's high-performance staff, Paul Turk. When Turk is interviewed by ASADA, he tells them he knew nothing about Hexarelin before the release of the ACC report.[33] ASADA is sceptical of Turk's evidence. He is recalled to a second interview and asked to explain this text message exchange with Dank on 1 April 2012:

> Dank: Hi mate. Ended up watching Western Bulldogs and West Coast. I am following West Coast for a few weeks as I think they are the team to beat. So I wanted to study them. If you want some Hexarelin and you are going back to the club after the reserves, text me when you are back at the club.
>
> Turk: OK sweet mate … on way back now … r u about?
>
> Dank: Yes mate. Let me know when you are in.
>
> Turk: At the club now.
>
> Dank: On my way.

During his second interview with ASADA, Turk admits the SMS exchange looks terrible but he insists he didn't know what Hexarelin was and still doesn't. He says he took no notice when Dank mentioned it in the text message.[34] ASADA is still not convinced by this explanation, particularly when the SMS exchange is read in the context of a text sent a week earlier by Turk to another Essendon coach, Justin Crow, after he'd checked out a local gym: 'Heaps of steroid monsters … there's plenty of Danksy juice getting around.'

The text message, although colourful, doesn't prove that Turk knew Dank was supplying banned drugs. Like Robinson, Turk is entitled to take whatever peptides he wants. However, Turk's responsibilities at Essendon extend beyond his personal use of training supplements. During the 2012 season, he was paid part of his club salary to live with and supervise some of Essendon's younger players in a shared house. Their parents would blanch at the idea of performance enhancing peptides being kept in the fridge.

At Windy Hill, the Danksy juice flows to coaches, administrative staff and even the property steward. Simon Goodwin was an assistant coach at Essendon. He is a celebrated figure at Adelaide, where he played 275 games, and highly regarded by Melbourne, the club that poached him from Essendon at the end of the 2013 season as an understudy to senior coach Paul Roos. He is quizzed at length by ASADA about a series of text messages he sends to Dank in 2012. On 28 June: 'Don't forget the good gear today buddy.' On 4 July: 'Don't forget the good gear mate.' On 10 July: 'Bring some of the good stuff in buddy.' What was the Goodwin good stuff?

Goodwin says Dank described it to him only as vitamins and amino acids. He maintains he doesn't know what the amino acids were.[35] Goodwin also took Melanotan II. At the time, he was living with Xavier Campbell, an Essendon manager and a future club chief executive. Goodwin tells Campbell about Melanotan II. Then he gives him some, showing him how to inject it into a pinch of skin.

Carmelo Gervasi, a volunteer property steward, gets to know Dank in February 2012 when Essendon are in Perth for a pre-season game against the West Coast Eagles. Gervasi and Dank share a room and hit it off. Gervasi tells the sports scientist about himself. He mentions that he sometimes wishes he had a little more energy. Dank says he has something back in Melbourne that might help. When they are back at Windy Hill, Dank injects Gervasi with a Selective Androgen Receptor Modulator. SARMs are used by gym junkies as a safer alternative to steroids. They are banned by WADA. They are also renowned as a powerful aphrodisiac. Gervasi becomes a regular visitor to Dank's office.

ASADA suspects Hird was given Hexarelin by Dank. This is based not on text messages secured by the investigators but interviews given by Dank to two journalists in April 2013. In an off-camera comment, Dank tells ABC *7.30*'s Caro Meldrum-Hanna that he injected Hird with Hexarelin twice a week for much of the 2012 season.[36] He repeats the claim in an on-the-record interview with Nick McKenzie, a journalist with *The Age* newspaper in Melbourne.[37] Hird denies the allegation publicly and during his interview with ASADA. Dank has never withdrawn the allegation; Hird has been consistent in his denials. Like Goodwin, Hird says he was injected with an unspecified amino acid by Dank when, in March 2012, the senior coach was seriously ill. Some mornings he struggled to get out of bed. Some afternoons, he had to pull his car over on the way home from Essendon's training ground to his Toorak house and rest before he could complete the journey home. Reid had twice ordered blood tests and found nothing amiss. When Hird mentioned all this to Dank, the sports scientist says the coach's immune system was probably depleted and suggested Hird try an injection of amino acids. Hird agreed. He says he receives two injections in total and claims the accusation he took Hexarelin is 'an absolute out and out lie'.[38]

The only Essendon official other than Hobson who admits to being injected with Hexarelin is Sue Anderson. Anderson is part of the Essendon football department but she isn't a coach or a member of the high-performance staff. As an administrative co-ordinator, her job concerns more immediate tasks: making travel arrangements for coaches and players, making sure the families of players get the tickets they need to see their boys play, working through a succession of mostly thankless duties that are essential to keeping a football club happy and harmonious. She has worked at Essendon for seven years. She is well liked and valued at the club.

For anyone at Essendon concerned about diet or body weight, Dank was an obvious person to talk to. He is introduced around Windy Hill as an expert in nutrition. He is running the club's supplement program. When Anderson decides she'd like to lose a few kilos, she goes to see Dank. He is happy to help. He says he has just the thing for her. He shows her a little brown vial and explains that if she takes it regularly it will help her lose weight and give her more energy. Anderson isn't worried about needles. In Dank's basement office, the sports scientist pierces a syringe through the rubber cap on the bottle and shows Anderson how to inject it. Anderson doesn't ask many questions. She trusts Dank in the same way she would trust Bruce Reid, the club doctor. She takes the vial home and over the next few weeks, injects herself a couple of times. When the bathroom scales tell her the treatment is having no effect she stops. She doesn't think about it again until the blackest day in Australian sport arrives. Then she remembers the label on the bottle.

The Danksy juice flows beyond Essendon staff. Across town at Princes Park, home to the Carlton Football Club, John Donehue is the tackling coach. He is a prominent instructor in mixed martial arts, the boom sport that now rivals the NFL for popularity in the United States, and a highly sought-after bodyguard for visiting dignitaries and celebrities. He is also recovering more slowly than he'd like from shoulder surgery. Donehue can't do his job with his arm in a sling. He gets in touch with Dank, whom he knows from his previous work at AFL and NRL clubs. According to ASADA, Dank supplies him with a buffet of banned substances: growth hormone, SARMs, Hexarelin, Mechano Growth Factor and CJC-1295. Another client of Dank's is John Deeble, the coach of Australia's national baseball team and a regional scout for the Boston Red Sox. Deeble, a near unhittable left-handed pitcher in his playing days, has been retired from the game for ten years. He is introduced to Dank when he goes to Essendon to talk to the club about recruiting. When he explains to the sports scientist that he has got a chronic knee injury, Dank suggests he try a couple of peptide creams. In March 2012, Dank mails to Deeble a cream containing Hexarelin and another containing CJC-1295. When Deeble checks the substances with a sports doctor, he urges him to send the products back. ASADA investigators accept Deeble's explanation that he didn't use the peptides or pass them on to anyone else.

Coaching staff who used banned substances before 1 January 2015 did not breach the World Anti-Doping Code. Under changes to anti-doping laws introduced by WADA, they would now. However, it was an anti-doping offence then, as it is now, for Dank to supply banned drugs to anyone while he was employed as a sports scientist at Gold Coast or Essendon. In 2012, the mandatory penalty for a first-time trafficking or related violation is a four-year ban from sport. A repeat offender can be banned for life. Of ASADA's thirty-four anti-doping charges against Dank, all but seven relate to his dealings with coaches at Essendon, Gold Coast, Carlton and the Australian baseball team. When Suki Hobson walks into the ASADA interview room on 21 February 2013, the investigation into Essendon is just two weeks old. By the time she walks out, they have Stephen Dank.

4

WHAT'S IN THAT BLOODY DRUG?

AUSTRALIA IS ON holiday. At the beach. Gone bush. Watching the cricket. At the WACA Ground in Perth, Dave Warner is at play. He bats like the hero of a kid's summer daydream, pounding good balls into the fence, launching bad ones into a sunburnt crowd. The Indian bowlers trudge back to their marks, resigned to their fate. They hate this little man with his Popeye forearms and breeze-block bat. In Melbourne, the tennis will soon start, with its baseline rhythms and brassy stars. At AFL clubs, football is already back to work, the remaining weeks of the pre-season a countdown to the first match of the year. At Windy Hill, the training is intense. Dean Robinson and his high-performance staff are driving the players harder than they have ever experienced. The Weapon is rebuilding Essendon from the boots up; massive leg weights for strength and power, lung-busting hypoxic training to improve endurance. The players are responding; the coaches are pleased with what they are seeing. Bruce Reid is not.

A week into 2012, Reid returns from his summer break on the Murray River to rumours that, since before Christmas, the club's sports scientist Stephen Dank has been injecting Essendon players with AOD-9604. Reid remembers Dank talking about this substance but he hasn't approved its use. He hasn't read about it. He doesn't even know if it is permitted under the World Anti-Doping Code. Reid is alarmed by what is happening at Essendon. Robinson's push to use Actovegin, the Tribulus episode, unapproved visits to an osteopath and now unauthorised injections of God knows what. Reid feels he is being deliberately marginalised. He only works part time at the club. He can't keep up with what's going on if people are intent on going around him. For the first time in thirty years, he wonders if he can remain club doctor.

Reid takes his concerns to James Hird. He also goes to see Mark Thompson. Neither is in charge of the football department but they are the dominant personalities at the club. A Sunday meeting is called, an intervention planned. Hird and Thompson are there from the coaching staff, Robinson and Dank from the high-performance team, along with Reid and football manager Paul Hamilton. The mood is tense. There are denials and conflicting accounts of what has taken place. The divide between the medical and high-performance staff is laid bare. Whatever has happened at Essendon, it is clear that people haven't been talking. No one seems to be in charge. But amid the confusion a consensus emerges. For the first time, Dank and Robinson talk in detail about the treatments they want to give the players, the substances they have in mind. Dank assures Reid and the coaches that AOD-9604 is approved by WADA and safe to give the players. Thompson says the meeting, by its end, is strangely productive.

'It worked out that they had all these plans,' he says. 'We didn't know what their plans were. We sat down, we heard all their plans, what they wanted to do. Out of that, there was a supplement they wanted to use, AOD-9604. We wanted proof that it was safe to use.'[1]

A protocol is agreed to. The rules about supplements at Essendon are made clear: any new substance to be used at Essendon must not contravene the World Anti-Doping Code, must not be harmful to the players and must be approved by Dr Reid. Before he can approve any substance, Reid must be provided its common and scientific name, a summary of the literature about it including possible side effects, a statement from Dank that the substance does not contravene any WADA guidelines and any further information he needs. Once Reid has this information, he will consider it and report his decision back to Hird, Robinson and Dank. Before any player can be administered with a new supplement, they must sign a letter of consent. The program is not mandatory and players can refuse supplements at any time. If they do take part, they must agree not to talk about the program to anyone outside Essendon, to protect the club's competitive advantage.

The protocol appears sound at the time yet its weakness is now glaring. Essendon believes Dank has been injecting footballers with a substance without medical authorisation, a substance for which no one has seen WADA approval. Yet the new supplements protocol maintains Dank as the club's WADA gatekeeper. So long as the club doctor is content that a supplement is not potentially harmful, anti-doping compliance rests on the word of Dank. Reid writes the new rules out in pencil. Robinson types them up and emails them to all parties. Hird is satisfied with the protocol and sends Robinson a short note in reply:

> Sounds good Deano, You know my thoughts on supplements.
> 1   It must not harm the player.
> 2   It must not be illegal (according to WADA and the AFL drug guidelines).
> 3   We must get player consent.
> As long as we stick to those guidelines and you and Steve think it will help us then lets go for it.
> See you tomorrow.
>
> Hirdy.[2]

Reid is far from satisfied. Later that day, he starts researching AOD-9604. He discovers it is a fragment of growth hormone developed to combat obesity and diabetes. Its main purpose seems to be reducing belly fat; not something elite footballers need. The substance is still in development. Reid can't find any record of Therapeutic Goods Administration approval. An internet search takes him on a disturbing tangent, to body building sites and forums where gym junkies extol the virtues of the peptide. This is unfamiliar, uncomfortable territory for Reid. He has seen enough; the injections must stop.

On the Tuesday morning he returns to work at his private practice. He calls in his personal assistant Joan and says he needs to dictate a letter. It is addressed to Paul Hamilton, the Essendon football manager and Robinson and Dank's boss, and James Hird. The letter is rough. Reid is animated, talking faster than Joan can type. There are typos and words missing. Yet with each paragraph, the doctor's frustration is evident:

Dear Paul/James,

I have some fundamental problems being club doctor at present.
This particularly applies to the administration of supplements.
Although we have been giving supplements for approximately three months, despite repeated requests as to what exactly we are giving our players and the literature related to this, have at no time been given that until last Sunday. Last week the players were given subcutaneous injections, not by myself, and I had no idea that this was happening and also the drug that was involved.
It appears to me that in Sydney with Rugby League the clubs do not answer to the governing body (e.g. A.F.L). It seems that their whole culture is based on trying to beat the system as are close to the edge as one can. It is my belief in A.F.L that we should be winning flags by keeping a drug free culture.
It is all very well to say this is not banned and that is not banned but for example, the injection that we have given our players subcutaneously, was a drug called AOD/9604, is an

Oligomeric Peptide. This drug is derived from the growth hormone. The molecule has been constructed so it has removed what we call IGF-1, which is part of the growth hormone that causes muscle and organ growth and bone length and photosynthesis.

It is at the moment used for fat metabolism but also bone strength in children and may have some side effects that may be beneficial in bone growth. This to me just seem ludicrous at this stage where the only trials I have got are on how to lost weight and fat around the abdomen.

If we are resorting to deliver this altered growth hormone molecule, I think we are playing at the edge and this will read extremely badly in the press for our club and for the benefits and also for side effects that are not known in the long term, I have trouble with all these drugs.

I am still not sure whether AOD/9604 is approved by the drug authorities in Australia at this stage. Just because it is not classified as illegal, doesn't mean that it can be used freely in the community, it cannot. The other interesting thing about AOD/9604 is that its market in America is body builders. This also should raise a red flag if we are worried about perception.

When it comes to Actovegin, this has been used around the world for many years. There is some flimsy evidence that it may help in speeding up the healing of tendons when they are damaged, though after speaking to radiologists, the recent opinion is that platelets and one's own blood, probably does a better job.

We are claiming that we should use it as a recovery agent. To me it seems ludicrous that a few mls of calf's blood spun down, is going to give you a concentration of growth factors and other factors that would speed up recovery.

I am frustrated by this and now feel I am letting the club down by not automatically approving of these things. I need to collect my thoughts as these drugs have been given without my knowledge.

I am sure Steve Danks believes that what we are doing is totally ethical and legal, however, one wonders whether if you take a long stance and look at this from a distance, whether you would want your children being injected with a derivative hormone that is not free to the community and whether calf's blood, that has been used for many years and is still doubted by most doctors, is worth pursuing.

Kind Regards

Dr Bruce Reid
M.B.B.S.
Senior Medical Officer[3]

What happens next shows the dysfunction within Essendon that allows Dank's work to expand into something that ends careers, threatens others, engulfs a football competition and unleashes a series of corrosive forces.

Reid prints out two copies of his letter. One he keeps. The other he takes to the club. He walks into the office of Hamilton, the man in charge of the Essendon football department, and puts it on his desk. It is the last that anyone at Essendon remembers seeing it until the night of Hird's birthday dinner, more than a year later.

Hamilton is well liked at Essendon. He is one of theirs. He went to school at the local Catholic boy's college and played more than a hundred games for the Bombers. His playing career dovetailed with Hird's, in 1992, when Hamilton was playing out his final season at Essendon, and Hird was playing his first. He played between premiership eras, his one grand final appearance for Essendon climaxing with an all-in brawl and ending in an eight-goal flogging by Collingwood. At a time when such a positions still existed, Hamilton was a back pocket player in a team of more famous names—Tim Watson and Paul Van Der Haar, the Daniher brothers, Simon Madden, Paul Salmon and another local kid who would captain the club to its next flag, Mark Thompson.

Football then wasn't a full-time job. Throughout the week, Hamilton worked for an insurance company. His area of speciality was WorkCover, administering claims of people injured at work and advising employers about their responsibilities. With tertiary qualifications in commerce and international business, a lucrative career beckoned away from football but he couldn't give up the game. A coaching stint in Tasmania led to one in South Australia and, eventually, brought him back to the big league, at North Melbourne then the Adelaide Crows. In 2008, he returned to Windy Hill as general manager of football operations. Essendon was a football club, if not in turmoil, then in dramatic transition. James Hird, the teenage boy he brushed past sixteen years earlier, had achieved it all and played his last game. Kevin Sheedy, Hamilton's old coach at Essendon, had just been shown the door, politely but firmly. Matthew Knights, an untried senior coach, was the new face in the senior coach's office. He was bequeathed the impossible task of following a legend.

Hamilton has been running the Essendon football department for three seasons when Hird and Thompson, heroes of Windy Hill, return to the club. Hird brings Danny Corcoran with him. Corcoran is twenty years older than Hamilton and more experienced as a football and sports administrator. He was doing Hamilton's job at Essendon when Hamilton was still a player and had done the same job at Melbourne and he had run Athletics Australia. It did not take long for Hamilton to realise that the new senior coach and Thompson, Hird's influential assistant, want Corcoran back in charge. Hamilton is a smart, capable administrator but, as a manager, he lacks authority. He knows Hird and Thompson are undermining his position but he is unable or unwilling to protect his turf.

'The moment I walked into Essendon I could see that it wasn't set up properly,' Thompson says. 'No one was managing. Everyone was just allowed to do their own thing. Who pulled up Stuey?[4] Who got the high-performance manager and coach in front of each other to sort it all out? There was no presence there. So Dean

Robinson comes in and, my God, if you employ this man you have got to manage him because he will look for a hole in the fence and he will go out and run all night. I don't know how many times Hirdy and I told Evans and Robson that he [Hamilton] is not the right man. It ended up costing us. He was too compliant. We would have preferred if he walked in and said no, I'm footy manager, everything has got to come through me.'[5]

At the end of the 2011 season, club chief executive Ian Robson sits down with Hamilton and Corcoran to define their respective jobs. The result is a recipe for overlapping responsibilities and administrative chaos. Hamilton is to remain general manager of football operations, Corcoran accepts the nebulous title of people and development manager. Hamilton is given responsibility for reporting to the chief executive, overseeing player contracts and managing player payments, senior football staff and public relations. He is also responsible for dealing with the AFL and player welfare. Corcoran is to manage eight football department staff and assist Robinson and Hird in their duties. He is supposed to mentor Hird, assist both Hird and Robinson, liaise with fitness and coaching staff and help manage the playing list and player payments. He is also responsible for players' welfare. In practice, it means while Hamilton is managing up, Corcoran is managing down. Hamilton is the boss of the football department but not all its staff. Corcoran is to work closely with Hird and Robinson but isn't the boss of either. When prominent corporate director Ziggy Switkowski is commissioned by Essendon chairman David Evans to review the club's governance failings, he portrays the football department as a managerial basket case:

> In particular, there was a lack of clarity about who was in charge of the football department. There were two separate roles, with fuzzy lines of responsibility. The responsibilities of two key staff overlapped, and the new fitness team was able to largely ignore their attempts at direct management. Added to this is a senior coach in his first coaching role.[6]

Into this black hole of football bureaucracy, Bruce Reid's letter disappears. Hamilton does not recall reading the letter but remembers a meeting with Reid in which the club doctor made clear his concerns about what was going on with the club's use of supplements. He says he was sufficiently worried about what the doctor told him that he reported it immediately to chief executive Ian Robson.[7] Robson says he has no recollection of Hamilton doing this or of seeing Reid's letter. He maintains no one raised with him any concerns about substances being given to players before the scandal broke.[8] Hird encouraged Reid to write the letter but didn't read it. The discrepancy between Hamilton and Robson remains unresolved. Hamilton quits Essendon at the end of the 2012 season; Robson resigns in May 2013, two weeks after the release of the Switkowski report. Neither has spoken publicly about what went on at Windy Hill.[9] Paul Hamilton says he has a clear conscience;[10] Robson says he accepts responsibility for his and the club's failings.[11] As for Corcoran, throughout much of this his mind was far removed from the problems of Windy Hill.

Danny Corcoran remembers the day football was no longer important. It is Sunday, 2 October 2011, the day after the AFL grand final. Maxine, his wife of thirty-three years, has just returned home from training her athletics squad. She says something isn't quite right, that she doesn't feel good. On the drive home, she struggled to keep the car on the road. Everything was off-balance, out of kilter. Corcoran is immediately concerned. His wife is a fit, strong woman. Rarely sick, always on the go. Now she is so unsteady on her feet, she can barely stand. He helps her to the car and starts driving towards the Epworth Hospital. On the way, she goes into seizure. Terrified, he takes her straight to emergency. The diagnosis is grim. That night, she undergoes surgery to remove brain tumours that are killing her.

Maxine Corcoran ran the quarter mile. When she was at the height of her athletics career, she ran it faster than any woman in Australia. In 1978 she ran in Edmonton, Canada, as part of

Australia's 4 × 400 metres relay team and returned home with a Commonwealth Games silver medal. Four years later, she ran at the Commonwealth Games in Brisbane. She never really stopped running. After racing she discovered a passion for coaching and sports administration, which she shared with her husband. She became vice-president of Athletics International. She managed the Sport Australia Hall of Fame. She coached a generation of young athletes. She raised three children. For two months the children sit with Danny Corcoran next to their mother's hospital bed, watching this vibrant, active woman they all loved fade from life.

Throughout his wife's illness, Corcoran spends his days at Essendon and his evenings in hospital. Football clubs are good places to be distracted from real life. When he needs someone to talk to, there are people at Essendon—Hird and Bruce Reid and club reverend Allan Dunn—whom Corcoran has known for twenty years. But the work doesn't matter. Corcoran says that throughout October and November 2011, the months when Robinson and Dank began work at Essendon and the first signs emerged there might be a problem, he was sleepwalking through the job.

'It wasn't that I didn't care but I had no focus on work,' he says. 'It just pales into insignificance.'[12] The first two weeks of December are taken up with funeral preparations, then Christmas comes and Corcoran realises he needs time to grieve in private. In mid January, he flies to Europe. The day Bruce Reid dictates his letter to his secretary Joan, Corcoran is in the southern France town of Aix-en-Provence, his thoughts immersed in a foreign place and another language. The football club is a distant concern when its troubles reach him by text message from Hird:

> No stress but need to organise a meeting with you, me Reidy, Danksy and Weapon the day you get back. Reid has stopped everything which is getting a little frustrating. Need to get your United Nations skills back into action.

Corcoran replies, urging caution:

> You know I read a book on world doping while away and once lay people start injecting players there are always issues!! We must be careful here for a host of reasons.

Hird assures him he doesn't want to push boundaries:

> Just need to make sure we are doing everything we can within the rules. As the other clubs are a long way ahead of Reidy and us at the moment.

Corcoran reads the message then returns to his French tapes, pursing his lips around the romantic vowels. He is in no hurry to get back.

For three weeks there are no injections at Windy Hill. Reid has ordered a halt to all supplements until he is satisfied that AOD-9604 is safe to use. A delegation of senior players led by captain Jobe Watson also raises concerns about unfamiliar substances being administered. The players have no reason not to trust Dank. He is the club sports scientist. It is his job to know what various supplements do and what can and can't be taken under anti-doping laws. Yet around the locker room there is unease at what is happening. The experienced players are used to taking supplements in sports drinks or protein powders. They haven't had so many injections before. The younger players don't know what to think. Dank seems to know his stuff but he talks in scientific jargon. They want more information about what they are being given.

On 16 January, the player leadership group of Watson, Mark McVeigh, Heath Hocking, Michael Hurley, Brent Stanton and David Zaharakis meets with James Hird and Jonah Oliver, the club psychologist. McVeigh, Hird's teammate throughout nine seasons, is blunt: 'What the hell's this new supplement program that we're doing? What is it? These injection shit, I don't like it. Where's it coming from?'[13] The players ask for a presentation setting out precisely what they are taking and why, and confirmation that it is WADA approved. Hird thinks it is a good idea.

The next the players hear of it is on 8 February, when they are called into the auditorium at Windy Hill by the high-performance staff. It is a Wednesday. Neither Bruce Reid nor Brendan De Morton, Essendon's other doctor, are at the club. Reid rarely is on a Wednesday. Everyone within the football department knows this. One of the players recalls Hird being there but the coach insists he wasn't. The players take a seat and Dank takes over, guiding them through a PowerPoint presentation. They are told what supplements are involved in the program, how they work, why they will help their training and given assurances that they are approved by WADA. The players understand that what they are being asked to take is at the limits of what is permitted in sport. Ricky Dyson, an experienced player preparing for his ninth season in the AFL, recalls a dramatic metaphor used by Robinson in the meeting: the program would drive to the edge of a cliff but not over.[14] Consent forms are handed out, reiterating the assurance that nothing being administered is in breach of anti-doping rules. A total of thirty-eight Essendon players sign the forms, giving written consent to be treated with four substances: AOD-9604, Thymosin, Tribulus and Colostrum. The player signatures are witnessed by Robinson and Oliver. The forms are countersigned by Dank.

Only one Essendon player refuses the program. David Zaharakis, a midfielder nearing his twenty-second birthday, has a thing about needles. He later takes AOD-9604 in a cream instead. Others don't sign straight away. Stewart Crameri, a hard-running forward preparing for his third season of AFL football, takes the consent forms home to his mum. Mandy Crameri is a retired schoolteacher. She and husband Bernie have raised three children in the Victorian Goldfields town of Maryborough and Stewart is their youngest. At the kitchen table, mother and son go through each substance, researching what it does and checking it against the WADA banned list.

'Stewart and I went through that together and I ticked them all off. I said that is fine, that is fine, that is fine, that is fine. So I have always been happy in my mind that what he was administered was okay in terms of what you would take in a supplement.'[15]

For the players that sign up, the proposed treatment regime is: one weekly injection of AOD-9604 throughout the season; one weekly injection of Thymosin for six weeks then monthly injections for the rest of the season; two grams of Colostrum, twice daily; one tablet of Tribulus Forte daily. Bovine Colostrum, a pre-milk substance produced by lactating cows, is known to many of the players. It is supposed to improve their immunity and comes in a tablet. Tribulus they recognise from the start of the pre-season. They are told that Thymosin and AOD-9604 are amino acid treatments that will help their recovery from heavy training sessions and games. They are told the substances are most effective when delivered by injection. They are not told that either is a peptide. They are also not told that one form of Thymosin, Thymosin Beta 4, is banned by WADA.

The players leave the auditorium meeting reassured. They believe the club doctor, Reid, has approved the use of everything they will be given. He hasn't. The first time he sees one of the forms is twelve months later. What the players don't know, and can't be expected to, is that the consent they have just given is farcical. The form has been downloaded from the internet by Jonah Oliver. He is a psychologist and doesn't have a medical degree. He doesn't have any expertise in pharmacology. Beneath Dank's signature there is the following claim: 'I base this recommendation on the visual examination(s) I have performed, on any X-rays, models, photos and other diagnostic tests that have been taken, and on my knowledge of your medical and physiological history.' Dank isn't a doctor. He isn't qualified to read an X-ray or conduct a diagnostic test and, even if he could, he hasn't done this with any of the Essendon players. He doesn't have access to their medical records. These are kept by the two club doctors, Reid and Brendan De Morton, neither of whom are present in the auditorium meeting and neither of whom have signed the consent forms. The forms are supposed to be vetted by club and external lawyers. They aren't. Sydney University endocrinologist Professor David Handelsman, called by ASADA as an expert medical witness in the doping case against the players, describes the form as 'alarmingly inadequate.'[16] As for the assurance that 'all components of the intervention/s are in compliance with current WADA anti-doping policy and guidelines', it is a sham.

Bruce Reid rises from his dining table, opens a briefcase and pulls out a thick manila folder. In it lays the history of Anti-Obesity Drug 9604. As with many scientific discoveries, AOD-9604 emerged after years of dedicated work spent looking for something else. It was the 1990s and Monash University researcher Frank Ng was carrying on the life's work of his late mentor Joe Bornstein, the university's founding professor of biochemistry. Bornstein was fascinated by the relationship between growth hormone and insulin. He believed that within the 191 amino acids of the growth human molecule there might be a cure for diabetes. For twenty-five years Frank Ng explored this theory, breaking up growth hormone into its fragments and studying what they do. When he came across the last strand of fifteen amino acids on the growth hormone chain, he found something unexpected: a polypeptide chain that metabolised fat. It wasn't a cure for diabetes but Ng realised it could be something just as useful and perhaps more profitable: a chemical treatment for obesity. Frank Ng patented the discovery on 4 September 1998. Two months later Metabolic Pharmaceuticals, a joint venture to develop AOD-9604 involving Monash University and a biochemical company called Circadian Technologies, was floated on the stock exchange.

For the next ten years, pre-clinical and clinical trials were conducted on AOD-9604 in Australia and the United Kingdom. Metabolic, headquartered in Melbourne, spent $50 million chasing its dream of developing the world's first, bona fide fat pill. That dream crashed in 2007 after a clinical trial, led by Royal Adelaide Hospital endocrinologist Gary Wittert, declared AOD-9604 a bust. The substance was safe but it didn't work. It was a failed anti-obesity drug, Professor Wittert concluded.[17] Metabolic abandoned AOD-9604 for the next two years. Then, in 2009, company chief executive David Kenley revived the moribund project. He discovered that although the development of AOD-9604 had ceased, its use had not. In California, a subculture of ageing body builders had started injecting AOD-9604 as a way of burning stubborn tummy fat. The effect was temporary but for body builders looking to reduce body fat before competition, it was liquid gold.

'You can imagine what happened,' Kenley says. 'It spread like wildfire through the body building industry and moved into the weight loss area and, from there, started to get into the sports arena.'[18]

Metabolic didn't make AOD-9604 but dozens of biochemical companies, mostly in China, were manufacturing the stuff and exporting it to a growing black market. Metabolic was more intrigued than alarmed to discover AOD-9604's secret double life. The company contracted a Hong Kong–based corporate investigator to report on what was going on. The findings of the investigation, announced to the stock exchange in December 2010, were staggering; up to $US20 million worth of AOD-9604 was being sold every month from Shanghai manufacturers to buyers in the United States, Canada, Australia, Russia, the United Kingdom and Germany. The substance was being shipped in single-dose, 2-milligram vials. Buyers were paying between $3000 and $30,000 a gram, depending on purity. Metabolic announced its discovery of a black market for AOD-9604 to the stock market in March 2010. Soon after, Kenley received a tip-off from a shareholder. He'd heard that Manly, an NRL club, was using AOD-9604. The person to talk to about it was a bloke named Stephen Dank.

Metabolic could do little to stop the black market trade. In Australia, the substance was entirely unregulated, with online businesses importing it from China and selling direct to gym junkies. In China, the manufacturers were too small and varied to hit with patent breaches. What excited Kenley was the possibility that the body builders had discovered something about AOD-9604 that researchers had missed. He commissioned further pre-clinical trials and the results were promising—it appeared that AOD-9604 had a healing effect on damaged cartilage and muscle. Had Frank Ng, all those years ago, actually unearthed a treatment for osteoarthritis?

The more Reid looked into AOD-9604, the more he understood why Dank thought it might help Essendon players. Between 2001 and 2007 the substance was subjected to six human clinical studies, including one in which patients were injected intravenously. The studies involved nearly a thousand patients and had not triggered any safety concerns.

AOD-9604 had provisional GRAS (generally recognised as safe) approval to be used in diet drinks and supplements in the United States and was an active ingredient in a cosmetic cream available from David Jones department stores in Australia. It hadn't been approved by the Therapeutic Goods Administration but it was legally available, on prescription, through compounding pharmacies. Reid thought it sounded like a good treatment option for footballers with stress fractures and early arthritis. It was part of the growth hormone fragment but it didn't have anabolic properties. The substance was safe, legal and might just work. The only question was whether WADA allowed it. This was the question Dank promised to answer.

World Anti-Doping Agency approval for AOD-9604 is something plenty of people at Essendon remember seeing yet nobody actually read. In truth, it never existed. Dank certainly sought approval for the peptide. In early February, he exchanged emails with a WADA official in Montreal about AOD-9604.[19] The correspondence provides insight into how Dank operates. He doesn't set out to break anti-doping rules but he is forever looking for a loophole. He acknowledges the role WADA plays but is disdainful of how it carries out that role. He thinks he knows more about peptides than WADA does. On 2 February 2012, Dank calls and then writes to WADA's manager for research and prohibited list, Irene Mazzoni, seeking confirmation that AOD-9604 is not on WADA's prohibited list:

> Good evening Irene,
>
> I'm hoping to obtain confirmation on a polypeptide that is part of a topical cream marketed for weight loss. The polypeptide is AOD-9604. There is no anabolic activity associated with the peptide. The peptide has been shown not to have any effect on I-GF1 or any androgenic effects within the body. The peptide or any related compound does not appear on the WADA prohibited list. I believe that this would confirm that it is not a prohibited substance. The company with the licensing rights – Metabolic Pharmaceuticals – indicates that the peptide is a nutraceutical. It is not considering it as a pharmaceutical substance. They are currently applying for it to be registered as an over the counter nutraceutical with the FDA. I am hoping for clarification on its allowed use.
>
> Regards,
> Stephen Dank[20]

Dank's email reveals his principal concern about AOD-9604 is whether it is banned under WADA's S2 category covering peptide hormones, growth factors and related substances. Mazzoni advises Dank to direct his inquiry to his local anti-doping authority, ASADA. She also cautions him about another category on WADA's list that prohibits the use of any substances that haven't been approved for therapeutic use. On 1 January 2011, WADA introduced a new, S0 category of banned substances designed to capture performance-enhancing drugs not yet approved by health authorities.[21]

Dear Steve,

Thank you for your inquiry. As I mentioned during our telephone conversation you should contact your National Anti-doping Organization (in this case ASADA) as certain drug preparations may differ between countries and also because some drugs are manufactured in one or a restricted number of countries and little is known about them outside those jurisdictions. Such seems to be the case with AOD9604. In addition, please be aware that there is a section in the Prohibited List, 'S0' that deals with non-approved substances. Therefore, even if the substance or similar substances do not appear listed, it does not automatically mean that the substance is permitted.

I hope this helps

Kind regards
Irene.[22]

In response, Dank verbals Mazzoni.

Dear Irene,

Thank you for your reply and confirmation that the product or any related product does not appear on the prohibited list. ASADA have already confirmed with the manufacturer that it does not appear on the banned list. The peptide is available within the weight loss cream BodyShaper Cellulite Contour Creme that is marketed and thus S0 would not apply as the peptide is a constituent of an approved product. I appreciate your prompt help in this matter.

Regards,
Steve[23]

WADA writes back to Dank. This time, Mazzoni has done some checking on AOD-9604. She emphasises her earlier caution.

> Dear Steve,
>
> Just to clarify, I was generalizing when I said that "even if the substance or similar substances do not appear listed". I should have said "even if a substance…" because as a matter of fact the constituent is reported to be a synthetic modified C-terminal of HGH, and GH is on the List. It does not seem to bind the GH receptor though.
>
> As for whether this product would fall into S0, I could not find that it had been approved by any government health authority. That's why I say to contact ASADA to check its status in Australia, where it seems to have been developed.
>
> I hope this clarifies my point.
>
> Irene.[24]

Shortly after this correspondence, Dank approaches senior club officials during a training session and announces that WADA has approved the use of AOD-9604. If any Essendon officials read the document that Dank is brandishing, they don't do so carefully. Rather, the senior coach, football manager and club doctor all take Dank at his word about what the document states. James Hird recalls being shown something on WADA letterhead but not what the text said. Reid has a similarly vague recollection of events. Other club officials have told Reid that Dank showed him the WADA correspondence as they were standing on the boundary line at Victoria Park, Collingwood's old suburban ground where Essendon was training that day. Reid remembers the training session but cannot say with certainty whether Dank showed him the documentation or not. Robinson remembers Dank showing the documents to Reid inside the Victoria Park change rooms.

On two things Reid is clear. The first is that he approved AOD-9604 without taking any steps to verify what Dank told him. Reid admits this is a significant failing on his part. The second is that neither Dank nor anyone else asked him to approve the other substance that Dank injected into Essendon players with their consent—a peptide called Thymosin.

Over the weeks that follow Essendon players are injected with peptides by sports scientist Stephen Dank in his basement office at Windy Hill. There is no ceremony and not much system. Some players drop by Dank's office for their shot, others he collars in a corridor or the weights room and tells them to come and see him. Once inside, it is a three-minute thing: Dank prepares a needle from one of his little vials, they lift up their training jumper and he injects them into their stomachs, just below the surface of the skin. Most of them don't ask questions. They'd been to the information session, they'd signed the consent forms, they'd been assured that Doc Reid had ticked off on everything and had it in writing that all the supplements were WADA compliant. Some remember Dank talking about a substance called AOD. Others have a recollection of being given Thymosin. Most players remember being treated from bronze vials; others remember seeing clear vials in Dank's fridge. One of the few players who presses Dank for more detail is the Essendon captain, Jobe Watson.

Jobe Watson is nobody's lab rat. When the AFL introduced rule changes on the eve of the 2011 season that, potentially, would dramatically increase the physical demands of the game, it was Watson who led a player protest. The rule change—a reduction of the interchange bench from four players to three—meant midfielders like Watson who rely on regular breaks on the interchange bench to regain their breath would need to do more running with less rest. During a meeting with AFL football operations manager Adrian Anderson, attended by Watson and the other AFL captains, the Essendon skipper hotly challenged the decision to introduce the rule with little warning, consultation or studies into what the downstream impacts on player health and welfare might be. When he didn't get the answers he wanted from Anderson, Watson floated the idea, albeit briefly, of a sit-down strike at the first bounce of his club's opening match against the Western Bulldogs. When Watson walks into Dank's office early in the 2012 season, he wants to know more about the Thymosin substance the sports scientist is planning to administer.

'I talked to Stephen about Thymosin and he said there is a bad one and a good one. That was my understanding of that. He said there is one that is banned that we can't take but there is one that is not banned and we can take and obviously we are taking the one that is not banned.'[25] It is not until after the blackest day in Australian sport that Watson learns the banned form of Thymosin is called Thymosin Beta 4. It is this form of Thymosin that ASADA suspects thirty-four Essendon players of taking.

The greatest test of high-performance manager Dean Robinson and his recovery guru Stephen Dank is Essendon's ANZAC Day game against Collingwood. The 25 April match between the two clubs is the biggest day in football outside the grand final. The game is worth four premiership points, the same as any other regular season match, but the stakes are dwarfed by the occasion. After Australia's war veterans and their descendants march up St Kilda Road to Melbourne's Shrine of Remembrance, some diggers go home, others to the pub and those with a ticket to the MCG. At about 2.30 p.m., the cavernous arena heaves with anticipation, then falls quiet for 'The Last Post'. First-time visitors are awestruck by the silence of so many, the lingering beauty of the final bugler's note. Footballers are remembered for what happens over the next two hours.

For the people responsible for preparing Essendon's team to play against Collingwood in 2012, ANZAC Day is also a ridiculous ask. With it falling on a Wednesday that year, there are only three days between Essendon's Saturday afternoon match against Carlton and the ANZAC Day game against Collingwood. Three days is not enough time to recover from an AFL match and prepare to play another. Some high-performance coaches will tell you a full week isn't long enough. If the AFL really wanted its teams fully fit to play every match of the year, they would spread the season around fewer matches, a minimum of ten days apart. As it is, the season is a six-month campaign of attrition, with players accumulating minor injuries each weekend and carrying them into the next. In April 2012, three days between matches is a cruel joke, a high-performance nightmare. The only consolation for Robinson and his staff is that Collingwood has no more time to prepare.

Robinson and Dank have a plan for ANZAC Day. Dank has spoken to Mal Hooper, a chiropractor who runs Hypermed, a hyperbaric treatment centre in the Melbourne suburb of South Yarra. Hooper is happy for the players to come in and get as much hyperbaric treatment as they want before the Collingwood match. Hooper is also arranging for VacuMed treatment to be available. Robinson is told that Hooper won't even charge the club. He's happy to provide the service so long as he can spruik his association with the club to other prospective clients. Hyperbaric treatment, in which athletes are placed in an oxygen-rich environment to stimulate healing and recovery, has been used for decades by AFL players. Television footage of footballers spending grand final week in a pressurised, Perspex cubby in the hope of recovering from a torn muscle or ligament is a September perennial. VacuMed is lesser known but has also been around for a while. It has its origins in 1960s technology developed by NASA and German scientists to emulate gravity and help astronauts maintain their circulation when in space. Used on athletes, it creates intermittent pulses of negative atmospheric pressure. This is said to improve the flow of oxygen to the body. More oxygen, so the theory goes, means faster recovery and healing.

Not everyone at Essendon thinks the treatments are a good idea. Thompson believes hyperbaric theory is rubbish and that most of all, tired footballers need to sleep and a chance to clear their heads.

Thompson doesn't know the half of it. The other part of Dank's Hypermed plan involves injecting the players with two substances. One is called Cerebrolysin. The other doesn't have a name. It becomes known as substance X.

Cerebrolysin is a treatment for stroke, dementia and Alzheimer's. It contains a series of peptides extracted from the brains of pigs. It is approved for therapeutic use in some Asian and European countries but not in the United States or Australia. Cerebrolysin is a substance well known to Mal Hooper, the owner of the Hypermed clinic. Hyperbaric oxygen therapy, in which pure oxygen is breathed in a pressurised environment, is used as an alternative therapy for people with traumatic brain injury. Hooper uses Cerebrolysin and other peptides to augment his treatments. Dank's theory is that Cerebrolysin might help restore the brain function of mentally fatigued footballers and allow them to make better decisions during a match.

In early April Dank sends information about Cerebrolysin to the two club doctors, Bruce Reid and Brendan De Morton. He also texts the senior coach: 'We have Cerebrolysin. Will reoxygenate and recirculate the brain.' Hird doesn't respond to the text but Reid remembers talking to Dank at length about the substance. As Reid explains, at his age he is interested in anything to do with Alzheimer's.[26] He says when he and Dank discuss the peptide, he doesn't realise the sports scientist is planning to use it on players. Nor does he give approval for it to be used. When Dank approaches De Morton at training to talk about the substance, De Morton is dismissive.

'How in the hell could you possibly extrapolate it for AFL footballers?'[27] Despite this, Robinson believes the doctors have approved Cerebrolysin. He says Reid and Hird both know what Dank has planned.[28] No one other than Dank supports this claim. Hird says when he visits Hypermed the morning after the Carlton game, all he sees is footballers receiving hyperbaric treatments.[29]

Substance X is a multi-vitamin amino acid and mineral. It is contained in a half-litre brown jar with a peeling label that has sat on a shelf in Hooper's South Yarra clinic for at least twelve months. It was bought over the counter at a chemist in El Paso, Texas. The man who bought it is a regular client of Hooper who has a form of muscular dystrophy, a genetic muscle-wasting disease. He is a successful, second-generation business owner with enough money to travel overseas for experimental treatments that aren't offered in Australia. He brought a couple of jars of substance X back from the United States and left one at Hooper's clinic. Hooper says he injected substance X into thirty-three Essendon players, some of them multiple times.[30] None of the players knew what the substance was.

Essendon loses to Collingwood on ANZAC Day by a point. The final score from the Hypermed debacle takes months and years to tally. Despite Dank's promise of free treatments, Hooper charges Essendon $61,000 for his services, an invoice the club haggles over for the rest of the season until Hooper deducts the unapproved 'injectables' from the final bill. Of greater cost to Essendon and concern to its players is the club's failure to determine exactly what they were injected with at the hyperbaric centre. Substance X marks Essendon's disgrace. Mal Hooper's disgrace is confirmed a year later, when the Chiropractic Board of Australia cancels his registration after upholding misconduct and unprofessional conduct allegations against him in an unrelated case.[31]

Dank and Hooper are not accused of breaking anti-doping rules at Hypermed. Cerebrolysin is not banned by WADA. ASADA investigators do not suspect substance X contained a banned ingredient either. For reasons that have nothing to do with doping, what happened at Hypermed remains the most disturbing episode within the entire drugs scandal. Dr Paul Spano, a hair transplant surgeon who runs a clinic near Windy Hill, shares Dank's interest in peptides and is intrigued by the work that Dank is doing at Essendon. Throughout the 2012 season, Essendon players are also treated at Spano's Skinovate clinic under Dank's direction with intravenous vitamin injections. Vitamin injections are permitted under doping rules and used by other AFL clubs but the Skinovate treatments and Spano's dealings with Dank are closely scrutinised by ASADA. When Spano drops by Hypermed one night in the lead-up to ANZAC Day to say hello to Dank and the players, he is sickened by what he sees.

'Steve very proudly marched me around and showed me all the boys, whatever, and then he produced this big bottle with a very ripped-up label … the rubber stamp on the top of this bottle had been pierced about a hundred thousand times … he said, "They're all getting a shot of this," and my stomach just turned, because I couldn't even read the label.'[32]

Spano fears Dank is out of control.

To make a bad story worse, ASADA investigators confuse their geography. They place El Paso on the wrong side of the US border. When they tell Bruce Reid, nearly a year later, that Essendon players were administered an unknown substance bought by a muscular dystrophy patient at a Mexican pharmacy, the club doctor is distraught.

'Please tell me they're all right … it's disgraceful, it's a year old, you don't know what's in it and everything … it's just, it's mind boggling … am I allowed to ask you, do you know what's in that bloody drug?'[33] When news of the mysterious 'Mexican' drug leaks from the investigation, it is cited as further, incontrovertible truth that Essendon has gone loco.

When David Evans first hears ASADA's full account of what it believed Essendon players were given during the 2012 season, the blood drains from his face. It is 4 April 2013. He is sitting in a meeting room in the old East Melbourne offices of Evans and Partners, a boutique investment firm he founded and chairs. Alongside him are Essendon's two Pauls: Paul Little, a self-made billionaire who turned Toll Holdings from a medium-sized trucking company into a logistics leviathan, and Paul Brasher, a former chairman of accounting giant PricewaterhouseCoopers. Both are Essendon directors. Within three months they will take control of the club. Also seated in Evans' office are the AFL's deputy chief executive Gillon McLachlan and integrity services manager Brett Clothier and, from ASADA, chief executive Aurora Andruska, investigators John Nolan and Paul Simonsson, and others. The meeting is cramped, with about a dozen people squeezed into the room.

Nolan has the floor. Deliberately, methodically, the former police detective reads through a list of substances that ASADA suspects were given to Essendon players. It includes AOD-9604, Cerebrolysin, Tribulus and the 'Mexican' drug, substance X. The full list runs to seventy different substances. There is Lube All Plus, an equine supplement administered from a bottle clearly marked 'for animal use only'. There is Thymosin Beta 4. There is also Thymomodulin, another form of Thymosin peptide.

'They were shocked,' says Andruska. 'I was shocked, because I was hearing it all for the first time. All of it not fit for human use.'[34] Paul Little and the other Essendon directors are blown away by what they are hearing.

Says Little: 'It was pretty unnerving and I was having trouble believing, even at that early stage, that there could have been so much going on behind the scenes that we as a board knew nothing about. That is the thing that even to this day I can't explain.'[35]

Within a few weeks of Essendon's ANZAC Day loss to Collingwood, Bruce Reid learns of just one substance that has been given to players, Cerebrolysin. An Essendon footballer complains about a sore bum. When questioned by the doctor, he reveals the cause of his discomfort is an intramuscular needle he was given at Hypermed. Reid starts asking more questions. Someone mentions Cerebrolysin. The Essendon doctor is furious.

'You know, I'm ripping my hair out by this stage,' he says.[36] The protocol that everyone agreed to, that was prompted by Reid's earlier concerns, is being ignored. Again Reid takes his concerns to Hird and Thompson. For a second time the coaches intervene. They talk about sacking their sports scientist. They decide to give him another chance. Another meeting is called with Robinson and Dank. Thompson does the talking. There is no discussion of keeping to protocols, of adhering to processes; Dank is simply told the injections must stop.

On a scale of ten, Thompson rates his admonishment of Dank after the Hypermed episode as a seven. Two weeks later the coach's anger is dialled up to nine. He discovers that Dank has ignored his directive and injected a player inside his basement office. Thompson, Hird, football managers Danny Corcoran and Paul Hamilton, club psychologist Jonah Oliver and Reid all confront Dank and Robinson. Thompson delivers the message. Reid, Essendon's club doctor throughout the 1980s and 1990s, was on the sidelines for nearly every one of Thompson's 202 matches for the Bombers. He says the blast Thompson delivers to Dank, leaning across his desk with his face contorted in rage, is as loud as he ever heard Thompson shout on a football field.

'This has got to stop. There's no more. It's out of control,' Thompson screams. There is a pause, an uncomfortable silence.

'Okay, son,' the scientist says.[37] It's not okay. The injections don't stop. Not until Dank leaves Essendon.

Robinson offers a different recollection of these events. He was interviewed at length by ASADA, on multiple occasions in 2013 and 2014. His account to investigators is: Bruce Reid approved all substances administered to players, including Thymosin and Cerebrolysin; there was no club edict to stop the injection regime until July 2012; the club's only concern about the treatments given to players at Hypermed was the cost of the bill; Thompson's fearful dressing down of Dank never took place. This account is consistent with what Robinson says in a paid television interview[38] and what he maintains throughout his protracted employment dispute with the club, which was eventually resolved in a confidential settlement for breach of contract. In Robinson's take on 2012, Hird is the driver of everything at Essendon; good and bad. Robinson trains and conditions the Essendon players to meet the coach's needs, he challenges the conservative orthodoxy of how things were previously done at the club because this is Hird's wish, he supports Dank in his work, knowing that Hird wants the club's sports scientist to give his team the edge. Robinson saw what happened to Stuart Cormack and he sees what is happening to Paul Hamilton; he knows how it ends up for people at Essendon who don't meet the expectations of the senior coach. Robinson is at his third AFL club in as many years. He needs his stint at Essendon to be successful. He needs to be on the right side of James Hird.

On a key point, Robinson is supported by Dank, who insists that all substances he gave Essendon players were known to and approved by the club medical staff. To believe Robinson, however, is to accept that everyone else at Essendon was involved in an elaborate conspiracy; that everyone from Danny Corcoran to Paul Hamilton to Mark Thompson to Bruce Reid to Brendan De Morton to James Hird all lied to ASADA with the intention of shifting the blame for what happened during 2012 to Robinson and Dank. An alternative explanation is that Robinson is deluded; that he genuinely believes James Hird and Bruce Reid approved all the injections despite the absence of any rational basis for this. This would help explain what happens next.

Twice Dank has been upbraided by Thompson. As Dank's boss, Robinson should be chastened. Instead, he proposes a new supplements regime, with weekly injections of yet more stuff, to run through to the end of the season. On the Friday of Essendon's bye weekend, when most of the club has gone away for a mid-season break, Robinson emails his proposal to the two club doctors, Bruce Reid and Brendan De Morton. It includes subcutaneous injections of an immunity boosting peptide, Thymomodulin, two days before every game and injections of Cerebrolysin, the porcine peptide dementia drug, every two weeks. Players are also to receive monthly intravenous vitamin treatments and a widely available supplement called ubiquinol. The other supplements listed—Arginine, Creatine, Colostrum, Tribulus—are to be taken in tablet form.

Robinson says he is doing what he has been told to do, adhering to Bruce Reid's protocol. At a glance, his email to the two club doctors can be seen as the high-performance manager trying to do the right thing. Yet, within the detail of the email, there is an anomaly. The proposed list of supplements reaches De Morton but the address for Reid is incorrect. Where the high-performance manager has previously sent correspondence to Reid at his Epworth Hospital email address, he sends his list of proposed supplements to an Essendon email address. Reid doesn't have an Essendon email address. At the time Robinson sends his proposal, Reid is away in London, visiting family. He doesn't see the email until ASADA investigators produce it during his second of two interviews on 26 March 2013. If not for Robinson's previous attempts to circumvent the Essendon club doctor, typing in an incorrect email address would be seen as a careless mistake at the end of a long working week. Reid believes it is a deliberate deception.

'Dean Robinson knows my email,' he says. 'I've never had that address but everyone could see it was sent to me so that is deception again.'[39] When De Morton reads Robinson's supplement list, he defers to the club's senior medical officer, telling the high-performance manager that he needs approval from Reid. Robinson never seeks it. After Reid returns from London, Robinson does not raise his proposal with him. Eight months later, when Reid is given a copy of Robinson's proposal by ASADA investigator Aaron Walker, he describes its contents as, 'Pathetic. Bullshit. Just absolute bullshit.'[40]

Mark Thompson doesn't believe Stephen Dank set out to cheat. He certainly doesn't think he intended to harm the players. Reid offers a similar assessment of Dank and Robinson. He remains angry that they went behind his back; that they thought they knew better than the club's medical staff. He is furious at Robinson, in particular, for claiming he approved substances that he didn't.

'I personally think they were rogues,' he says. 'That is a bad word to use. I think they couldn't give a stuff what I said.'[41] Yet, despite this, Reid believes they did it only to help players recover from the physical toll of football.

'They thought they were doing a good job,' he says. 'They believed it.'[42] In this, Robinson and Dank had a powerful co-conspirator: the AFL ladder.

Football clubs are the best and worst places to be around, depending on the score. When the team is winning everyone is happy, optimistic and purposeful. At these times, few questions are asked of anyone. When the team is losing, gloom spreads from the change room floor to the coaches' office to the front-of-house staff working in marketing and membership and media. At these times, all sorts of questions are asked. Keep losing for too long and, inevitably, a football club puts itself under review. Then the questions never stop. Midway through the 2012 season Essendon was winning. It was more than winning; it was heading for a top-four finish, the place from where premierships are won. Hird, Thompson, Reid, Corcoran, Hamilton—they had all made clear to Dank that they weren't happy about Hypermed and that the injections had to stop. But for the most part, Essendon didn't want things to change.

'You have got to remember the euphoria of the start to the season,' Corcoran says. 'Being 10–3, thinking of grander visions. Dank and Robinson could have written their own story.'[43]

In one regard, Stephen Dank did. After the Hypermed episode, Reid insists that records be kept of every supplement administered by Dank to Essendon players. Dean Wallis, one of the club's assistant coaches, is tasked with ensuring an electronic spreadsheet is kept up to date. Wallis was a tough, uncompromising defender in his playing days for Essendon. His effort at manning-up Dank is laughable. As Wallis explains it, at the end of each week he receives an email from Dank listing the supplements he has given to players. On Monday mornings he sits down with the sports scientist to check if there is anything else that needs to be added. Dank's invariable reply is, 'No, son.' Wallis then sends the information to someone in the club's IT department to update the spreadsheet. In this way, one of the few records of Dank's supplement regime at Essendon is ghostwritten by Dank.

It is only after the club stops winning that it starts asking more serious questions of Dank and, particularly, Robinson. By the middle of winter, Essendon's early season euphoria has faded. As spring approaches, Windy Hill is a desperate, foreboding place. The 10–3 win–loss record has slumped to 11–11. The team slips out of the top four and then out of finals contention. The reason is clear to everyone: the players keep getting injured. Predictably, blame is sheeted to the high-performance manager. Where football clubs are usually willing to write off twisted knees and fractured ribs to bad luck, torn muscles are considered preventable injuries, evidence of bad management; someone's fault. The raw statistics for Essendon's 2012 season are: thirty hamstring tears at nearly treble the ten-year season average, eight calf injuries, eight torn quadriceps, a total of 258 matches missed through soft-tissue injuries.[44] Right on cue, chief executive Ian Robson calls a review. On his ample shoulders, Dean Robinson feels the entire weight of a football club bearing down.

Within this climate of missed matches and loathing, the players also begin to question Robinson and the eccentric sports scientist he has brought to the club, Stephen Dank. Robinson is a chest-out manager. The players tolerate his alpha-manner while they are fit and the team is winning, less so when they are on the sidelines icing a torn hamstring, watching their finals aspirations dim. Robinson has come to the club with new ideas and a new, aggressive approach to training. Where he was embraced at Geelong, he feels like an outsider at Essendon. Jason Winderlich, a footballer who has spent ten years in the AFL, becomes furious when he rips a hamstring the day after Robinson asks him to do an exercise that places a heavy load on the muscle group. Scott Gumbleton, his lower back and season shot, mutters darkly about the squat exercises Robinson insisted he do. Robinson can be engaging but his combustive temper tests the loyalty of staff. A disagreement with Hird earlier in the season about how best to run a training drill results in an imprint of a Weapon-sized fist in a Windy Hill wall.

The players also grow wary of Dank's mad professor approach. They question why he doesn't keep records, why he doesn't seem to know whom he has injected with what on any given day. Club captain Jobe Watson believes Dank is knowledgeable and experienced. The sports scientist has worked for many years in professional sport within NRL and AFL clubs; he is supposed to be an expert in dietary supplements.[45] Watson also says that as the season drags on, the players begin to question his methods and results.

'We lost faith,' he says. 'The lack of reporting was concerning, his lack of, I suppose when he would come and say to you, "Oh, look, you need to have your shot today," and you'd say, "No, you did that to me yesterday," and he'd just walk off ... I think the players started to, as they do, just started to question a little bit and then also the fact that the injuries that we were sustaining, the performance that we were sustaining as well, meant that I lost faith in the program.'[46] Reid puts it more bluntly: 'At the start they thought he was a guru who was helping them. By the end they thought he was a madman.'[47] Even Robinson, previously Dank's strongest supporter, no longer trusts him. Robinson believes what Dank says about the substances he gave Essendon players but he is disappointed that Dank misleads him about other things and leaves him with a trail of unexpected and unpaid bills. At the end of the season, when he hears that rugby league clubs are asking about Dank's services, Robinson warns them off the sports scientist.

The club, meanwhile, is busy accounting for some of the financial outlays associated with its cultural revolution. The final bill from Hypermed is negotiated down to $50,000. The bill from Skinovate, Paul Spano's clinic where players were given intravenous vitamins, comes to nearly $15,000. On the advice of Dank and Robinson, the club spends $40,000 on an ultrasound machine. Dank and Robinson say it will help improve the immunity of players by stimulating their pineal glands. It breaks down after a week. Peter Memete, the owner of supplements supplier Advanced Sports Nutrition, says he is still owed $10,000 for protein powders and other supplements that Dank used to pick up on Friday afternoons in a white van. Dank says the bill is Essendon's to pay, Essendon says it is Dank's. More than two years later the unpaid invoice sits on Memete's desk; a reminder never to do business with either again.

Near the season's end, with Essendon's spectacular early bloom gone to seed, Danny Corcoran takes over the running of the football department from Paul Hamilton. He decides that Robinson has to go. The senior coach, James Hird, can no longer work with him and the senior medical officer, Bruce Reid, also refuses to work with him. Brendan De Morton has told the club that if Robinson is there next season, he won't be. Corcoran seeks advice from the club's HR manager, Hailey Grimes. She tells him the club doesn't have grounds to sack Robinson, that it can only issue a warning. Corcoran, Hird and Reid take the case to club chief executive Ian Robson and chairman David Evans. With Essendon's football department already haemorrhaging money, Robson baulks at paying out Robinson the remaining two years of his $290,000 per season contract. Essendon ends up paying all that and more when it settles Robinson's lawsuit two years later. In September 2012, Robinson is stripped of responsibility but kept on until the scandal breaks. When Essendon turns to the question of Stephen Dank's employment contract, the club discovers he hasn't even signed one. There is no personal file attached to his name. Whatever traces there are of his work at Essendon disappear with him.

Bruce Reid falls quiet. The Essendon doctor has been reliving this story for two years. He remains incredulous about parts of it, deeply embarrassed about others.

'When I look at my own evidence I think no one is going to believe this,' he says. 'How can a doctor be so dumb?' He is angry at ASADA, disillusioned with the AFL and frustrated that his memory of certain events is not clearer. He is hurt by his own failings. The biggest one, he says, is that he didn't go straight to the players when the club declared an end to all injections.

'I've thought, no, I won't worry the players on this. I should have gone to the players and said no one has an injection.' The doctor thumps the dining table with his hand. 'That is where I failed. In my mind, that is where I failed.'[48]

5
PEPTIDE ALLEY

THE BUSINESS PLAN is simple enough; sell peptides and lots of them. A full blown, drugs-in-sport crisis means there is big money to be made. Gym enthusiasts, grey-haired executives and even middle-aged mums are asking for the stuff that makes you younger, slimmer, stronger, tanned, more virile. The peptides that ASADA suspects of being used by professional footballers have gone from obscure acronyms to pharmaceutical rock stars. In a small, upstairs office in the aptly named Vogue Shopping Plaza, Stephen Dank and Robin Willcourt stand at a whiteboard doing their sums. Dank, the nation's most notorious biochemist, scrawls a round number on the board. Willcourt, an anti-ageing doctor with a fervent belief in the power of peptides, stands back and smiles broadly. $16 million. That's what they are looking at. A loosely regulated, rampaging market worth $16 million a year to whoever can supply it.

The street below is Melbourne's Peptide Alley; a stretch of Chapel Street, South Yarra, near the corner of Toorak Road. Body sculpting, botox treatment, liposuction, laser therapy; a promenade of glass-fronted clinics holds the promise of no more wrinkles, blemishes or fat. It is the perfect location for Willcourt, a Mount Gambier-born physician who trained in Hawaii and experienced his 'aha' moment, as he calls it, in Las Vegas, Nevada, at the 2006 World Congress on Anti-Ageing. A qualified obstetrician and gynaecologist, Willcourt runs Epigenx, a Chapel Street anti-ageing clinic that specialises in hormone replacement therapy and the treatment of andropause, the male menopause. He also prescribes peptides. If Dank is right about their business plan, it may soon be all he does. Around the corner is the Como Compounding Pharmacy run by Nima Alavi. Under a loophole in the Therapeutic Goods Act, Alavi and other compounding pharmacists can tailor-make medicines that aren't otherwise approved for human use and dispense them to patients with a script. So long as he has the ingredients, Alavi can compound any peptide that Willcourt prescribes: growth hormone-releasing secretagogues like Hexarelin, CJC-1295 and GHRP-6, anabolic agents like SARMs, the mysterious growth hormone fragment AOD-9604 and Thymosin Beta 4, a ubiquitous, regenerating peptide that is said to repair everything from heart muscle to eye cornea. Across the road is Hypermed, Mal Hooper's treatment centre where you can have pure oxygen pumped into your lungs while rejuvenating peptides are injected into your system. Hooper's clients are sometimes referred by Dank. They get their scripts from Willcourt and their peptides from Alavi.

Stephen Dank isn't a doctor or a pharmacist. He can't prescribe pharmaceuticals and he can't compound them. But as the sports scientist at the centre of the AFL and NRL drug scandal, he is a peptide rainmaker and crucial to the business plan. It is Dank who will bring customers to Willcourt, Willcourt who will consult and write the scripts, and Alavi who will dispense the peptides. They talk about ten-minute consults, done by Skype, with the potential for national reach and distribution. All legal, all above board, and all very lucrative. They also believe in what they are doing. They believe peptides are good for people. They will keep their customers younger, healthier and disease-free, and they will get rich doing it.

'If we could form a company somewhere down the line I would have stepped out of medicine and just done online peptides,' Willcourt says. 'Why wouldn't you? It was all guesswork but it was a huge market. It wasn't greed. It was just a fantastic income based on not having to do very much.'[1]

In the end, they don't make millions. Within months, their plans disintegrate amid claims and counter claims of theft, forgery, fraud and a police investigation by Victoria's gang-busting Purana Taskforce. Accusations of double-crossing course down Peptide Alley, fracturing personal relationships and severing business ties. Amid this wreckage, the shadow story behind the Essendon scandal is revealed.

Nima Alavi-Maghadam has arrived at Peptide Alley after a remarkable journey. Alavi was born in Iran in 1979, the year of the Islamic Revolution. For a child of Baiha'i parents, it was a dangerous time and place. The Baiha'i are followers of Baha'u'llah, a nineteenth-century Tehran-born prophet. Under Ayatollah Khomeini's theocratic rule, the Baiha'i were declared heretics. The lucky ones were kicked out of university or sacked from their jobs. Those less fortunate were murdered in the streets. When Alavi was four years old, his parents realised there would be no life for him in Iran. In the middle of the night his family climbed aboard a small, leaky dinghy and sailed across the inky waters of the Strait of Hormuz. They landed on a stretch of coast near the United Arab Emirate of Ra's al Khaimah, where one of Alavi's aunts lived. He was only a small child but the images from that night have stayed with Alavi: his father and another man bailing water out of the bottom of the boat as they crossed, walking with his family down a dirt track and being surrounded by the glare of four-wheel-drive headlights and soldiers armed with machine guns. In the confusion of the night they landed on the wrong beach. They were loaded onto the back of a truck and thrown in jail.

Alavi's family was well connected on both sides of the Persian Gulf. His grandfather, a wealthy merchant in the Iranian port city of Bandare e Abbas before the revolution, used to do business with Sheikh Zayed bin Sultan Al Nahyan, the ruler of Abu Dhabi and a central figure in the establishment of the United Arab Emirates. When Alavi's aunt discovered his family was in prison, she got word to Abu Dhabi. Alavi remembers being shifted from one jail to the next, invariably in the middle of the night, before his family reached Abu Dhabi. Even then, they came within minutes of mistakenly being put back on a boat to Iran—and almost certain death—before a high-ranking government official intervened. Once safe, they emigrated to New Zealand as refugees. When Alavi was fourteen years old, his family crossed the ditch to Brisbane, where he finished high school, went to university and married. Alavi and his wife later moved to Melbourne, where he worked as a pharmacist before opening his own compounding business.

Alavi remembers the day he first meets Stephen Dank. It is springtime 2011, and a paunchy, middle-aged man wearing shorts and a t-shirt walks into Alavi's Toorak Road pharmacy and introduces himself as the sports scientist for the Essendon Football Club. Alavi doesn't follow football. He can't tell you what colours the Essendon players wear. He doesn't know the name James Hird. But he takes an interest in Dank and what he might have to offer. He soon realises that Essendon is only a small part of Dank's work. Dank explains that he needs training supplements for Essendon. Alavi can certainly help him with that. Dank also tells him about the work he is doing in Sydney with a business called the Medical Rejuvenation Clinic (MRC), a spin-off research body called the Institute of Cellular Bioenergetics, and private customers. Dank and Alavi have a shared interest in peptides. MRC deals in them and Alavi has plans to start compounding them. They also have an associate in common, a self-styled fitness, nutrition and lifestyle adviser named Shane Charter. Charter runs the Dr Ageless anti-ageing clinic. Charter is looking to join the peptide business.

Charter is charismatic and intelligent. A fit, powerfully built man with a shaven head and a neatly trimmed goatee beard, Charter would look at home guarding the velvet rope of a Chapel Street nightclub. The impression is deceptive. A power-lifting biochemist with a post-graduate qualification in exercise physiology, he is as comfortable around burettes as he is barbells. For ten years he sold pharmaceuticals for a company that specialises in drugs for asthma and hypertension. He was good at it, a natural salesman. He'd grown up on a farm outside a town of less than five hundred people in Victoria's central highlands and could talk the leg off a chair. Plus he knew his stuff. The customers liked him; the bosses valued him. After a few years on the road, they made him state manager. It was an easy gig. In his spare time he moonlighted as a private fitness consultant to high-profile footballers. His clients included AFL star Shane Woewodin in the year he won his Brownlow Medal as the competition's fairest and best player. In 2003 he advised another Brownlow medallist, James Hird, an association that would return to haunt the Essendon coach. Charter met with the Essendon captain about once a month to tell him what to eat and what dietary supplements to take. Before Hird took anything, he checked it with Essendon's experienced fitness coach John Quinn. Charter's clientele wasn't restricted to footballers. He was welcomed in the boardrooms of some of Melbourne's largest companies, where he advised executives on how best to eat, exercise and manage stress. He was married to a pretty woman. They had two young kids. Friends said he was a great dad. He was a poster boy for good, smart, clean living. Or so his friends and family thought.

Charter also knew the underbelly of the fitness industry: the 24-hour gyms frequented by bikies and methamphetamine-fuelled meatheads, the traffickers who could get you the best steroids and the latest party drugs. For years he had used and abused steroids. In his powerlifting days he took them to compete. Then he took them to stay big. He got tired of having to pay inflated prices and started sourcing his own, direct out of China. Once his body was wrecked by 'roids, he discovered testosterone as a way to repair it.

He imported that, too. He got in deep. On the night of 18 April 2004, Victoria Police pulled over Shane Charter on a stretch of Normanby Road in South Melbourne. Unbeknown to Charter, they had watched him drive out of a nearby hotel car park they had under surveillance in a sting operation with customs. They found a briefcase containing 105,688 pseudoephedrine pills in his car, boxes of steroids at his house and half a million dollars in cash in a safety deposit box registered to his drug-dealing pseudonym—Arnie.[2]

In April 2004, Melbourne's gangland war was raging. Nik 'The Bulgarian' Radev had been shot dead in his Mercedes-Benz and Jason Moran was gunned down before terrified children at an Auskick clinic. Benji Veniamin was fatally shot in the kitchen of a pizza parlour and Mick Gatto, the man who emerged with the smoking gun, was in Barwon Prison facing a murder charge he'd eventually beat. Crime patriarch Lewis Moran went for a beer at the Brunswick Club and never came home. He was assassinated at point-blank range next to a row of blinking pokie machines. The Victoria Police's Purana Taskforce was up and running, tasked with solving gangland murders and stopping the bloodshed. Amid the carnage, Shane Charter was expanding a sophisticated, highly profitable drug importation business without anyone taking much notice.

Charter was no accidental criminal. He planned carefully and left little to chance. In October 2003, he travelled to Kuala Lumpur and introduced himself to a local pharmacist. He said he wanted to buy pseudoephedrine for clients who worked in banking back home. Charter used a false name, Arnold Mills—'Call me Arnie,' he'd say. The pharmacist put Arnie in touch with an associate of his, Chris Lau. Lau provided Arnie with the product he needed. Charter provided Lau with plastic bottles in which to pack the pseudoephedrine, a thousand pills to a bottle. He told Lau to label the drugs 'Vitamin B Complex' and to seal the bottles into boxes and mail them to Australia. In each package they included a letter, written by Charter, on behalf of a fictitious health company spruiking the benefits of the mislabelled pills. Charter gave Lau a series of addresses around Albury, Bendigo, Mildura and Melbourne, belonging to friends he knew from the gym scene. He involved forty-three people in his operation, almost all of them as unwitting accomplices. One of his few knowing helpers, a family friend for twenty years, had previously helped Charter import steroids from China. He agreed to let Charter use his gym and house as a delivery point and accepted steroids as payment. Lau was happier with cash.

Charter transferred $32,215 into the account of Lau's wife between November 2003 and February 2004. In return, he received 124 packages from Malaysia, each containing between five and seven bottles of pseudoephedrine falsely labelled as vitamin B. From his home in Hillside, on Melbourne's northwestern suburban fringe, he tracked the progress of each bottle on a laptop computer. He communicated with Lau by encrypted email and untraceable phones. He even went to the trouble of sending the empty pill bottles back to Lau to recycle. All in all, it was a considered, well-concealed, environmentally responsible criminal enterprise. He was dead unlucky to get caught.

The customs officer simply noticed the similarity of the packages. There were eight of them—all small, white FedEx boxes, and all lobbed in on the same day in the Qantas Mail Handling Unit near Sydney Airport. Curiosity aroused, the officer saw the name of the sender was the same on each package, a Chris Lau from Kuala Lumpur. The recipient addresses were spread around the Albury area but the name of the householder and telephone number on each box was the same. Three of the boxes were opened. The pills tested positive for pseudoephedrine. A joint customs and police investigation began.

The night Charter was arrested in Melbourne he lied to police about his involvement. Inside an interview room at the Victoria Police St Kilda Road headquarters, he told the detectives he'd gone to meet a friend and didn't know how a briefcase full of illegally imported pseudoephedrine got into his car. Police knew he was no naïf. The pills imported by Charter were about 50 per cent pure. The various shipments they traced to him contained 11.5 kilograms of pure pseudoephedrine. Pseudoephedrine is a decongestant. It is also a key ingredient in the manufacture of methamphetamine, a highly addictive stimulant that, at the time, was fuelling Melbourne's gangland killings. Charter had brought in enough pseudo to manufacture methamphetamine with a street value between $13 million and $30 million. While Charter was being questioned, detectives searched his house. On a shelf above the garage roller door they found $25,000 in a Sportsco bag and a further $33,800 in a Westpac money bag. They found lab equipment. They found the same plastic bottles the pseudoephedrine had been shipped in and spare vitamin labels. Near the lab equipment they found boxes of testosterone and steroids—Nandrolone, Trembalone, Boldenone, Oxymetholone. They found two books, one titled *Clandestine Drug Laboratories* and another titled *Secrets of Methamphetamine Manufacture*. Charter's secret was out.

A successful sales rep, fitness adviser to the stars and model dad, Charter was looking at a long stint in jail. For more than two years, through preliminary hearings, he denied all allegations. Even after a co-conspirator pleaded guilty and went to jail, Charter still maintained his innocence. But as his trial date loomed, Charter abruptly changed his story. He decided to confess his involvement and something else; for the chance of a lighter sentence he would throw two long-time friends under a bus. Charter struck a deal with prosecutors. He was willing to plead guilty to three counts—one of importing pseudoephedrine, one of trafficking in a commercial quantity of pseudoephedrine and one of trafficking in steroids. He would also provide a statement and appear as a witness against one of his accused co-conspirators and another man who was not part of the police case. Charter's evidence against the co-accused was rejected by a jury and his allegations against the other man never made it to trial but, for Charter, his testimony served its purpose. Justice John Smallwood, an experienced County Court judge with a Harry Potter Dumbledore beard, told Charter that if not for his co-operation with police and guilty plea, he would have given him at least ten years. Instead, the judge jailed Charter for four years with a minimum of two.

'I accept that your prospects of rehabilitation are good,' Justice Smallwood told Charter. 'I accept from the sworn evidence in front of me that you are genuinely remorseful and indeed, are ashamed at what you have done.'[3] Charter indeed learned a lesson, though perhaps not the one the judge hoped for.

It is Nima Alavi, an entrepreneurial compounding pharmacist, who convinces Robin Willcourt to come to Melbourne. In mid 2011, Willcourt is working in Adelaide at the Queen Elizabeth Hospital. For the past two years, he has worked there as the medical director of the Pregnancy Advisory Centre, consulting women with pregnancy complications. It is a homecoming of sorts for Willcourt, who had left South Australia forty years earlier to train and work in the United States. His work has taken him to Honolulu, Louisville in Kentucky, Reno in Nevada and Newport Beach, California. A hand injury has left him unable to operate so the non-surgical job at the Queen Elizabeth is a good fit. He also dabbles in anti-ageing medicine on the weekends although, in this area, he sees Australia as years behind the United States. For instance, he is the only physician in Australia licensed to prescribe hormones according to the Wylie protocol, an alternative to traditional hormone replacement therapy. This is why Alavi is on the phone. Alavi has met TS Wylie, the namesake of the protocol. He wants to start compounding oestrogen and progesterone hormones for women interested in the treatment. He needs a doctor who understands the protocol to see patients and write scripts. Would Willcourt be prepared to consult in Melbourne? For the next few months, Willcourt works with Alavi as a fly in–fly out consultant. During the week he works in Adelaide at the hospital. On the weekends, he bases himself in a little office in Alavi's South Yarra pharmacy.

During these weekends the doctor and the pharmacist talk about another passion of Willcourt's, the relationship between elite athletes, injury, performance and hormones. While in Adelaide, Willcourt has met a young man, Trent Croad, who was once an AFL footballer and is now plagued by a debilitating foot injury. Croad tells him about playing for Hawthorn in the AFL with painkilling injections to numb the pain from his fractured foot. He recounts the moment in the 2008 AFL grand final when he was running across the MCG and suddenly felt his foot snap. Hawthorn won the premiership, Croad never played again. There is nothing that Willcourt can do to fix Croad's foot but his story stays with him; evidence, as he sees it, of the folly of conventional sports medicine. He is angered by doping rules that allow athletes to play with local anaesthetic jabbed into their joints while prohibiting the use of substances such as growth hormone, which help the same joints heal. Willcourt relays Croad's story to Alavi.

'If only we could get all athletes at peak performance with their hormones, then they would heal up, they wouldn't injure themselves as often,' the doctor tells the pharmacist.

'I have got just the person you need to talk to,' Alavi replies. 'You'll really get on with him.'[4] And so Robin Willcourt is introduced to Stephen Dank.

In November 2011, Willcourt and Dank meet at Alavi's pharmacy. They talk about athletes. They talk about hormones. Together, they pose the question: is there anything we can do for them? Dank has begun work at Essendon. Willcourt tells Dank about Croad. They wonder out loud whether there might be an untapped market in Melbourne working with retired athletes. There are ten AFL teams in Victoria, an NRL and a rugby team, and soccer is on the move. When Willcourt next talks to Croad, the retired Hawthorn star is enthusiastic about the idea. He knows lots of people across the different football codes. He can make the introductions.

'A whole lot of things were happening,' Willcourt says. 'There was all this stuff with Wylie, there was Trent and a whole other group of people and in the middle of this mix was Stephen Dank, who was working at Essendon. It's a sign.'[5]

No sooner than Willcourt shifts into his newly rented premises in Peptide Alley, Stephen Dank has work for him. The Essendon sports scientist explains that he is conducting a study at Windy Hill. He wants to better understand the relationship between elite sport and physiology. His plan is to take regular blood tests of all the players throughout the season and future seasons to show the impact that training for and playing AFL football has on hormone levels, cholesterol, white blood cell counts, liver function and other measures. Dank says there is just one hitch: the Essendon club doctor Bruce Reid is too busy to request the blood work. Would Willcourt be willing to do it? Willcourt thinks the study is a brilliant idea. Without seeing any Essendon players, he fills out the pathology requests for Dank. How can a doctor sign a pathology request without seeing the patient? It is a question that Australia's health regulator, the Australian Health Practitioner Regulation Agency, has since asked Willcourt to answer. The doctor's response is that as long as the cost isn't billed to Medicare, which only issues rebates for pathology tests with a legitimate medical purpose, it isn't a problem. You don't even need to be a doctor to sign off on a pathology test.

'The problem is lumping all these things together and having Medicare pay for it,' he says. 'The government is paying for unnecessary testing. That is called fraud.'[6] It is also based on a falsehood. Reid says he had no idea the blood tests were being done.

Willcourt says Dank never told him he was planning to give Essendon players peptides. Rather, it was the opposite; they discussed peptides at length and agreed none of them could be given to footballers covered by the World Anti-Doping Code. They didn't agree with the code but its rules were clear enough: CJC-1295, Hexarelin and GHRP-6 were definitely banned, Thymosin Beta 4 was probably banned, and AOD-9604 could well be banned. Even if Willcourt could rewrite WADA's rules he still wouldn't give footballers peptides—he'd give them growth hormone and testosterone and be done with it. In any event, peptides were a no-go at Essendon.

'We had already discussed ... the peptides, they were out of the question,' Willcourt says.[7] Besides, there were plenty of other customers out there. It is time to get down to business.

Of Dank, Alavi and Charter, the sports scientist is the only person established in the peptide business. Dank has an extensive client base. Through his interest in the Medical Rejuvenation Clinic, he has a ready-made distribution network. Through the Institute of Cellular Bioenergetics, the research spin-off of MRC, he can sidestep the health regulations governing peptides, lax though they are. The peptides at the centre of the Essendon and Cronulla scandals don't have therapeutic approval but they can be used for research. Most importantly, Dank is the Essendon sports scientist. It says so on his business card. This association will open doors, particularly in Melbourne, that a Toowoomba-born biochemist would otherwise find shut. Essendon is a cash cow. It is one of Melbourne's richest sporting clubs and happy to spend money on new ways to win. Dank's business card is an affirmation of his bona fides and a potential lure; to Willcourt and Charter he dangles the possibility of jobs at the club, to Alavi the promise of a steady income stream. Alavi needs reassurance on this front. He needs to spend $50,000 on lab upgrades before he can start compounding peptides.

Alavi and Charter are in business discussions of their own. Charter says he knows his way around the biochemical scene in China. He is willing to travel there, to Shanghai, to find a reliable source of peptide materials for Alavi. He also knows people who can help Alavi expand his business. He tells the pharmacist that an associate of his, Tom Karas, is a financier. He suggests that Karas will lend him the money he needs for lab upgrades. He doesn't tell the pharmacist that Karas is suspected by the Purana Taskforce of helping gangster Tony Mokbel conceal proceeds from his drugs empire. In one of his better decisions, Alavi declines Charter's financial advice and borrows the money from a bank. Charter claims he enters into a formal business arrangement with Alavi to supply materials for peptides.[8] Alavi says it never gets that far; that when the drug importer draws up a contract he declines to sign.[9] Whatever the truth, their business dealings are short-lived.

On 26 November 2011, Charter flies to China with a shopping list of peptides. Who they are ultimately for is a matter of significant dispute. When he arrives in Shanghai, Charter looks up an old jailhouse friend, Cedric Anthony. The same year that Charter was sent to prison for his drug convictions, Anthony was settling his own account in the Victorian County Court for inducing an ANZ bank employee to advance him a series of secret loans. The Sri Lankan-born businessman is an entrepreneur. Educated and well versed in international trade, finance and property, he is, like Charter, charismatic and persuasive. For the cost of a swanky lunch, an $8000 betting account and a trip to Sri Lanka, he convinced a bank worker of twenty-six years standing to funnel $7.4 million of loans into his clothing importing business over nine months.

Once Charter and Anthony are together behind bars, it is inevitable these two unusually intelligent, creative inmates hit it off. Within the minimum-security confines of Dhurringile prison, a nineteenth-century homestead south of Shepparton previously used as a Presbyterian orphanage, there is ample opportunity for inmates to get to know one another. During this time, Charter also befriends an ageing crook with a bung hip. His name is George Williams. George's son is Carl Williams, a drug dealer, murderer and a central figure in Melbourne's gangland war. Charter introduces himself to Carl's dad as a fitness adviser and nutritionist. He advises the older man on what to eat and how to exercise without aggravating his bad hip.

'He was quite a good help to me,' George Williams says. 'He wasn't no standover or bully. He was just a nice man.'[10] The friends that Charter implicates in his drug dealing beg to differ.

After Anthony is paroled from Dhurringile, he is soon back in business. He establishes Austgrow, a fabric manufacturer headquartered in Guangdong Province, China, with branch offices in Melbourne and Shanghai. When Charter comes to China in search of peptides, Anthony offers him the use of a desk and a computer in his Shanghai office. According to Anthony, Charter has big plans.

'All over China he wanted to do Dr Ageless. He was setting up everywhere.'[11] Anthony says he has no involvement in Charter's peptide dealings in Shanghai. He maintains the only thing he imported for his friend was an empty medicine cabinet; 'Other than that I have never touched anything.' Charter offers a different recollection.

GL Biochem is a cavernous biochemical research and manufacturing company south of Shanghai's international airport. Its twin research and development facilities are spread over more than 32,000 square metres, it employs more than a thousand scientists and it specialises in synthetic peptides. When Charter is given a tour of the sprawling, spotless facilities by GL Biochem sales manager Vincent Xu, he is impressed by what he sees. Charter tells his guide he owns a pharmaceutical company and needs peptides for research. Xu provides him with samples to take home, a small amount of the growth hormone releasing peptides, GHRP-6 and CJC-1295, an anabolic agent called IGF1-LR3 and 0.25 grams of Thymosin Beta 4. He later emails Charter a price list for various peptides that GL Biochem can provide. The list includes two variants of Thymosin peptides—Thymosin Beta 4 and a substance referred to only as Thymosin. The distinction is small on paper but enormous when considering the fate of Essendon players. Thymosin Beta 4 is banned by WADA. Thymosin Alpha is not. Whether either peptide manufactured by GL Biochem finds its way to Windy Hill and, if so, which ones, are two questions that will vex ASADA investigators, lawyers representing the thirty-four players, an AFL anti-doping tribunal and ultimately, the World Anti-Doping Agency and the International Court of Arbitration for Sport.

If Charter is good for his word, the Essendon players wouldn't have a case to answer. On 8 December 2011 he emails Vince Xu and orders 2 grams of GHRP-6, 0.5 grams of CJC-1295, 1 gram of Melanotan II, 0.5 grams of Mechano Growth Factor and 0.25 grams of Thymosin Beta 4. Five grams of Hexarelin is added to the order a week later. The total cost quoted to Charter is US$3570. He bills Alavi $14,025 plus GST for the same peptides. For Charter, it is a profitable venture but it requires one further deception. Before GL Biochem can supply the peptides, it needs a written assurance they won't be administered to any people. Xu is insistent on this. His company provides peptides for research purposes only. On 8 December, Charter signs and dates the following statement:

> I and my affiliation/employer are quite clear that all your products have been restricted to laboratory research purposes, excluding clinical research on human body ... They cannot be applied for human usage without proper handling and some appropriate registration and approval.
> You have our commitment as follows,
> The products outsourced to your company will not be directly applied for usage in a human body without appropriate requirements satisfied.
> And precautionary measures, if applicable, will be adopted to ensure that the products will not be used improperly by third party during the process of disposal, transfer or alike.
> My affiliation/employer and/or I will take all the responsibilities caused by the improper usage of the products by ourselves or any third party.[12]

Within two weeks of Charter providing the signed undertaking, the goods are ready to be picked up. According to Charter's version of events, it is here that his old jailhouse friend Cedric Anthony, a businessman whose previous claim to sporting fame was opening the first indoor cricket centre in Sri Lanka, plays a small but essential role in the great doping scandal. Charter says Anthony arranges for one of his staff to pick up the order of peptides from GL Biochem. He stores them in a fridge in his Shanghai office and once instructed by Charter, sends them by international courier to Nima Alavi's South Yarra pharmacy. Charter says that before the peptides are mailed to Australia, Anthony ensures that all identifying material tracing the peptides back to GL Biochem is removed—the batch numbers for the peptides and the certificates of analysis provided with the powdered chemicals. Charter did this with the earlier samples he carried back to Melbourne. The reason, Charter explains, is so the pharmacist can't deal direct with GL Biochem and cut him out of future deals. When Alavi opens the package, he finds among the peptides one quarter of a gram of a substance labelled only with a single, hand-written word: Thymosin. There is no other information. What kind of Thymosin is it? Alavi will never know for sure. Neither will ASADA.

Who were the peptides for? When ASADA begins pursuing suspicions of doping at Essendon, its investigators assume everything Charter ordered from GL Biochem was destined for Windy Hill. It is a reasonable starting point. Dank had just started a full-time job as Essendon's sports scientist. The club was aggressively trying to develop bigger, stronger players. Dank's direct boss at Essendon, high-performance manager Dean Robinson, used peptides himself. Charter knew Dank was working with Essendon. He believed, though he never knew, that whatever he was sourcing in China, Dank planned to use on Essendon footballers. It was no great concern to Charter either way; he was on the ground floor of what he saw as a potentially huge, new drug enterprise. It might even be legal. He had used steroids and other prohibited substances throughout his adult life. He was hardly going to judge Essendon footballers for doping.

In its starting assumption, however, the ASADA investigation is blinkered. Essendon was only ever a small part of what Dank, Charter and Alavi were up to. There was a far bigger play going on down Peptide Alley. There were deals within deals, with each using the other to get what they wanted—cheap, reliable peptides to feed a highly profitable, growing grey market. Dank says the peptides sourced by Charter in China were not intended for Essendon at all. He says the customer in the China deal was the Medical Rejuvenation Clinic.

'Under no circumstances did we ever deal directly with Shane on anything in relation to the Essendon football club. The early order referred to in the emails related to business transactions for the Medical Rejuvenation Clinic.'[13] Dank doesn't tell this to ASADA. He refuses repeated requests by ASADA to be interviewed and MRC does not hand over any company records. Given this, Dank's claims deserve scepticism. Yet on this point, there are three pieces of evidence that support Dank's account.

The first is email correspondence between Charter and an MRC director, Edward Van Spanje, two days after Charter arrives in China. On 28 November 2011, Van Spanje asks Charter to get a quote from his Chinese supplier for a large order of peptides. Van Spanje, the MRC director most involved with the day-to-day running of the clinic and its online peptide store, Best Buy Supplements, tells Charter he needs a hundred bottles per month each of CJC-1295, GHRP-6, IGF-1 and SARMs. With summer fast approaching, he also needs two hundred bottles a month of the tanning agent Melanotan II. He asks for the peptides to be put into amber glass vials. This small detail will become important as events unfold. The second piece of evidence is Charter's notes taken of an 11 September meeting he had with Dank when the pair discussed sourcing peptides. On the file note the word 'Ed' is circled. Charter says it is a reference to the probable customer for the peptides, Ed Van Spanje.[14]

The third piece of evidence is contextual. At the time Charter is sourcing peptides from China, he and Dank are talking about merging their respective businesses. In effect, they are in the same line of work—they run anti-ageing clinics, they consult with private clients on diet and fitness, they advocate the use of peptides. With Dank shifting from Sydney to Melbourne to work with Essendon and looking to expand his MRC client base, it makes sense for Dank and Charter to co-operate rather than compete. Charter has done well with his Dr Ageless clinic but he would like to be bought out by someone with deeper pockets. He and Dank discuss this with Laurie Williams, a well-known obstetrician and prominent figure in several private health ventures in Melbourne's western suburbs. Williams has read about Dank, Essendon's new sports scientist. Charter introduces himself to Williams as James Hird's fitness adviser, an association ten years out of date. Williams decides he doesn't like the look of the peptide business but he employs Charter as a health and fitness adviser at one of his clinics, where Charter works with chronic disease patients. As with most relationships formed along Peptide Alley, it ends badly. On the blackest day in Australian sport a journalist calls Williams for a comment about Charter and the obstetrician sacks the drug importer on the spot.

The Medical Rejuvenation Clinic, not Essendon, is at the centre of Charter's relationship with Dank. Charter initially tells ASADA the peptides he sourced from China were for Dank, not Van Spanje. He later withdraws this and says the order was for Van Spanje to fill a pre-Christmas peptides shortage at MRC. In reality, Dank and Van Spanje cannot be separated. Not when it comes to peptides. ASADA's case against Essendon relies on the provenance of twenty-six vials of Thymosin at a time when Alavi's pharmacy is preparing to supply MRC up to 2455 vials of peptides a month.[15] As for Charter, it makes no difference to him who the peptides are ultimately for. As far as he understands his China trip, he is there to source peptides for Alavi, who will in turn compound them for Dank and other customers. What Dank does with them is Dank's business. And the business interests of Dank are many and varied.

The package from Shanghai arrives at the Como Compounding Pharmacy on 28 December 2011. Three days later, with the nightclubs and bars along Peptide Alley gearing up for another raucous New Year's, Alavi is hard at work inside his newly fitted, sterile laboratory. This is the first batch of peptides he has ever compounded. Charter is again playing middleman, running progress messages between Dank and Alavi. Charter hasn't been paid yet, so he needs to stay useful. He tells Alavi, 'Steve wants the Hexarelin by Monday.' Then he wants the Thymosin Beta 4 and CJC-1295. With no certificates of analysis to guide him, Alavi can't be sure what he is compounding. Peptides are chains of amino acids. The number, make-up and order of the amino acids on the chain are all variables that determine what kind of peptide it is. Normally, peptides delivered from a biochemical company would come with a certificate of analysis clearly stating the name of the peptide, molecular weight and chemical structure. Alavi doesn't have any of that information. All he has are handwritten labels.

Thymosin can refer to any number of thymic hormones. There is Thymosin Alpha, a substance permitted by WADA and Thymosin Beta 4, a substance that is banned. There is TB500, a banned synthetic analogue of Thymosin Beta 4 and Thymomodulin, a permitted, immunity-boosting substance used clinically since the 1970s. They all have substantially different chemical structures and when administered, do different things. For example, Thymosin Beta 4 is made up of forty-three amino acids in a precise order. Thymosin Alpha has twenty-eight amino acids, TB500 a mere seven. To suggest a pharmacist would prepare medicine without knowing exactly what it is invites ridicule yet in this case Charter deliberately kept Alavi in the dark.

'The confusion here is a compounding pharmacist doesn't make up the actual drug itself,' Alavi says. 'We receive the drug in its raw form and then we compound it into a dosage form. For instance, in the case of Thymosin, we would receive the Thymosin raw ingredient and then dissolve it, stabilise it, put it into a particular concentration which is appropriate for injecting, then we'd sterilise it. And then we would prepare it for use. At no time do we actually make the Thymosin itself. So I can tell you every step of the process and what we did and I am 100 per cent across it, except for that initial supply of Thymosin that we received. That Thymosin is made in a big, pharmaceutical manufacturing facility in China. To double-check their work the only thing that I can do is test it using a mass spectrum. A mass spectrum is going to tell me whether or not it actually is Thymosin, how stable it is, whether it has got any unknown organisms in it. That is really the only way. That part of the process is very important when you are receiving a powder from outside Australia. When it is in Australia we can usually assume that quality control measures have been used and whatever is on the certificate of analysis, we can pretty much rely on that. When it is something from overseas it could be anything.'[16]

The Thymosin peptide that Alavi compounds in January 2012 is never tested. This is crucial to understanding why the doping case against Essendon players is so difficult to prove. Alavi says that, under pressure from Dank and Charter to deliver the peptides on a tight deadline, he is unable to find a laboratory that can test them. He contacts a US-based lab he has previously used for other drugs but the quoted cost is prohibitive. When he mentions this to Dank, the sports scientist says he is a customer at Mimotopes, an international biochemical company headquartered in the Melbourne suburb of Clayton. He says if Alavi gives him the peptides he will take them to Mimotopes and have them tested. With time pressing on his other work, Alavi agrees. On 19 January, Dank comes to the pharmacy. Alavi gives him two small Eskies. Both contain clear, identical glass vials filled with the compounded peptides. One Esky is marked Thymosin, the other is marked Hexarelin. Alavi doesn't see the peptides again. The next time Alavi hears from Dank is more than week later. Dank says he took the peptides to Mimotopes and they were 'fried' from exposure to the light. He admonishes Alavi for compounding them into clear vials, against the instructions of Van Spanje. He tells the pharmacist and later insists to me that he threw the peptides away.

'I have never denied that we took those vials but I've also said to you the vials were destroyed because they were in clear vials, not amber.'[17]

Alavi doesn't believe Dank. He is suspicious that Dank is trying to cheat him out of $15,000 worth of peptides. His suspicion deepens when he learns that Mimotopes has no record of Stephen Dank testing anything at its lab in January 2012. Mimotopes managing director Sonja Plompen confirms this. Her company records show

Dank did have peptides analysed at Mimotopes in 2012 but not before April. She has since stopped dealing with Dank.

'We only supply peptides for research and development, not for human use,' she explains. 'We sell to universities, we sell to biotech companies. We don't sell to people off the street.'[18]

Dank maintains he told Alavi the truth; that the peptides Alavi gave him were spoiled by light exposure, that this was confirmed by Mimotopes, that they were destroyed and not injected into anyone. ASADA, like Alavi, does not believe him. Essendon weights coach Suki Hobson described injecting herself with Hexarelin from a clear, glass vial. Some Essendon players remember being administered something called Thymosin. Others remember clear vials in Stephen Dank's fridge at Windy Hill. Essendon players signed consent forms to be administered with Thymosin. It all fits, almost.

What about the Hexarelin Dank gave to Sue Anderson, the Essendon admin worker? It came in a bronze vial. It is not from one of Alavi's Eskies. What about the players who recall being administered Thymosin from a bronze vial? Dank says the Hexarelin was part of a later batch supplied by Alavi in March, along with vials of Thymomodulin, a permitted form of Thymosin. Alavi says he never supplied Dank with Thymomodulin. Is Dank referring to another, mysterious delivery of Thymosin sourced from China on 18 February? The only trace of it on Alavi's books is a handwritten note from his lab assistant Vania Giordani: '1g Thymosin.' This one comes with an unauthored, undated certificate of analysis and no batch number. So what's in the vials? The molecular weight is close to Thymosin Beta 4 but there is no breakdown of the chemical structure.

Professor David Handelsman, a leading endocrinologist at the University of Sydney and ASADA's expert witness in the doping case against the Essendon players, tells an AFL tribunal he wouldn't place any trust in such shoddy documentation.[19] Nonetheless, ASADA is convinced that Dank picked up the first batch of peptides from Alavi's pharmacy and used them on Essendon players and staff. For Alavi the implications of this go well beyond doping allegations.

'For something to be used on humans it has to be dispensed and labelled properly. Because these vials were unlabelled they were still halfway through the compounding process. They hadn't been completely finished yet. It is similar to someone coming into the pharmacy and buying some Betadine or some Dettol and then taking it and re-labelling it as a soft drink and giving it to someone to drink. That is essentially what Dank has done; he has taken something that wasn't supposed to be used on humans—or not yet anyway—and he has made someone drink it. Dank is the person who has put the human therapeutic stamp on it.'[20]

It is a shaky foundation for a lasting business relationship. Alavi suspects Dank of cheating him. Dank accuses Alavi of incompetence by putting stuff in the wrong vials. Charter suspects he is at risk of being cut out of the loop and he duly is, with Alavi soon finding a cheaper supply of peptide materials from another source. The business discussions between Dank and Charter go nowhere. The sports scientist and the drug importer soon go their separate ways. Meanwhile, there is another problem; no one has been paid. The nominated customers for the December batch of peptides are the Medical Rejuvenation Clinic and the Institute of Cellular Bioenergetics. Dank is a director of both. He is also the Essendon sports scientist. Alavi gives Dank the peptides but where should he send the invoice? The final decision is taken by Alavi's lab assistant, Vania Giordani. Over the summer, Giordani has become used to the sight of Dank. He is a regular visitor to the pharmacy and seems fascinated by every aspect of the work they do. Alavi permits Dank to move freely around the backrooms of the business. On the last day of January, when Giordani is finalising the month's accounts, she mistakenly bills the Essendon Football Club for twenty-one vials of Hexarelin and twenty-six vials of Thymosin. Dank is given the invoice.

Throughout February, Alavi chases Dank for his money. So does Charter, who won't get paid until Alavi does. Eventually Alavi discovers the billing error. He credits the cost to Essendon and bills MRC for the peptides. Another month passes without any payment from MRC or Dank. MRC has become a significant customer of the Como Compounding Pharmacy. Alavi is spending an enormous amount of time responding to emails and phone calls from two MRC directors, Van Spanje and Dank. But, as he complains to Charter, he can't keep giving them peptides for free. He tells Charter he is seriously considering dropping their business and moving on. It is only after Alavi threatens to cut off Dank from any more peptides altogether that the MRC account is settled.

Dank is interested in more than treating footballers and private clients. He also has research projects on the go. The blood testing at Essendon is continuing. So are Dank's discussions with David Kenley, the chief executive of Metabolic. Metabolic owns the rights to AOD-9604, the tiny fragment of growth hormone so befuddling to ASADA investigators, WADA, the AFL and Essendon in the early months of the doping scandal. Kenley and Dank first met in 2010, when the Metabolic chief was looking for ways to rekindle development and investment in the peptide. They remained in regular contact. At one point they looked at trying to establish another clinical study in Sydney. That fizzled into something less ambitious: a proof of concepts outline for a study involving two obese people and two people with bone fractures. When Dank goes to work for Essendon, he is still completing the draft proposal for Kenley. AOD-9604 soon takes him further afield. In April 2012, he travels to Qatar, with the approval of Kenley, to pitch the idea of a major clinical trial involving AOD-9604 as a preventative medicine for obesity and type 2 diabetes.

Qataris are among the fattest people in the world. According to Qatar's National Health Strategy, seven out of ten people in the United Arab Emirate are overweight. As of 2012, 43.2 per cent of women and 39.5 per cent of men were considered obese.[21] Unsurprisingly, Qataris are disproportionately diabetic. The health implications of this are grave but for an Australian sports scientist trying to find investors in an anti-obesity drug, the opportunities are great.

Dank flies to Doha to discuss AOD-9604 with Dr Peter Fricker, a prominent Australian sports physician then working at ASPETAR, Qatar's dedicated orthopaedic and sports medicine hospital. Andrew Moufarrige, a former colleague of Dank's from a job he briefly held selling GPS data to NRL clubs, including Cronulla, is also at the meeting. Fricker isn't sold on the idea but he is interested enough to invite Dank back for a second meeting in November. This time, Dank brings Kenley with him. Kenley believes that if not for the drug scandal, he and Dank could have landed a substantial new investment in AOD-9604.

'It all fell over when the February announcement was made, the darkest day in Australian sport,' Kenley laments. 'The people who were introducing us were expats and everyone essentially ran for the hills as soon as that announcement came out. They weren't sure what sort of mud was flying and who it was going to stick to.'[22]

ASADA suspects Dank and Kenley of being party to a secret clinical trial involving AOD-9604 and Essendon players. The allegation is based on four things: the blood tests of the Essendon players that Dank orders; Dank's association with Kenley and advocacy of AOD-9604; the proof of concepts outline that Dank completes for Kenley after he begins working at Essendon; and a series of case studies involving the use of AOD-9604 that Dank produces for Kenley shortly after he leaves Windy Hill. In particular, ASADA investigators are suspicious of four case studies documenting the use of AOD-9604 by professional footballers. Kenley is adamant that AOD-9604 was not trialled at Essendon. If anything, the drugs scandal cost Metabolic its best chance of securing a trial in Qatar. He confirms that Dank, after he left Essendon, was commissioned by Metabolic to write a series of case studies documenting his work with AOD-9604. He says Dank produced twenty-five case studies, the majority of which related to obesity patients. The four footballers were not injected with AOD-9604. They were treated with a cream containing the peptide.

'The ASADA people are trying to look at that with the beauty of hindsight and say because there were case studies there was a clinical trial going on,' Kenley says. 'The fact was there was never a clinical trial.'[23]

Kenley is principally interested in Essendon as a potential source of investment. If Kenley is going to fund a new series of clinical trials into the regenerative properties of AOD-9604, he needs new financial backers. Through Dank, Kenley sounds out James Hird, who in turn arranges a meeting with his club chairman David Evans at Evans' East Melbourne office. As a favour to his coach, Evans agrees to meet with Kenley and another representative from Calzada, the parent company of Metabolic, in February 2012. The Calzada reps give their usual investor spiel about AOD-9604 and another Calzada property, an experimental polymer used to treat burns victims. Dank also comes to the meeting. Evans listens politely and isn't interested. Calzada is looking for capital raising; Evans and Partners isn't a capital-raising firm. The most curious thing about the meeting is no one mentions that AOD-9604 is being used at Essendon.

Whatever is going on at Essendon in 2012, things are heating up along Peptide Alley. Trent Croad has joined the peptide business and is working for Robin Willcourt at his Epigenx clinic. Croad's title is business development manager and his job is spruiking peptides to sporting figures. Croad is a charming retired footballer with a premiership to his name. With a strong handshake and a gleaming smile, he knocks on the doors of football clubs and racing stables, offering the promise of supplements that will make horses, dogs and people all run faster. One night when Willcourt is working back late, Croad bursts into his office in a panic. The former Fremantle and Hawthorn footballer is sweating, his face the colour of egg whites. He is rambling, barely coherent.

'The fucking Comancheros!' he exclaims. 'Fucking Comancheros!' Willcourt tells him to slow down, to tell him what happened. Croad explains that he has just come from The Olsen, a swanky hotel bar and restaurant next to Mal Hooper's Hypermed clinic. He was there to meet some people about a peptide deal. One of them, a patched member of the Comancheros Outlaw Motorcycle Club, had a bag of money, a paper bag with $250,000 in cash. The bikie demanded to know if Croad had the peptides. Croad didn't. The bikie got angry and threatened him.

Willcourt looks at Croad. He doesn't know whether to believe a word of it but he can see Croad's fear is real. He suspects Croad has been cooking up a side deal with someone, and that he is in way over his head. Willcourt also realises that whatever Croad was up to, he wasn't planning to include his business partner in it. He is fond of Croad but doesn't feel he can trust him. Trust is becoming scarce in this little corner of Melbourne. By the end of the 2012 football season, Willcourt and Croad's association is at an end. Croad quits the peptide business and goes to work for a landscape gardener.

By this stage, the Australian Crime Commission has Peptide Alley in its sights. One by one, they are hauled in before an ACC examiner: Stephen Dank, Nima Alavi, Shane Charter, Robin Willcourt, and even Trent Croad. When they receive a summons, they have no choice but to attend. They can bring a lawyer but some choose to go alone. Once inside the windowless ACC examination room, the interrogation is like a scene from a Franz Kafka novel. The examiner has no name. They can address him as 'Sir'. He sits perched on a raised dais, protected by a thick metal rail. The examination subjects are seated in the middle of the room. They feel small, like a bug under a microscope. An ACC lawyer sits off to one side, calling out questions from an exaggerated distance. There is another witness behind them, face obscured. They never know who is there. They must answer all questions. They must produce any documents the examiner asks for. If they lie to Sir they risk five years in jail. None of them are accused of a crime but the ACC suspects something very dodgy has taken place. They think Essendon is in the middle of it all.

Dank, when returning to Melbourne from his second trip to Qatar, is detained by customs officers. They tell him they need to inspect his phone, that they are looking for illegal pornography. It is a ruse. They are looking for evidence of peptides, not porn. Customs is working with the ACC as part of Project Aperio. As soon as Dank hands over his phone, the ACC downloads his text messages with Charter, Robinson and Hird. The blackest day is coming.

Throughout the dramatic events of February 2013, Alavi, Dank and Willcourt stay in business. Thanks in no small part to the drugs scandal, it has never been better. On the same day that Senator Kate Lundy and Justice Minister Jason Clare release the findings of the ACC report into Project Aperio, the Therapeutic Goods Administration sends a letter to Edward Van Spanje, Dank's fellow director at the Medical Rejuvenation Clinic. It is a detailed, politely worded warning. The TGA knows that Van Spanje is selling peptides online for human use. The peptides are those at the centre of the drugs scandal—AOD-9604, SARMs, Melanotan II and the growth hormone releasing peptides Hexarelin, CJC-1295 and GHRP-6. None of them are included on the Australian Register of Therapeutic Goods. None of them can be legally imported, manufactured or sold as therapeutic goods:

> Our records indicate that these products are not included in the ARTG in respect to you or your company as required by law. You are therefore to cease any importation or manufacture along with advertising and supply immediately of these products ...[24]

The drug regulator has belatedly discovered what every gym junkie has long known; that peptides are being illegally sold all over Australia with the click of a mouse.

Van Spanje knew this day was coming. His only surprise is that it has taken so long. The TGA attention will be enough to close down some rival websites and perhaps push some smaller peptide sellers into another line of work. This will mean more business for the MRC, which can legally channel sales through a loophole in the Therapeutic Goods Act; a provision that exempts compounded medicines from regulation. All you need is a script and a pharmacist willing to compound peptides. After the blackest day in Australian sport, Van Spanje and Dank need Willcourt and Alavi more than ever.

More a marriage of convenience than chemical attraction, the relationship comes to an end in the winter of 2013 over the case of the missing peptides. On 5 July 2013, a well-informed, very wealthy customer hobbles into the Epigenx office of Willcourt. He has been referred to Willcourt by Dank after looking up the sports scientist at the centre of the peptides storm. The man is a millionaire many times over and stricken with a permanent, muscle-wasting disease. He has been taking growth hormone for years and is the full bottle on peptides. Rich and incurable, he is the perfect customer. Willcourt prescribes the shop: Testosterone, a form of human growth hormone called Scitropin, Hexarelin, the muscle-building protein Follistatin, Folic Acid and AOD-9604. He also gives repeats for the lot. It is a year's supply of drugs and a $12,000 sale for Alavi, Willcourt's compounding pharmacist of choice. The man climbs carefully into his chauffeur driven car and is not seen down Peptide Alley again.

It is some weeks later that the man becomes suspicious. He is reading his credit card statement and notices the $12,000 charge by the Como Compounding Pharmacy. He didn't go to the pharmacy himself. With his mobility restricted, he asked his personal assistant to take care of it. It seems like a lot of money for the drugs he received. He searches through his files and finds the receipt. It is only then that he realises that he's been fleeced. He hasn't received many of the drugs he paid for and he has been prescribed way more than he needs. He has spent half his life seeing doctors. He knows they are duty bound not to overprescribe medicine. He also knows that pharmacists are ethically required to make sure any medicines they dispense reach the patient they are intended for. The man knows he's been ripped off.

When Alavi receives the angry phone call, he immediately suspects Dank. He remembers Dank picking up medicine for the wealthy customer. Did he keep some of them for himself? He accuses Dank of stealing peptides. Dank rejects the accusation. The customer sides with the sports scientist. As the customer reasons, it was Alavi with his credit card details, not Dank. The customer's personal assistant was supposed to pick up the drugs. Dank had nothing to do with it. Alavi is mortified. He flies to Sydney and pleads his case to the wealthy customer. The customer is not impressed. Alavi is incensed. He has one more call to make.

Inside the St Kilda Road Victoria Police headquarters, the detectives of the Purana Taskforce are a little bored. The gangland war is over. Almost all the bad guys are dead or locked up. In the hullabaloo that followed the ACC report into Project Aperio, the taskforce has been given additional responsibility to investigate issues to do with integrity in sport. When a pharmacist named Nima Alavi cold-calls a taskforce detective with information about Stephen Dank, the detective is immediately interested. He visits with the pharmacist. He views video footage that Alavi provides from his store's security cameras. It is not the only complaint about Dank the Purana Taskforce receives.

One Saturday morning, Robin Willcourt unlocks the door of his South Yarra office. He switches on the light and notices a stream of paper in the tray of the fax machine. He picks up the faxes and sees they are referral letters and requests for blood work. The letter is to a Sydney doctor, purporting to be from Willcourt, referring to clients of Dank and MRC. The blood requests also carry his signature. He has no recollection of writing the letter. He does not recognise any of the names of the patients on the blood requests. He examines his signature more closely. On many of the forms, it is identical. Now deeply suspicious, he goes to his filing cabinet and pulls out the blood request forms he authorised for the Essendon footballers. He finds an exact match. Has his signature been photocopied? Suspecting forgery and fraud, he sends copies of the paperwork to Medicare and also to the Purana Taskforce.

Beneath the surface of a national drugs scandal, the Purana Taskforce investigates the allegations against Stephen Dank. It also takes an interest in Shane Charter. In an undercover sting operation, a police detective poses as an athlete and books an appointment with Charter, asking him what substances he might be able to supply. Several months later, Charter is detained at Melbourne Airport and taken to the Victoria Police St Kilda Road headquarters for questioning. He is released without charge but it is a temporary reprieve. He is eventually charged with one count of trafficking steroids, two counts of possessing steroids and a further seven counts of possessing growth hormone and other schedule four poisons. The amounts of drugs involved are small. Charter suspects something larger at play and vows to fight the charges.[25] Meanwhile, Dank receives a knock on the door. It is Purana Taskforce detectives. They want to talk to him about missing peptides and phoney signatures.

Dank is livid at the arrest. Even more so when news of it leaks within hours. He is questioned and never charged. He denies all allegations of wrongdoing. What's more, he knows that Alavi and Willcourt, the pharmacist and the doctor, have ratted him out.

6
GET THE BIGGEST STICK YOU CAN

THE MOMENT JAMES Hird opens his front door the relief is immediate. For days on end, TV crews and journalists have laid siege to his Toorak home. Collecting the morning papers, putting the kids in the car for school, heading to the shops for milk and bread; every mundane outing is greeted with the whirr of camera shutters and the same pressing questions: Will you step down? Have you taken banned drugs? What do you have to say to Andrew Demetriou? This Saturday afternoon, 13 April 2013, there are no thrusting microphones or squinting cameras on his doorstep, just a small, white-haired man with a grandfatherly smile. Bill Kelty, Australia's most influential union leader, confidant to Labor prime ministers and a Bombers supporter since John Coleman ruled the goal square in the 1950s, shakes the hand of the Essendon coach and steps inside.

As Australian Trades Hall Council secretary for nearly twenty years, Kelty was party and witness to seismic events in national affairs: the accord between the Hawke Government and the unions; the Kirribilli prime ministership succession agreement brokered then broken between Bob Hawke and Paul Keating; the epic industrial dispute on the waterfront. When he retired from the ACTU, Kelty was asked to nominate his greatest regret. Rather than picket lines or politics he thought of a drop punt: Tony Lockett's after-the-siren, long-range bomb for the Sydney Swans, which put Essendon out of the 1996 grand final.

'Jeez, I felt bad for two days,' he says.[1] Kelty was appointed to the AFL Commission in 1998, the year his great friend Ron Evans was elevated to chairman. He also chaired the advisory board of David Evans' private investment group, Evans and Partners. When the drugs scandal broke, he recused himself from any deliberations on his beloved football club. As he explained, David Evans is like a son to him; he can't sit in judgement of the Bombers. But as the consigliere to AFL chairman Mike Fitzpatrick and a mentor to Demetriou and Evans, Kelty remains uniquely placed to influence events.

Around the Hirds' dining table, they talk first about football. Essendon's match the previous night against Fremantle was a cracker. Kelty shakes his head in wonderment as the coach reflects on the comeback, the resolve of the players. Kelty has seen countless Bombers games and rarely a better win. The conversation then turns serious. Kelty tells the Hirds about a telephone hook-up between AFL commissioners two nights earlier. He reveals that during the discussion, AFL deputy chief executive Gillon McLachlan put forward arguments for why Hird should be stood down from his job—if not by Essendon then the AFL. James and Tania Hird listen carefully, the blood boiling in their ears. Hird is being publicly portrayed as the architect of the Essendon drugs regime. People are likening him to Lance Armstrong. They are calling for his head. All this before anyone from ASADA or the AFL has heard Hird's version of events. Kelty assures the coach the AFL will not force Essendon's hand. He has made this point strongly to his fellow commissioners during the conference call: if Hird goes without due process, the clamour will be for the AFL chief executive to go next.

Kelty, throughout all his years on the commission, has championed the principle of natural justice in causes less popular than

James Hird. Even when St Kilda footballer Stephen Milne is charged with rape midway through the 2013 season and there is a desire around the commission table to take a strong stance against violence against women, Kelty cautions the commission against dispensing summary judgement. The AFL is neither judge nor jury in criminal matters. Let the courts do their job, he counsels. Milne is allowed to play out the final season of his career while waiting for his day in court. The rape charges are later dropped when Milne agrees to plead guilty to a less serious charge of indecent assault.[2] Kelty's advice to the Hirds this day inside their Toorak house is simple. Don't stand down for any reason, he tells them. Get a lawyer. Get the biggest stick you can.

It is a football truism, long-held, that there are two kinds of coaches: those sacked and those about to be sacked. Depending on which newspaper you read, Hird is both of these. He could wallpaper his kids' bedrooms with newsprint clippings declaring that he should be sacked, cover the garage floor with those reporting he would be sacked, and frame the one, published briefly on *The Age* website in October 2014, stating that he had in fact been sacked. Throughout the scandal, Hird thinks many times that he is going to be sacked. The first of those times is 10 April 2013.

At Essendon's still-to-be-completed replacement headquarters at Tullamarine, Hird is taking the players through their main training session of the week. The assignment is one of the toughest in football: a road trip to Perth to play Fremantle. The Dockers are the AFL's best defensive team. They harass, chase, pressure. They hit hard. Their coach Ross Lyon is a tactical savant. He doesn't always win but coaching against him makes for a four-quarter migraine. To play the Dockers at Subiaco Oval you need fresh legs, clear resolve and a head free from distractions. Two days out from the game, while the Bombers are running through their drills, Hird's telephone rings. It is his barrister, Tony Nolan QC, a sports law expert who has deliberated on and appeared as an advocate in countless anti-doping cases. He tells Hird he has just spoken to the Essendon club solicitor, Tony Hargreaves. Hargreaves has learned that two investigative reporters from *The Age* newspaper, Richard Baker and Nick McKenzie, are planning to publish a story making a series of allegations against Hird. The most damaging of these allegations is that Hird was injected by Stephen Dank with the banned peptide Hexarelin throughout the 2012 season.

Hargreaves is Essendon's legal adviser and in-house investigator. He has interviewed Hird and other club officials at length about what went on the previous year at Windy Hill. He speaks daily to Evans, who is receiving regular updates from ASADA about the progress of its investigation. Evans knew this story was coming. A few days earlier he had called Hird to his house and told him that ASADA had evidence that Essendon's senior coach used Hexarelin supplied by Stephen Dank. Evans and his board believe the AFL will move against the coach. They don't think he can survive the allegations. The club directors are concerned that if the AFL sacks Hird, it could trigger a members' revolt and spill of all board positions. This is the last thing that Essendon needs in the middle of a drugs scandal.

Hargreaves suggests to Nolan that in the circumstances the best move for Hird is to pre-empt any AFL action and stand down until the storm passes. It is not just Hargreaves' view. When Nolan relays the message to Hird, the coach fears he is about to lose his job. He turns to Sean Wellman, one of his assistant coaches.

'They are trying to get rid of me,' he says flatly. Hird's next call is to football manager Danny Corcoran, who is back at Windy Hill. He tells Corcoran that he needs time to find out what is going on. He is worried that if he goes back to the club he will be sacked on the spot and escorted off the premises. They come up with a plan. Corcoran picks up Hird's computer and meets him in a side street near the club. Hird has gone from Essendon hero to football fugitive.

As Hird drives home he knows his immediate fate rests in the hands of David Evans, his friend and club chairman. He thinks back to a strained conversation they had two weeks earlier, when they were talking about Hird's looming interview with ASADA. The club's publicly stated position is for all staff and players to fully co-operate with the joint investigation being conducted by ASADA and the AFL and truthfully answer all questions. Evans suggests that Hird should be less forthcoming. The Essendon president is fretting about the phone call from Andrew Demetriou on the night of Hird's fortieth birthday. Evans has already been interviewed by ASADA and didn't tell the investigators about the Demetriou call. He wants Hird to do the same. He is worried what the ramifications will be if ASADA suspects the AFL tipped off Essendon.

'Tell the whole truth to ASADA but not the bit about what Andrew Demetriou said to me,' Evans allegedly tells his friend.[3] Hird is uncomfortable about where this is heading. He tells Evans that he can't lie to ASADA but if he isn't asked he won't tell. Since Evans disappeared into another room to take that phone call from Demetriou, the relationship between Hird and Evans has changed. The Essendon coach perceives, for the first time he can remember, a distance between them. Has his friend decided that, for the good of the club, Hird must go?

When Tony Nolan hands Hird a printed copy of Nick McKenzie's questions, he expects the Essendon coach to slump in his chair. McKenzie and Baker are two of Melbourne's most accomplished investigative reporters. They have a reputation for tackling big, difficult stories. They have trusted sources within Victoria Police, the Australian Federal Police and the ACC. Evidently, extensive information about the Essendon drugs scandal has come from a very good source: Stephen Dank.

The reporters have provided Hird seventeen questions, all of them heavily loaded, including, 'Why did you consider it appropriate to support Steve Dank's sports science program given it involved giving players (via regular injections or other means of administration) a range of substances with uncertain scientific, health and performance enhancing properties?' 'Why did you allow yourself to be injected with Hexarelin given it is most likely banned by ASADA under S2 of the WADA code?' 'Why did you take Melanotan II?' 'How do you respond to claims by Steve Dank that you asked him to order Human Growth Hormone for your personal use?' 'Why do you consider it appropriate that you remain as senior coach?' They have given him a close-of-business deadline to respond.[4] Hird reads the questions carefully. Rather than slump in his chair, he rallies. He knows what the allegations against him are. He knows what he is fighting. There is no way he will stand down now.

Other people at Essendon are less convinced. Chris Heffernan, a club director, calls Hird. The two men were Essendon teammates. In the club's near perfect season of 2000, when Essendon won the pre-season competition, the premiership flag and lost just one match throughout the entire year, Heffernan was a star of the Bombers' midfield. As the only contemporary of Hird on the Essendon board, it is Heffernan's task to sound out his celebrated former captain's intentions. Hird is immovable. He tells Heffernan he has done nothing wrong.

The next person to call Hird is David Evans. Evans does not like confrontation. Even though he wants Hird to stand down, he will not compel the coach to do so. They talk it over and Hird again makes it clear he is not going anywhere. He tells his chairman that now they know what the allegations are they can work through it. Evans has another concern. The club has received notification from ASADA that Hird's interview will be next week. Again Evans broaches the thorny subject of the Demetriou phone call. This time Hird's response is more forceful.

'You are asking me to lie, I am not going to lie.' Evans insists that is not at all what he is asking Hird to do. He tells Hird that his telephone conversation with Demetriou has been misconstrued, that the AFL chief didn't mention the ACC, that it was questions Demetriou and his deputy Gillon McLachlan refused to answer over many conversations with Evans, rather than any single thing they told him, which convinced him that Essendon was under investigation.

James and Tania Hird arrange to meet with Tony Nolan at his house later that evening. Liz Lukin, the crisis management expert hired by Evans to advise the club through the doping scandal, is also there. At Hird's request, she will write a press release for the club to issue in response to the story about to be published by Fairfax newspapers. Again, the issue of Hird standing down as senior coach is discussed. Nolan advises against it. As he explains, anti-doping investigations are often long and complex. Any eventual case will be heavily contested and, potentially, subject to appeal. It may take years to resolve. Stand down now and it is unlikely you will ever come back. Lukin disagrees. She thinks it is best for everyone—for the club, for Hird—if he offers to stand down. Tania Hird is fiercely dismissive. Before Lukin can finish speaking, the adviser is told to butt out.

'We are not standing down under any circumstances,' Tania says flatly. A different story is already running on radio and social media. As the Hirds drive home and Lukin issues her press release, Twitter is alive with rumours that Hird is already gone, that he won't coach Essendon against Fremantle.

The next day arrives with the force of Mark McVeigh's knee back in 2002. The headline on the front page of Melbourne's *The Age* newspaper on 11 April is big, unambiguous and immensely damaging: 'Hird Injected Drugs'. The inside pages hit just has hard. There are details about players being injected with a menagerie of substances—peptides extracted from pigs' brains, colostrum from cows and sheep placenta. The paper's chief football writer Caroline Wilson declares Hird must quit or be stood down by the board. Her prognosis for the senior coach is bleak:

> The best-case scenario now for the highly paid coach who is emerging as a central figure in the club's doping investigation is that he was incompetent and naive to the point of delusional. The worst case is that he has been uncooperative

at a time when the Australian sporting landscape is demanding full disclosure.[5]

Hird's position is pronounced untenable. It becomes a familiar refrain.

It is a rolling, bruising story. Across the city, news reporters are woken by frantic chiefs of staff. Journalists and photographers are sent to Hird's house in Toorak, to Dank's house in Ascot Vale, to the Essendon Football Club, to AFL House. Hird is encircled by TV cameras as he leaves home and again as he arrives for work at Windy Hill. He looks shattered. He says the allegations are upsetting but he can't address them in detail before he speaks to ASADA and the AFL. On the club room steps, David Evans falters through a prepared statement. He already knows about the various substances—he was sitting in his East Melbourne office with Lukin and AFL officials a week earlier when ASADA investigator John Nolan listed them in sickening detail—but Dank's allegations against Hird give the scandal a new dynamic. It is now Hird, alongside Dank, at the centre of Essendon's shame. Evans says anyone who failed in their duty of care to players will be dealt with appropriately. The Essendon chairman adds a cautionary note that the board won't be making decisions based on newspaper reports.

'James and the others will be afforded the opportunity to talk to ASADA and the basic right to natural justice.' He is not convincing. When asked whether Hird should stand down, Evans turns his back and walks inside, leaving the question hovering over his football club.[6]

The Essendon players gather at Windy Hill for a light training run. The hares are running faster still. In Sydney, AFL boss Andrew Demetriou is door-stopped by reporters. He speaks emotively about bad things being injected into young men. Two things he makes clear: Hird will get his chance to speak to ASADA, and a day of reckoning is coming.

'As a parent, and not just as the chief executive officer of the AFL, the issues as reported surrounding the potential use of various substances are something that are disturbing. They are very disturbing. We don't conclude investigations on the basis of newspaper reports and James Hird will have an opportunity, I'm sure, to answer the questions that are put to him by ASADA. Notwithstanding that, it is very clear that, and I support the words of the chairman, David Evans, if any coach or official puts the duty of care of their players at risk then they will be held accountable.'[7]

Demetriou's words were chosen carefully and with brutal effect. In the space of twenty-four hours, the parameters of the drugs scandal are redrawn. Demetriou and Evans, the AFL and Essendon are aligned against the drugs scourge. James Hird is cast in the company of Dank. And there is still more to come.

'And now to our top story,' says Leigh Sales that night. With dramatic effect, the camera slowly pans in on the host of *7.30*, the ABC's flagship current affairs program. In Perth's Crown Plaza Hotel prior to the match against Fremantle, Essendon officials watch in their rooms, wondering what is coming next. Outside his hotel window, Hird can see one television van after another pulling onto the grassy verge of the Swan River. Text messages that customs officials lifted from Stephen Dank's mobile phone at the airport are now in the hands of the ABC.[8] They include texts between Dank and Hird between March and May 2012, the peak period of Essendon's injection regime. The messages between the coach and the sports scientist do not contain any reference to a banned substance. Nor do they support Dank's claim that he injected Hird with Hexarelin. Read closely, removed from the fast-moving events of April 2013, they don't implicate Hird at all. Yet, still, their release is damaging. They show the Essendon senior coach was given details about the injection program that not even club doctor Bruce Reid knew. They portray Hird as an overseer and keen supporter of Dank's needle work.

The messages are telling in another respect. Between 7 March and 11 May, the pair exchanged forty-two texts of interest to ASADA. Of those, all but fourteen were sent by Dank. They ranged from the perfunctory to medical gobbledegook. Sometimes they elicited a brief response from Hird, often none at all. If Hird was reading Dank's messages carefully, he would have known by early March that Dank was planning to administer a substance called Thymosin to Essendon players and that Dank was considering by early April the use of Cerebrolysin, the peptide extracted from pigs' brains. The coach's generic responses suggest he wasn't reading them closely at all. It is Dank seeking to draw Hird into his work, rather than Hird seeking to influence Dank. The sports scientist understands that Hird is the power at Essendon. The best way for Dank to guarantee his tenure is to convince the senior coach he is getting results. Hird wrongly assumed that whatever Dank was telling him he was also telling club medical staff. Hird didn't try to hide his text exchanges with Dank. He volunteered them to the AFL on 5 February before the press conference at AFL House; he offered them to David Evans shortly after the blackest day in Australian sport; he told Tony Hargreaves about them when he was interviewed by the club solicitor on 12 February; he offered them to Liz Lukin the day before the ABC story went to air. In the debate that rages, such subtleties are lost.

The chorus is now deafening. A new dawn brings more calls for Essendon to punt Hird. Patrick Smith, an influential sports columnist with the ear of the AFL chief executive and the Essendon chairman, argues the coach must go. He writes in *The Australian*:

> The text messages ... leave no option but for Hird to stand down. It is a question of his judgment, both personally and professionally. If he doesn't, Essendon chairman David Evans must demand he does.[9]

Smith reports that even Hird is convinced of this. The columnist writes that on the Wednesday night before *The Age* story is published, Hird decided to hand over coaching duties to Mark Thompson before changing his mind.

This report is denied by Hird, who suspects it has been maliciously leaked from the AFL, his own club or both. Then Andrew

Demetriou lowers the boom. During a radio interview with Neil Mitchell on the morning of the Fremantle match, the AFL boss all but confirms damning allegations against Hird in *The Age*.

'I think you'd appreciate that I have briefings that are more advanced than what is in the public domain … and I think it is terribly important that we now get the investigations finalised as quickly as possible.' You know things there that we don't, that are really concerning you? 'I think the things that are allegedly in the public domain now, I mean they are very fine reporters the fellows from *The Age*, Baker and McKenzie, I don't think people print things like that unless they are pretty sure about their facts.' Should Hird stand down? 'I think as he goes through his thought process, Neil, which I'm sure is a very stressful time for him and his family, that is an option he has to consider.'[10]

Game time. There are nearly 36,000 people at Subiaco Oval on that Friday night in Perth. The national television audience peaks at a whopping 1.3 million. Some have tuned in for the footy, others for a funeral. At half time, James Hird is a dead coach walking. The Bombers are down by six goals. They have kicked one goal for the entire night. Essendon appears drained of energy and purpose. The Bombers are overrun, both by the relentless Dockers and a rampaging scandal. Surely, the senior coach will have to go now. If the Essendon board won't sack Hird in the name of player welfare they will do it to win more football games. As absurd as this sounds, everyone in football knows it to be true—Hird better than anyone. If Essendon gets belted tonight he doesn't expect to coach again.

In the next hour of football a remarkable thing happens. The Essendon players, cast variously as hapless victims or negligent participants in a doping regime, turn Subiaco upside down. With one surge followed by another, the score line narrows. With two minutes to play, the teams are locked. What's left of the match is played out in chaotic free-form. The coaches can only watch, their chance to influence at an end. Near the Essendon goals, Bombers forward Stewart Crameri is given a moment's space, and then he kicks the ball into the purple blur of a Fremantle body. The rebound lodges into the hands of Paddy Ryder, the Essendon ruckman, who has his back to goal. He pivots and kicks in one motion, a balletic, left-foot hook that twists and tumbles through the mouth of goal. At the opposite end of the ground Fremantle's final chance is in flight. From 15 metres out Fremantle forward Chris Mayne watches his kick hit the post. He collapses onto the grass, his head in his hands. Essendon is celebrating. Madly, joyously. Players, coaches, supporters. All but the club's exhausted chairman, David Evans. Walking around the boundary, the Essendon chairman looks as though he has been to a funeral after all.

After the game, the Essendon coach walks into a small, airless room filled with television crews and journalists. There are microphones and a bottle of water on a table. He wants to make a statement. He wants to hit back, to refute things written about him that aren't true, to denounce those who have called for his head before he speaks to ASADA. He wants to blow the joint up. He wants to, but he doesn't. He has been told by those he still trusts to resist the temptation, to talk to ASADA first. Then he can have his say. When the inevitable question comes up during the press conference, he hints at how he'd like to respond but holds back.

'How do I say this? People say things and they are untrue and you know you have got truth on your side, you go hard and, when you get your opportunity, you tell the whole truth. And when the truth comes out I think I will be in a very, very good position and so will this football club.'[11]

On the red-eye flight back to Melbourne, Hird cannot sleep. He suspects the AFL of leaking against him but doesn't know why. He suspects someone at his own club is undermining him but he doesn't know who. He fears it may be one of the men he trusts most. Against all reason the Bombers are winning. Essendon is about to be split in two.

David Evans believed he had an agreement. It was not written down. It was not even a handshake. But it would hold as long as Essendon did the right thing. This was what the AFL kept telling him. This was what he kept telling his fellow club directors. Evans was told that if Essendon allowed ASADA to do its work, if the club investigated and accepted its own failings of governance and management, if it accepted whatever AFL sanctions were necessary and took tough action against club officials who allowed Stephen Dank through the door at Windy Hill, ASADA would spare the players. This was the grand bargain that shaped the management of the drug scandal throughout 2013, both at Essendon and within AFL House. The AFL believed it had an understanding with ASADA. The AFL Players Association believed a deal was in place. The Essendon board believed it would be painful but wouldn't end badly for the players.

'We understood that whilst this was obviously very serious and certain investigations needed to and should occur, it would never culminate in infractions notices,' says Paul Little, the Essendon director who will later replace Evans as club chairman. 'We were told that at board level. That was an understanding. I wouldn't go so far to say it was a deal.'[12]

The Essendon players were told as much. As the team was waiting to fly to Canberra back on 11 March to play a pre-season match against Greater Western Sydney, Hird received a call from Evans: 'Tell the players it will all be okay.' Evans has met with the AFL, he's met with ASADA, and the players don't have anything to fear from the doping investigation. In the Virgin Lounge at Melbourne Airport, the coach duly gathered his players and passed on the message. Whatever ASADA was doing, whatever they were reading about, David Evans has assured him it is all sorted. This was two months before the first Essendon player was interviewed by ASADA. The players were relieved, although perhaps a little confused.

The trouble is, it was nonsense. There was no deal, no agreement, only misunderstanding. ASADA's investigators were sympathetic to the Essendon players but this didn't mean they would ignore evidence of doping if they found it. ASADA chief executive Aurora Andruska believes it was essential for her organisation to work closely with the AFL but this didn't mean she'd dog a prosecution if ASADA established a case worth running.

'It was never in my head,' she says. 'That makes no sense to me. Maybe it was in their head. They are businessmen used to doing deals.'[13]

To understand the bargain the AFL thought it had, imagine the reckoning from the entire doping scandal as a basket of punishment. Within the basket there is a finite amount of punishment, all of which has to be meted out to someone. The more the club cops, the more that club officials cop, the less there is to dish out to the players. In this ridiculous construct—a construct created by some of the smartest men involved in the running of the national football competition—James Hird is worth bonus points. He is the biggest name; he has the most to lose. Any punishment he cops will go a long way towards ensuring the players are not charged with taking a banned substance and hauled before an anti-doping tribunal. In fact, Hird is a non-negotiable in any deal acceptable to the AFL. These are the AFL's minimum terms: Essendon's exclusion from the 2013 finals series, and Hird's exile from football, at least for a while. If Essendon can satisfy these two conditions, it will have a team to field next season.

On a mid-winter's night at Hird's house, as coach, club chairman and team doctor sit around the dining room table sharing a bottle of red, Evans broaches the subject with a breezy casualness.

'You wouldn't mind taking three months, would you?' he asks Hird. Bruce Reid, a friend to both men, nearly chokes on his wine.

'For what?' the doctor wants to know. Evans also floats the idea of Essendon forfeiting its premiership points and its place in the final series. Hird is aghast. This is 25 June and the Bombers are in the top four. Exclusion from the finals would be a savage penalty, a penalty borne largely by the players, the group least at fault for what happened at the club. Hird cannot ask his team to do this. As he sees it, stripping a club of premiership points is a punishment for cheating—for rorting the AFL's salary cap, manipulating the rules of the draft, deliberate team doping. Reid says he can't believe what Evans is suggesting.

'I said, "This bloke wouldn't cheat." I didn't think Hirdy would ever cheat. So what are we taking a penalty for?'[14] Evans says the AFL wants to know what penalties Essendon will accept. He keeps talking of this deal between the AFL and ASADA. He is worried it is going to fall over. The previous night, club captain Jobe Watson admitted during a television interview that he was injected with the contentious peptide AOD-9604.[15] No other player has admitted this. Evans is furious. Immediately after the interview goes to air he calls Hird.

'Jobe has fucked it, fucked the deal!'

Watson has done nothing of the sort. Paul Simonsson, the ASADA investigator overseeing the twin probes into Essendon and the NRL club Cronulla, has already assured the players they have no case to answer on AOD-9604. The peptide had been declared banned by WADA, not because it releases growth hormone or has anabolic properties or enhances sporting performance in some other way, but because it hasn't been approved for therapeutic use.[16] The vagaries and timing of WADA's position, announced on 22 April, guarantee that any doping case built on the use of AOD-9604 during the 2012 season will be a nightmare to prosecute. On 6 May, Simonsson tells the players he'd be mad to try it.

'I'll go as far as to say I would have rocks in my head if I was recommending that we pursue something like that,' he tells them. 'It shouldn't have been on the WADA list and it shouldn't have been listed as a prohibited drug.'[17] There is a reason Simonsson can confidently say this to a room full of Essendon players, staff, coaches and lawyers. He has been told as much by Richard Young, a US-based anti-doping lawyer who helped write the World

Anti-Doping Code and a hired gun brought in by ASADA to advise on the Essendon and Cronulla cases.

Simonsson has come to Windy Hill on a momentous day in the doping scandal. A summary of the findings of businessman Ziggy Switkowski's damning, club-commissioned report into the governance failings at Windy Hill is about to be published. ASADA is about to start interviewing players about what went on in 2012. Simonsson's comments about AOD-9604 encourage the players to be open and honest about what took place in Stephen Dank's basement office. He makes no mention of Thymosin Beta 4. No one at this stage is talking about Thymosin Beta 4 or any other banned substances. Shortly after Simonsson finishes talking, Essendon captain Jobe Watson heads in to his interview, the first player to face the investigators.

As the 2012 season Brownlow medallist, Watson has more riding on the outcome of the ASADA investigation than any other Essendon player. He knows that if he is found to have taken a banned substance it will trigger calls for him to be stripped of his medal. At the very least, he will become the Brownlow winner with an asterisk next to his name, in the same way that Mark McGwire and Barry Bonds' season home-run tallies will forever carry a chemical qualifier. At the start of his interview, with Simonsson's assurance fresh in his mind, Watson freely admits that Dank injected him with a substance he said was AOD-9604. Having told ASADA this, Watson feels comfortable saying the same thing in a television interview nearly two months later. He doesn't expect any repercussions. He doesn't expect his admission to plunge Essendon into crisis all over again. He certainly doesn't anticipate the hoots and hollers that will come from opposition supporters a few nights after the interview is broadcast, when Essendon plays the West Coast Eagles in Perth. In one of the more shameful episodes of the entire scandal, the AFL does nothing to come to Watson's aid. They too are worried about the deal.

What are the origins of this deal, this grand bargain? They can be found scattered throughout Aurora Andruska's spiral-bound notebook, in the handwritten notations she made of things said in her meetings with AFL and Essendon and government officials when the drugs scandal was running at its hottest. Think back to the early meetings when the AFL wanted to talk about amnesties and player innocence and explore the possibility of a no fault or negligence defence. Think back to two days after the blackest day in Australian sport, when the AFL and Essendon bosses spent a Saturday with ASADA in Fyshwick. What did AFL deputy chief Gillon McLachlan want? According to Andruska's staccato notes: 'Come to arrangement. Players found to be innocent. Duped. This is the outcome … Sanctions against Essendon. Held responsible. Hold individuals to account.'[18] Think back to the terms of ASADA's 20 February written statement, negotiated between the AFL, ASADA and Gillard Government and read to the players by Paul Simonsson. It committed the anti-doping body, in a roundabout way, to do everything it could to help players who fully co-operate escape without sanction. Remember the meeting at AFL House on 4 June, when Andruska and Richard Eccles, the federal government's most senior bureaucrat responsible for sport, met with Gillon McLachlan and the Essendon chairman? This was where McLachlan revealed to Andruska the results of a survey showing that football supporters were losing faith in the game and made clear the AFL's overarching desire to take whatever steps necessary to protect the integrity of the 2013 finals series, to preserve the brand. At the time of this meeting, the Switkowski findings were in, Essendon chief executive Ian Robson had quit and McLachlan had made clear that football operations manager Danny Corcoran's head was on the block. David Evans did not quibble as the AFL's second most powerful man detailed his plans to carve up the Essendon Football Club. Evans accepted this was the price. This was the deal.

David Evans is a collector of people. He likes to be surrounded, supported, liked. He thrives on consensus, rather than conflict.

He is thoroughly decent but not always decisive. The deeper the Essendon crisis grows, the less trust Evans places in other people at his football club. He has taken leave from his business to manage the scandal unpaid, full time. His circle of advisers shrinks to Liz Lukin, the public relations consultant who had previously worked for unions, the ALP and the AFL, and solicitor Tony Hargreaves. Both are experienced professionals but outsiders at Windy Hill. Increasingly, Evans looks to his friends at the AFL for guidance—chiefly Andrew Demetriou and Bill Kelty—rather than his fellow Essendon directors or senior officials at the club. He has an open line of communication with ASADA investigators John Nolan and Paul Simonsson but his relationship with James Hird becomes more guarded. Before the drugs scandal, the strength of the Hird–Evans relationship was already a weakness at Essendon. Hird liked dealing directly with the club chairman and Evans encouraged the coach to come to him, even on relatively small issues. As a result, senior managers, like chief executive Ian Robson and football manager Paul Hamilton and other board members, were excluded from Essendon's ruling clique. Once the Hird–Evans relationship starts to fracture, it leaves the club chairman isolated.

'He tried to do it on his own,' assistant coach Mark Thompson says. 'I think it overwhelmed him in the end.'[19]

Evans believes he is protecting the club. He believes he is acting in the interests of the players. He is genuinely distressed by what he has learned from ASADA about Stephen Dank's supplement regime. He is convinced the scandal is too big for the club to try to handle on its own. It needs the help of the AFL and others. On 5 March he had asked Ziggy Switkowski, a business associate of his late father Ron, to report on what took place at Essendon. The idea of an independent report was suggested by Lukin, who argued the club needs to be seen to be doing something. Evans is convinced that if Essendon addresses its own mistakes it will count in the club's favour when its inevitable reckoning with the AFL arrives. Switkowski's brief wasn't to establish whether Essendon players took banned substances. As a former chief executive of Telstra and a prominent board director, Switkowski's expertise isn't in pharmacology or the complexities of the World Anti-Doping Code. Rather, his task was to examine the extent to which management and governance failures contributed to the scandal. His full report, prepared for the Essendon board, was not made public. A summary of his findings was published by Essendon on 6 May, the same day Paul Simonsson gives his 'rocks in my head' address at the club. The published summary, with its colourful turn of phrase and damning findings, lays bare the organisational dysfunction at Essendon throughout the 2012 season and provides the most quoted line of the entire drugs scandal: 'a disturbing picture of a pharmacologically experimental environment never adequately controlled or challenged or documented.'[20]

The full report, written for the eyes of Essendon directors only, is even more vibrant in its language. It portrays Stephen Dank as knowledgeable and experienced in elite sport and his work habits as appalling. Dank's boss Dean Robinson is cast as a well-intentioned, inept manager. Robinson's boss Paul Hamilton is depicted as too weak to preserve proper lines of reporting. Ian Robson, the chief executive, is adept at the commercial side of the business but pays insufficient attention to the goings on inside the football department. Switkowski is astounded by the lack of documentation kept by Essendon about the substances given to players. What records that were kept are ambiguous. For the same reasons that any doping case against Essendon players will be so difficult to prove, Essendon is condemned.

Switkowski's assessment of Hird is finely balanced. Switkowksi interviewed neither Dank nor Robinson, who was stood down by the club on 5 February, the day of the Essendon press conference at AFL House, and never returned to work. The decision not to interview Robinson was taken on the advice of Essendon's lawyers, who were facing a likely breach of contract lawsuit from the high-performance manager. The absence of testimony from anyone who worked in Essendon's high-performance department denies Switkowski an important perspective and limits the depth of his report. It also means his judgement of Hird is not clouded by either Dank or Robinson's claims about the senior coach. In Switkowski's view, Hird made serious errors.

The coach's instructions about all supplements needing to be approved by the club doctor and be WADA compliant were clear enough but Hird assumed, rather than ensured, that his instructions were followed. Switkowski is troubled by Hird's edict that high-performance staff should not 'cross the line', concluding that it is unwise and possibly reckless for a club to approach the boundary that separates banned substances from permitted substances. Switkowski also notes that responsibility for Hird's failings are shared by the club; that having appointed a first-time senior coach, the club took few steps to mitigate his inexperience and limit his mistakes. After spending six weeks at the club conducting his review, Switkowski is none the wiser about who is supposed to be Hird's boss. Mark Thompson was brought in as a mentor but Thompson saw his job as limited to football matters only. Anyone tempted to challenge Hird did so with the knowledge that he had a direct line to the chairman of the board.

The provision of the Switkowski report also exposes growing tensions within the Evans–Hird relationship. On the morning a press conference is called to release its recommendations, Evans, the adviser Liz Lukin, Hird and club director Paul Little haggle over the wording of the publicly available summary. Even as television crews are setting up their cameras at Windy Hill, calls are made to Switkowski about whether certain things can be rephrased. The points of contention relate to the depiction of Hird, who has spent the past month under intense pressure to stand down from his job. Any public criticism of the senior coach by Switkowski will lead to further calls for Hird to resign and trigger more instability at the club. Hird and Little want greater acknowledgement of the directive the coach gave to Dank and Robinson, that all supplements must be approved by the doctor and be WADA compliant. Lukin argues against this, insisting the summary should be kept in Switkowski's words. She has a room full of journalists next door. How would it look if it gets out that Essendon has doctored Switkowski's work to protect James Hird? Amid these divisions, Switkowski and Evans side with Lukin, against Little and Hird. Evans authorises the summary to be published as written and the full report made available to the AFL.

The AFL has broad powers to sanction clubs for any breach of player rules. Its weapon of choice is a sweeping provision contained in rule 1.6, which states:

> Where the Commission is of the opinion that a person (or club) has contravened the provisions of the Memorandum or Articles of Association or the AFL Regulations or the AFL Player Rules or has been involved in conduct which is unbecoming or likely to prejudice the interests or reputation of the AFL or to bring the game of football into disrepute, the Commission may deal with any such matter in such manner as the Commission in their absolute discretion think fit.[21]

By commissioning the Switkowski report and providing it to the AFL, Evans bares the throat of his club and coach. It is a fateful judgement about who his true friends are.

Hird is losing faith in Evans' ability to handle the drugs scandal. The day of Essendon's match against Fremantle, the day Andrew Demetriou publicly said Hird should consider standing down, the Essendon coach had a 90-minute telephone discussion that redefined the terms of his conflict with the AFL and attitude towards his friend and club president. Until this point, Hird had placed his legal affairs in the hands of Tony Nolan QC, an experienced sports lawyer. At the urging of Nick Harrington, a barrister Hird knew through his kids' school and neighbourhood sport, Hird sought the advice of Steve Amendola, an industrial relations lawyer who came to national prominence as Peter Reith's legal adviser during the waterfront dispute. Harrington's view was that Nolan is an accomplished sports lawyer and arbitrator, but Hird needed a bare-knuckle fighter. Amendola, a solicitor whose natural habitat is the fiercely contested ground between building companies and construction unions, would be a good candidate.

Within hours of Bill Kelty urging Hird to lawyer-up, the coach puts Amendola's firm Ashurst on a retainer. Amendola says Hird's case had immediate appeal.

'It was big, it was difficult, it could be a train wreck,' he says. 'I like that. And the fact that I thought he was being scapegoated.'[22] Having negotiated and litigated protracted disputes against the Maritime Union of Australia and the Construction, Forestry, Mining and Energy Union (CFMEU), Amendola also values an assertive public relations strategy. His new client was getting belted daily in the media, with Hird suspecting leaks from the AFL, ASADA and his own club. Ian Hanke, a cigar-chomping, battle-hardened Liberal Party spin doctor, known for shaving his head at the start of an election campaign, is brought on by Ashurst to level the playing field.

The shift in Hird's posture is immediate. Amendola is hired on 14 April and Hird appears before ASADA and AFL investigators on 16 April. In the two days between these events, Hird's bolstered legal team clashes with the AFL over its refusal to give a confidentiality undertaking ahead of the interview and over how many lawyers Hird can bring to his examination. It is a taste of things to come. During his nine-hour interview, Hird is asked about the meeting at David Evans' house on the night of his birthday. He recalls in full his understanding of the telephone conversation that night between Evans and Andrew Demetriou and his belief that the AFL tipped off Essendon about the soon-to-be-released ACC report. On the basis of Hird's testimony, ASADA recalls Evans the following day and quizzes him about his conversation with Demetriou. The Essendon chairman insists he wasn't tipped off. The disparity is accepted without further questioning by ASADA, but between Hird and Evans it represents a fundamental breach of trust. The moment Evans walks out of his second interview with ASADA his friendship with Hird is over. It is just that neither of them know it yet.

The *Herald Sun*, a newspaper not renowned for its patience, delays the story for a day. News Corp's Victorian managing director Peter Blunden has edited the paper for more than ten years. He understands Melbourne, he knows the damage an allegation like this could do to AFL chief executive Andrew Demetriou, a man he happens to like. News Corp is a commercial partner of the AFL. The *Herald Sun*'s football coverage is essential to sales. It does not lightly accuse the most influential man in Australian sport of a crime. Blunden and *Herald Sun* editor Damon Johnston are satisfied that the paper's two senior football writers, Michael Warner and Mark Robinson, have the story down pat. A first-hand witness has told them about the meeting at David Evans' house and Essendon's actions the next day are consistent with a football club that has been tipped off about a soon-to-be-released report. Getting out in front of a story, controlling the message, it's the AFL way. Yet, still, Blunden doesn't want Demetriou ambushed.

At its most serious, the allegation is that Demetriou has breached the ACC secrecy provisions. Robinson is to call the AFL chief first thing the next morning and give him an entire business day to respond. In the end, Demetriou doesn't need nearly that long. As soon as Robinson puts the allegation to him, Demetriou erupts. It isn't the first paint-peeling spray that Robinson has copped from the AFL boss but it is the daddy of them all. With slightly trembling hands, Robinson puts down the phone. Then he crosses the newsroom and plays the tape to his chief of staff to figure out what part of it, if any, they can use.

Before Robinson made his phone call to Demetriou, a frost had already formed on the *Herald Sun*'s relationship with the AFL. There are said to be more journalists accredited to cover football in Melbourne than politics in Canberra. Competition for stories is unrelenting. Within this willing mass of back-page reporting, no one is more critical of the AFL's handling of the drugs scandal than Robinson and Warner. Robinson is an Essendon supporter and a friend of James Hird. For years, he ghostwrote Hird's column for the *Herald Sun*. Amid the raging drugs scandal, he becomes a trusted confidant. Warner is unlike most football journalists. He shifted onto the AFL round after reporting on crime and politics. When he first started writing about football, an old hand in the *Herald Sun* newsroom warned him against taking on AFL House: you can't beat City Hall. It is advice Warner has steadfastly ignored.

The AFL saw both journalists as a problem. In particular, AFL boss Andrew Demetriou developed a deep animus towards Warner. Not long before the tip-off story breaks, Demetriou called News Corp chief executive Kim Williams demanding something be done about him. An AFL staffer had brought to his attention a tweet depicting a man with his head in the sand, referencing Demetriou. Warner had retweeted it. Kim Williams is sympathetic to the AFL boss. He is worried that both Robinson and Warner are becoming partisan actors in the drugs scandal. With his ear still hot from Demetriou's phone call, Williams rang Peter Blunden. The AFL wanted Warner sacked or stood down from reporting football. When Blunden refuses to take either action, the AFL denies Warner accreditation to cover the finals series. After Demetriou's off-the-record tirade at Robinson, the AFL chief accuses the journalist of playing a tape of his expletive-laden rant to people around town. Demetriou demands satisfaction. He gets none after an investigation by Adrian Anderson, a former AFL football operations manager who previously worked at News Corp, concludes that Demetriou's allegation is baseless. Kim Williams resigns from News Corp in August 2013 and joins the AFL Commission in time for the next football season.

The tip-off story, first published on 25 July, is central to understanding the Essendon scandal. After months of being pummelled by leaks from the ASADA and AFL investigation to Fairfax journalists, Hird has decided to attack. The previous week, *The Age* again led its morning paper with a story portraying Hird as the guiding force behind Essendon's use of peptides. The story is based on the meeting between the Essendon coach, ASADA investigator

Paul Roland and AFL integrity services manager Brett Clothier in August 2011. The meeting was prompted by Hird's enquiry to a drug-testing officer about the use of peptides in football. The story claims that, at the meeting, Hird was warned off the use of peptides by the AFL.[23] The claim is at odds with what Hird told ASADA about the meeting and the recollections of Essendon football managers Danny Corcoran and Paul Hamilton, who also attended AFL House that day. Hird suspects sensitive information was leaked by the AFL to Caroline Wilson, *The Age*'s chief football writer, who has taken a strong stance against the Essendon coach, repeatedly calling for Hird to be stood down or sacked from his job. Subsequent events suggest Hird's suspicions may be well founded.

Within hours of the story being published, Clothier adds new evidence to the ASADA–AFL brief against Essendon. It is a detailed account of the meeting with Hird, nearly two years earlier, and it goes well beyond what Clothier and ASADA's own investigator recorded in their respective file notes at the time. According to Clothier, he spoke to Hird at the end of the meeting and 'reiterated to Hird that peptides were a serious risk to the integrity of the AFL, in the same category as steroids and HGH.' He implored Hird to report to the AFL any information he received about peptides being used.[24] The brief, contemporaneous notes taken of the meeting by ASADA's Roland described the exchange as a 'general discussion'. The ASADA investigators treat it as nothing more until they read the story in *The Age*. When they query Clothier about this, he constructs from his memory and own brief notes an expansive description of his peptide 'warning' to Hird. ASADA's investigators accept Clothier's belated recollections without putting them to Hird, Paul Hamilton or Danny Corcoran.[25] The story isn't as damaging to Hird as previous claims about his use of Hexarelin but, in Hird's mind, it crystalises the forces at work against him: the AFL, ASADA and their willing media partner, Fairfax.

When Hird approves the release of the tip-off story to the *Herald Sun*, his target is Andrew Demetriou but he knows the revelation will leave his friend David Evans in no man's land. Evans knows this too. On the afternoon of 24 July 2013, the day before the story breaks, Hird receives a call from Evans. Demetriou has just been on the phone to Evans, livid about what is about to be published. Evans is distraught. Hird feels for his friend but he puts the hard word on the club president to back him up.

'Mate, you have to tell the truth. I'm a very good friend of yours, you must tell the truth. You will get caught out on this.' The problem is, Evans and Hird have not agreed on what the truth is. Hird insists that on the night of his birthday, Evans told everyone at his Hawthorn house that Demetriou had confirmed Essendon as the club under investigation for suspected doping. Evans says this interpretation goes beyond what was actually said. Hird does not believe him. Why did Evans ask Hird to withhold information from ASADA?

'In my office you said to me, "You can speak to them about anything but don't tell them what Andrew told me".' Evans is not for turning.

'I know I said this but I pushed Andrew Demetriou very hard. I read his body language on which club it was. I didn't say Andrew Demetriou said anything.'[26]

The decision to take on Demetriou and, if necessary, expose Evans, was carefully considered. Hird's lawyer Steve Amendola does not confirm his client as the source of the *Herald Sun* story but makes clear his view at the time: Hird would not survive as Essendon coach if Evans retained control of the board. Amendola and Hanke both perceive that Evans was compromised and was, perhaps unwittingly, furthering the interests of the AFL rather than those of his own club. They also suspect that Liz Lukin, Evans' handpicked public relations adviser, was fuelling the campaign against Hird. Lukin has since taken a job as the AFL's head of corporate affairs.

'You can't prove that the AFL was leaking but it was pretty bloody obvious they were leaking,' says Amendola. 'The most obvious thing was that Wilson article. Where else would she get something like that given it was the same date? My sense is the AFL thought something bad had happened and there is a lot of material to suggest that something bad did. They made up their mind. They were negotiating hard with ASADA for a protocol that effectively gives the players an out. Someone has to pay the price. If it ain't going to be the players it is going to be someone, and Hird is top of the list. My view was, and it had been for a while, that as long as Evans was president Hird was going. If Evans wasn't president, he may or may not go. When the story broke about the tip-off, that was the moment. If Evans had told what I consider to be the truth the whole thing would have gone in a different direction.'[27]

The tip-off story had another effect. Until now, Fairfax had led the coverage of the doping scandal in Melbourne. Its investigative journalists, Nick McKenzie and Richard Baker, had extracted important information from Dank and traced the threads of the scandal to drug importer Shane Charter, anti-ageing doctor Robin Willcourt, and David Kenley's Metabolic Pharmaceuticals. Caroline Wilson had been a prominent, influential voice calling for Hird to resign. The *Herald Sun* now owned the story behind the story. Two rival mastheads with competing narratives were locked in a furious media war. The consequence was that the biggest sports story in living memory, like so many political stories of recent years, was polarised. The middle ground, the place where truth usually resides, was elusive to both sides of a raging argument. James Hird was either the Lance Armstrong of Australian sport or the victim of a vast injustice. Public opinion was divided, not according to weight of evidence but depending on which newspaper you read and which team you followed. Radio callers were indignant, the Twittersphere crackled with conspiracy theories.

The *Herald Sun* published its story and Evans publicly supported Demetriou's account of events. The dispute between the Essendon coach and president about what took place that late summer evening is irreconcilable. The day after the story breaks, Evans again calls Hird. Evans and his wife Sonya have not slept. At 4 a.m. that morning, they are awake, bleary eyed, talking about what Evans should do. They decide he should resign as club president.

Evans tells Hird that Andrew Demetriou has asked him not to quit but his mind is made up, it is just a question of when. Evans also has a message from Demetriou to the coach: there is no personal vendetta against him, and the suggestion the AFL has already decided to strip Essendon of its 2013 premiership points is fanciful. On both these points, Evans is misled. Evans' tenure at Essendon, the club of his revered father Ron, is almost at an end, along with his friendship with Hird.

'I love you like a brother,' he tells the Essendon coach.[28]

That night Essendon plays Hawthorn. Just before the players run out, Hird seeks out Evans and the two men embrace. It is a scene laden with portent, part-Shakespeare, part Mario Puzo. The Hawks thrash the Bombers. At the final siren, David Evans is overcome with exhaustion and stress. He begins to cry and cannot stop. He feels ill. With the Essendon change rooms beneath the Docklands grandstand about to fill with footballers, supporters and journalists, he is led to a medical treatment area that smells of sweat and adhesive tape. He lies on his back and is comforted by his worried wife Sonya. In his resignation letter, he reveals it is friends rather than foes who have brought him down.[29]

7
IF THIS IS ALL THEY'VE GOT, YOU WILL WIN

THERE IS CERTAINLY no wink and a nod to the NRL, no tip-off to Cronulla. As the Australian Crime Commission prepares to release its report into alleged links between professional sport, crime and performance-enhancing drugs, it extends the same courtesy to Rugby League as it does the AFL. One day before Dave Smith is officially due to start his new job as NRL chief executive, the former Lloyds banking executive is summoned to Canberra for a meeting with the ACC, ASADA and government officials. In this meeting, however, ACC chief executive John Lawler sticks to the script vetted by his lawyers. There is no hint, tacit or otherwise, about which clubs are locked in the cross hairs of a national drugs scandal, there are no phone calls between Smith and Cronulla officials. The first time Cronulla chairman Damian Irvine learns the Sharks might have a problem is the morning before the blackest day in Australian sport, when he reads a story written by journalist Josh Massoud in Sydney's *Daily Telegraph* on 6 February 2013. There is one line, buried towards the bottom of an article about sports scientist Stephen Dank's previous history with Manly, that catches the chairman's eye: 'In 2011, Dank did some consulting for

Penrith and also took his expertise to the Cronulla Sharks.'[1] Irvine is perplexed. Cronulla, one of the most frugal clubs in the NRL, does not pay consultants often and never lightly. If Dank was on the books in 2011 he would have known about it. Until now, he has never heard the name Stephen Dank. Now that he has, he won't easily forget it.

If you need to know something about the football operations of the Cronulla Sharks there is only one place to go. Opposite the Andrew Ettingshausen grandstand on the leagues club side of Shark Park, there are two adjacent offices on the mezzanine level of an auditorium. In one sits Shane Flanagan, the Cronulla senior coach. In the other sits Darren Mooney, the club's football manager. Between the two of them, they look after every aspect of the club's core business: winning football games. In his two and a half seasons in charge of the Sharks, Flanagan has established himself as a highly regarded coach. Irvine, the club chairman who appointed him, envisages years to come with 'Flanno' in the coaches' box. Mooney, according to Cronulla's bare-bones management structure, is the club's most senior paid employee. Irvine, who does all his work for the club on a voluntary basis, spends more time at Shark Park than he can afford to. Even then, he is only ever there a few hours a day. In the absence of a chief executive, it is Mooney's job to run things. His responsibilities straddle the three pillars of the football department: coaching, recruiting and conditioning.

When Irvine walks into Flanagan's office on 6 February and asks about Stephen Dank, both the coach and the football manager assure their chairman there is nothing to worry about. Dank's only association with Cronulla was a fleeting involvement at the start of the 2011 season, when he came to the club a few times to help them calibrate some new GPS systems and software.

'He never had anything to do with any players,' the chairman is told. 'It is ridiculous that we are even mentioned in this. It is appalling. Do something to clear our names.'[2] Shortly before the jaw-dropping scenes in Canberra the following morning, when two federal government ministers and a parade of sports chiefs sternly address the TV cameras, Cronulla is one of half a dozen NRL clubs told by league headquarters to expect a visit from Deloitte auditors. They'll be going through their computer hard drives, servers, phones—the lot. Irvine thumbs an email from his phone to his fellow directors, telling them they have nothing to fear.

> Dear directors,
>
> Some media today and yesterday links our club with Steve danks who is currently being investigated for the Essendon doping scandal.
>
> I was at the club yesterday dealing with another matter when Shane Mattiske called to advise the NRL were doing a full audit /investigation. i advised that we would fully comply as per our obligations under asada andNRL rules.
>
> I spoke with Shane Flanagan and Darren mooney and advised them, both men clearly stated that danks was only consulted on which GPS equipment would be best to buy and was never part of our club, dealing with players or involved in sports science at all.
>
> NRL and Deloitte auditors attended the club and I asked Gy Wallace to work with them. Gy handled it well and will facilitate their audit but has askedfor some written documentation from them first.
>
> again, the coach and football manager could not have been any clearer in their assurances to me that this danks character was not involved in our club in any capacity that had him working with players or supplements
>
> Damian[3]

At the time he needs information about what has gone on at his club, Damian Irvine is badly misled. The suggestion that Dank did nothing more at Cronulla than fiddle with GPS units does not stand for long. On 8 February, Cronulla coach Shane Flanagan sends Irvine a clarifying email offering a very different recollection of Dank's involvement at Shark Park. It describes how he was introduced to the club through his work with GPS systems and then moved into supplying supplements to the players. It details concerns held by the club doctor, David Givney, about Dank's conduct and of 'alarm bells' ringing within the football department when it emerged that the sports scientist was treating players away from the club. Flanagan recounts how he and Darren Mooney stepped in to end the association midway through the 2011 season after Dank 'kept pushing the boundaries on supplements'.[4] Although the account is much closer to the truth than what Irvine was previously told by his coach and football manager, there is a crucial omission. There is no mention anywhere within Flanagan's 8 February email of Dank's supplement regime involving injections. Already, within twenty-four hours of the Canberra press conference, the force of the doping scandal has fractured Cronulla.

'It is fair to say that we were no longer working together as a team,' Irvine says. 'It is fair to say that he wanted us, and Darren wanted us, to circle the wagons, to be quiet and leave it in external hands. We felt that we had to act.'[5] The Cronulla directors, recognising the folly of trying to investigate their own club, commission Tricia Kavanagh, a former justice of the Industrial Court of New South Wales and an arbitrator with the Court of Arbitration for Sport, to find out what really happened.

As with Essendon chairman David Evans, the drugs scandal consumes Irvine. The difference is his ordeal while in charge of the club is mercifully short. Irvine resigns five weeks after the blackest day. The reason, ostensibly, is an ill-considered comment he makes to Phil Rothfield, another *Daily Telegraph* journalist, about Cronulla players being injected with horse drugs.[6] Irvine says he is in California, where it is 3 a.m. when Rothfield calls. Back at home, it has been a traumatic day for the football club. After receiving Tricia Kavanagh's report into the 2011 season, the Cronulla board stands down Flanagan as coach and sacks football manager

Darren Mooney, long-serving doctor David Givney, physiotherapist Konrad Schultz and head trainer Mark Noakes. Rothfield, a Cronulla supporter, is incredulous that the board has swung the axe against five popular club figures while Irvine, the board chairman, is overseas on a business trip. Over a long distance phone line, the journalist and the Cronulla president have it out like two cranky blokes in a front bar—Rothfield: 'Damian, this is your fault. I've told you for years you need a CEO. You should stand down.' Irvine: 'Mate, when paid staff fail to report … injecting players with equine substances, I can't help. Players deserve professional support, not people who risk their careers.'[7]

The equine substance Irvine suspects has been given to Cronulla players is TB500, a synthetic version of Thymosin Beta 4, the peptide at the centre of the Essendon drugs scandal. TB500 is used to reduce inflammation in racehorses. Irvine says he isn't told the conversation is on the record but when it is published in the next day's *Telegraph* it fuels the anger and betrayal of Cronulla fans. They are distraught that their coach has been dumped on the eve of a new season. They don't know what's in Tricia Kavanagh's report. Irvine and his board do but they can't make the details public. The board wants to do the right thing but it hasn't thought it through.

Within days, it is Irvine who goes and Flanagan is back in his job. What's left of the Cronulla board is spilled and a new one, elected on a jobs-for-the-boys ticket, reverses the decisions taken on the other staff. While the return of the coach is celebrated by Sharks supporters, Irvine is hounded by abusive phone calls and threats of legal action. The scandal races on but the walls close in around him. He is powerless and utterly alone. He checks himself into hospital and spends eight weeks in intensive treatment for depression. He grew up in the Sutherland Shire with sand between his toes and the Cronulla footy team in his heart. Once heralded as the club's financial saviour, he now says he would feel like an outcast if he walked through the gates at Shark Park.

The Cronulla players were excited about the arrival of Stephen Dank. Finally, they thought, the pauper club of the NRL is getting serious about sports science. The Sharks players are a talented group, fiercely led by Paul Gallen, one of the best forwards in the game. The Cronulla football department, with its chronic shortage of funds and staff, is considered an amateur outfit in a professional era. The Sharks' high-performance manager, Trent Elkin, says that among the bigger, richer clubs, Cronulla is a laughing stock.[8] Bruno Cullen, an experienced club chief executive brought in by the NRL to administer Cronulla through the early months of the drugs crisis, doesn't understand how anything gets done at Shark Park. At the Brisbane Broncos, a well-resourced club run by Cullen for eight years, he had twenty to thirty people to do the work that Irvine and a handful of board members are doing in their spare time.

'He and a couple of other guys there, their hearts were totally in survival mode,' Cullen says.[9] The only reason the players have a proper gym is because the coach organised golf days and fundraising lunches and squirreled away enough money away to refurbish the old one. At how many other professional football clubs would the senior coach come in during the off-season, roll up his sleeves and help with the tiling to reduce labour costs? When the scandal breaks, the private account Flanagan kept for fundraising is suspected of being used to funnel off-the-books money to Stephen Dank. Bruno Cullen says when he questions Flanagan about the account, the coach takes him on a tour of the gym facilities.

'From that point I didn't query it,' he says. 'There wasn't enough money to do what he had done, let alone paying Dank. I am not naive enough to say Dank never received anything but there is absolutely no proof that any money went to Dank through the Cronulla club and leagues club, and Flanno's work to provide the players with an up-to-date environment to train in looked pretty kosher to me.'[10]

Trent Elkin announces Cronulla's new recruit to the first-grade players in the middle of Shark Park on 18 March 2011. It is a Friday. Cronulla is due to play St George Illawarra in three days, at home, beneath the bright lights of Monday night football. After training, the high-performance manager sits the team down in the middle of the pitch. He tells them they've probably seen a new face around the club. His name is Stephen Dank. He's a top-notch sports scientist that Manly used for years. His services are wanted all over the world. He's the real deal. The players listen eagerly. They know some of the Manly players. They know rival clubs are doing all sorts of things that Cronulla can't afford in order to get their players fit and ready for games. If this Dank bloke is half as good as what Elks is saying he is, he will give them the edge they need. The Sharks have never won a premiership. It sounds like the club is serious about having a crack. Elkin then tells them the stuff Dank uses to help players recover needs to be injected. Among the group of footballers, a hand goes up.

'Did you say injections?' Elkin tells him not to worry. It has all been checked.

'I've checked it, the Doc's checked it. We have run it past ASADA, we have run it past WADA. Dank has been giving this stuff to the Manly boys for years. Have you ever heard of one of them testing positive? It is all good mate, don't worry.'[11]

The last training session before a game is known as the captain's run. The players trot out behind Paul Gallen, their refrigerator-shaped NSW State of Origin captain, Australian representative and heavyweight pug who has been menacing opposition teams for ten years. At the end of the short session, players are directed to the away team sheds, where Dank, Elkin and a wild-haired retired sprinter and supplements supplier named Darren Hibbert are waiting. Hibbert and Elkin perform the injections, which are administered into a pinch of stomach skin. The players are in and out in a few minutes. Dank doesn't administer the injections. He is mainly there to answer any questions the players have. He doesn't tell them exactly what is in the syringes. He doesn't mention anything about peptides.

'We are giving you aminos,' he tells the players. 'As a matter of fact, son, we are giving you the same stuff you normally take in your protein shakes, it's just that we are injecting it into you because it works better that way.' Dank has since told me he administered Cronulla players two peptides: CJC-1295 and GHRP-6. In 2011, both were considered substances banned by WADA. Dank didn't think they were. He still doesn't.

From the day of Elkin's introductory address in the middle of Shark Park to 29 May, when Dank is kicked out of the Cronulla change rooms after a Sunday afternoon game in Melbourne, the sports scientist's direct involvement with the club lasts about ten weeks. The club-sanctioned injections regime runs for only three weeks. The Cronulla team is injected for a second time before their next game against Penrith. Again, it is after the captain's run. Mark Noakes, the Cronulla head trainer and the club's NRL drug liaison officer responsible for ensuring that all supplements fall within the World Anti-Doping Code, brings a yellow sharps bin to the away team dressing rooms to dispose of the needles.[12] The players are not given any specifics about what is in the syringes. After the match, in which they flog the Panthers 44–12, they don't want to ask. In the lead-up to the next week's trip to New Zealand to play the Auckland Warriors, a third round of injections is administered. And that is it. Dank is never employed by the club, either on staff or as a consultant. Investigators find no evidence he received any money from the club. Dank's work at Cronulla is a neatly contained prequel to the program he runs at Essendon the following year. In Tolkien terms, Cronulla is a hobbit-sized scandal compared to the epic trilogy that unfolds at Windy Hill.

The similarities in how Dank operated at both clubs are instructive. At Cronulla and Essendon, he first won the trust of the high-performance manager and, for a time, the players, while sidestepping the scrutiny and scepticism of the long-serving club doctors. When describing his program to club staff and players, Dank was vague rather than misleading. He cloaked the substances he used in euphemisms and his methods in pseudo-scientific jargon. At both Essendon and Cronulla, the players were told to keep quiet about the program. Dank insisted this was not sinister;

he was merely trying to protect the competitive advantage of the clubs he worked for and the intellectual property of his work. Like the snake oil salesmen of the nineteenth century, Dank traded on mystique. His sales pitch was knowing something that others didn't. This was why, when current and former Cronulla players are investigated for suspected doping, most of them could honestly tell their lawyers and ASADA's investigators they didn't know what they were given. They also didn't know quite what to make of Dank. He didn't appear to keep records. He didn't seem to remember who he had injected and who he hadn't: 'Have you had your shot, son?' 'Yes, Danksie, Elks gave it to me twenty minutes ago.' They liked Dank but he seemed a little kooky. The plan, as explained by Dank, was that after they've been shown how to do the injections a few times, the players would be able to take the gear home, keep it in the fridge and administer it themselves. It never got to that.

The peptides used at Cronulla were dispensed by compounding pharmacists. ASADA believes Dank's principal source was Maged Sedrak, owner of the Belgrave Compounding Pharmacy in the Sydney suburb of Kogarah, just north of Cronulla. The Pharmacy Council of NSW has since revoked its approval for Sedrak's business. In 2014, the NSW Civil and Administrative Tribunal found Sedrak guilty of professional misconduct for improperly dispensing human growth hormone and testosterone in a case unrelated to Cronulla.[13] Once ASADA was armed with powers to compel people to produce documents and attend interviews, anti-doping investigators secured important testimony from Sedrak. He told them he provided both CJC-1295 and GHRP-6 to Hibbert, known by the Cronulla players as 'The Gazelle'. Sedrak provided ASADA with records showing batches of peptides that he says Hibbert picked up from his Belgrave Street pharmacy. To demonstrate to ASADA what was in the vials, Sedrak invites investigators into his lab and compounds a batch of both CJC-1295 and GHRP-6 while they are looking on. When the peptides are tested, they are shown to be the right stuff.

At Cronulla as with Essendon, intervention by the club doctor is crucial. Two days after Cronulla players were first injected in the away rooms at Shark Park, club doctor David Givney asked Trent Elkin to provide him the details of what Dank was planning. The vague answer he got back didn't inspire confidence. When Dank turns up unannounced at the Warriors game in Auckland, Givney is further troubled. Three days later he emails the coach and football manager calling for an end to the program. Shane Flanagan's response shows he knows it is the injections that Givney is most worried about. The coach replies: 'Doc thanks mate I will knock it on the head today. No injections, no anything. Thanks for your patience.'[14] Givney's concerns trigger a series of meetings. The first, at the Cronulla Leagues Club, is attended by Givney, high-performance manager Trent Elkin, physiotherapist Konrad Schultz, football manager Darren Mooney and Stephen Dank. Givney is furious at Elkin, whom he accuses of lying about Dank's program. Elkin pushes back hard. He believes the doctor is behind the times, that Dank is just what Cronulla needs. The doctor wins the argument. According to notes taken by Mooney, the understanding of everyone at the meeting is clear: everything had to be passed by Doc.

Later in the day, Mooney meets Flanagan to brief the coach on what has happened. He passes on the doctor's concerns about Elkin and reaffirms the new protocol. Flanagan then meets with Dank. The coach was a tough, honest footballer. He played for three NRL clubs before a knee injury ended his career before his thirtieth birthday. Just like Mark 'Bomber' Thompson at Essendon, the coach stares through the sports scientist as he lays down the law. There will be no more needles at Cronulla. Dank appears chastised.

'Okay, okay, I get it. Needles to stop and everything past the Doc. I get it.'

Cronulla doesn't get it. Despite Givney's suspicion of treatments being given to players under his care, Dank's association with Cronulla is allowed to continue. The injections are replaced by lozenges and, eventually, the lozenges with cream. ASADA says they all contain the same peptides, it is merely the delivery systems that change. The players are not convinced. They don't see how sucking a lolly can be cutting-edge sports science. Half of them toss the lozenges out. By the time high-performance manager Trent Elkin starts pulling out bright orange tubes of Danksy cream in the rooms before a game and rubbing it into their arms, most of the players aren't interested.

'They just didn't believe it and didn't go along with it,' says the players' lawyer Richard Redman. 'They thought it was bullshit by that stage.' Not all players lose faith with Dank, however. After the injection sessions in the visitors' rooms come to a halt, a group of players continue to see the sports scientist away from the club. When news of this reaches club physiotherapist Konrad Schultz, he tells Givney. The doctor's response, given his previous actions, is curiously passive. It takes another five weeks before Dank is shown the door at Cronulla.

In the aftermath of an embarrassing loss to the Melbourne Storm, they have it out in the visitors' rooms of Melbourne's AAMI Stadium. Givney says everything, all the injections, the homemade supplements, all of it, has got to stop. An angry Elkin says the players deserve more than a doctor who only turns up on game day. Givney threatens to quit; Konrad Schultz says if the doc goes then he's going, too. Faced with a divisive split between his high-performance manager and club doctor and the abrupt resignation of his medical staff, Flanagan makes a call. In full view of the players, Dank is told he is no longer welcome at Cronulla. The sports scientist leaves red-faced and furious, warning darkly about legal action as the change room door slams shut. He has no shortage of other clients. Before long, he'll meet a promising young Penrith footballer with a banged-up shoulder, Sandor Earl.

When Cronulla forward Wade Graham turns up to the first interview with anti-doping investigators on 29 April 2013 wearing a t-shirt, baseball cap and thongs, he is pilloried for his choice of wardrobe. In truth, it is ASADA, not Graham, that arrives for the interview underdressed. As Graham settles into his seat, he feels confident and relaxed. There are two reasons for this. The first is, he doesn't believe he has done anything wrong. The second is, he is armed with carefully considered legal advice. Where the AFL and ASADA are jointly investigating Essendon, ASADA is investigating Cronulla on its own. The NRL is willing to assist the anti-doping authority but has resisted pressure from ASADA to follow the AFL lead and become an investigative partner. No one from the NRL is sitting in on the Graham interview. Under the NRL's anti-doping policy, players are obliged to provide 'all reasonable assistance' to ASADA and to 'co-operate fully' with any investigation.[15] ASADA assumes this means that Cronulla footballers, like the Essendon footballers, will answer all questions when they are called to their interviews. On this, ASADA is wrong.

At the first question about anything that went on at Cronulla in 2011, Wade Graham refuses to answer. He also refuses to answer the next. Across the table, ASADA investigators John McNamara and Karen Smith become agitated. Graham's legal team, solicitor Richard Redman and barrister Andrew Coleman SC, explain their client is exercising his rights against self-incrimination. He can't do that, the investigators argue. Oh, yes he can. ASADA adjourns the interview to seek legal advice. It will stay adjourned for another three months. While ASADA considers its position, all player interviews are indefinitely placed on hold.

To ASADA's consternation, Graham has the NRL in his corner. The league's lawyers agree with Graham's legal advice; requiring a footballer to provide all reasonable assistance to an anti-doping investigation does not abrogate his rights against self-incrimination. The same right can be exercised by all Cronulla players suspected of doping. In this, the contractual arrangements between the NRL and its players and the AFL and its players are substantially different. The episode perpetuates a misconception about the two football codes and their attitude towards anti-doping.

'When I first came to ASADA people said you can trust the AFL, you can't trust the NRL,' former ASADA chief executive Aurora Andruska says.[16] Although the AFL was the last professional sports body to adopt WADA's protocols, when the drug scandal breaks it is the AFL rather than the NRL that is perceived to wear the white hat in anti-doping matters. On 7 February 2013, the use of prohibited peptides is assumed to be more widespread at NRL clubs than AFL clubs. The AFL has an in-house integrity unit in place, the NRL doesn't. ASADA has established a close working relationship with the AFL in a way it hasn't with the NRL. The AFL is more sophisticated than the NRL in the work it is doing developing blood profiles of players and gathering other anti-doping intel. By the time Aurora Andruska leaves ASADA, her view of the respective codes has changed entirely.

Although the AFL is quick to join ASADA's investigation into Essendon, Andruska soon doubts the league's motives. Where the NRL, for the most part, leaves ASADA to do its work, the anti-doping body feels intense pressure from the AFL to complete its investigation into Essendon before the 2013 finals series. In contrast to the AFL tactic of seeking to influence ASADA through government back channels, NRL chief executive Dave Smith and his deputy Jim Doyle hold weekly telephone hook-ups with Andruska and her senior staff every Friday. The NRL is kept informed of any developments in the investigation but do not meddle in ASADA's work. After ASADA's decision to provide an interim report to the AFL triggers a damaging falling out between the investigative partners and, very nearly, a Federal Court dispute, ASADA refuses a request from the NRL to provide a similar report. The NRL, not for the first time, is frustrated at perceived bias. However, it takes ASADA's advice and compiles its own report, which forms the basis of disciplinary action against Cronulla, its coach Shane Flanagan and its former high-performance manager Trent Elkin for failing to protect the health and welfare of footballers under their care.

'They did the right thing,' Andruska says. 'They produced their own report which they put to their board and their board made their decision. As we look back at the history of it, it has gone very smoothly for them.'[17]

The NRL, without the involvement of ASADA, imposes sanctions against Cronulla and its coach strikingly similar to those accepted by Essendon and, begrudgingly, Bombers coach James Hird. Cronulla is fined $1 million with $400,000 of that suspended. It is less than half the fine imposed on Essendon but, in relative terms, a higher cost for the cash-poor club to meet. Flanagan, like Hird, is suspended for a year. He is now back coaching the Sharks. Trent Elkin is deregistered, with the career-ending penalty later reduced to twenty-one months' suspension on appeal. The NRL's actions against Cronulla and its staff are dealt with entirely by the league's judicial system. There are no Supreme Court writs. There is no Federal Court case and appeal. No one challenges the legality of ASADA's investigation into Cronulla.

Throughout the doping scandal, the AFL is privately contemptuous of the NRL and its Welsh-born chief executive Dave Smith, a virtual unknown in Australian sporting circles before he is introduced to the nation on the blackest day in Australian sport. In a moment of characteristic hubris, AFL boss Andrew Demetriou describes the ASADA and AFL joint investigation of Essendon as a template for future anti-doping efforts. No one would suggest such a thing now. The strength of the NRL position throughout the doping scandal is its separation from ASADA. Its disciplinary procedures are not conflated with ASADA's anti-doping interests; its commercial interests are not blurred with anti-doping outcomes. The AFL instinctively, invariably, seeks to control. There are two lessons the AFL can learn from the NRL's handling of the doping scandal: how to accept the limits of your own influence, and when to let other organisations, particularly statutory government agencies like ASADA, do their job.

The doping case against seventeen members of the 2011 Cronulla football team should be a slam dunk. It takes Tricia Kavanagh, an experienced jurist, only a few weeks work to provide a rough outline of what happened. Her report is limited;

she does not interview any players and she does not interview Stephen Dank, Darren Hibbert or Trent Elkin, the three people with the most intimate knowledge of what Cronulla footballers were injected with. Yet through the recollections of Sharks head trainer Mark Noakes, Kavanagh identifies two banned peptides, GHRP-6 and CJC-1295, as the substances most likely administered at Cronulla under Dank's program. ASADA knows that Dank has told as much to the Australian Crime Commission. In stark contrast to the Essendon case, where Dank has denied both publicly and privately, in media interviews and under oath to administering Thymosin Beta 4 at Windy Hill, he does not quibble with the substances used at Shark Park. The five Cronulla officials interviewed by Kavanagh—the coach, the football manager, the head trainer, the club doctor and the physio—blame one another for what happened during 2011 but, amid the claim and counterclaim, a fairly clear picture emerges of what took place. Forget the creams and lozenges and other nonsense, the case against Cronulla case boils down to three lots of injections administered to the first-grade team in the away rooms over three weeks. ASADA's task should neither be complex nor especially difficult.

By any reasonable assessment, ASADA's management of the Cronulla investigation became a debacle. Noakes recanted his admission to Kavanagh and said he must have read about what was given to Cronulla players in the newspapers long after Stephen Dank left the club. Flanagan pointed the finger at Trent Elkin, Elkin at Dank, and Dank wouldn't talk to ASADA. ASADA asked Dank to provide evidence but did not compel him to attend an interview after it gained its coercive powers. When Wade Graham exercised his common law rights, the entire investigation ground to a halt. If ASADA had a back-up plan it never became clear what it was. When ASADA came knocking again at Shark Park three months later, nothing had really changed—ASADA's new powers did not enable them to compel professional footballers or anyone else to answer self-incriminating questions. Yet by this time, the players wanted to talk.

'The belief was we have got nothing to hide, we have done nothing wrong, we want to get our story out there so this can be finished,' Redman says.[18] Interviews are resumed and in most instances, players answer all questions. Some claim privilege on what substances were administered. For an entire year, there is complete radio silence between ASADA and Cronulla. Then, without warning, ASADA abruptly announces that seventeen current and former Sharks players have a case to answer. It is a case ASADA hopes it never has to run.

On Wednesday, 20 August 2014, the Cronulla players and their lawyers, ASADA and its lawyers and the NRL and its lawyers meet in the Pitt Street offices of Lander & Rogers, Richard Redman's law firm. The discussion is led by Darren Mullaly, ASADA's legal services director. Redman knows Mullaly well. He gave him his first job at ASADA when Mullaly was teaching law part-time at the University of Queensland. Mullaly says ASADA has completed its investigation and intends to charge the players with taking two banned substances, the growth hormone releasing peptides CJC-1295 and GHRP-6. He says ASADA will push for two-year bans against footballers found guilty of doping. He also has an offer. ASADA accepts that Cronulla players did not intentionally take a banned substance, that they were duped and doped. In exchange for a guilty plea, ASADA will accept a no significant fault or negligence defence and reduce the ban to a year. But wait… there is more.

Nearly two football seasons have been played since the blackest day in Australian sport. ASADA concedes the delays in its investigation have been unfortunate and not the fault of the players. ASADA's stop–start interview process, the distraction of the investigation into Essendon and the legal wrangle with the AFL, the change of federal government and sports ministers, the endless internal and external reviews of ASADA's work, the change of the ASADA chief executive, the loss of ASADA personnel—all of these things have conspired to delay justice for the Cronulla players. As a consequence, ASADA will backdate the start of a twelve-month suspension period to 1 November 2013. The NRL supports the deal and WADA will grudgingly accept it. It is both a plea offer and mea culpa for ASADA's stuff ups. For most players, the effective suspension on offer is three weeks—a hamstring strain. Any current player who pleads guilty can be back on deck in time for pre-season training. The players are given until 9.30 a.m. on Friday to take the deal. There's just one catch: ASADA's case doesn't look like much of a case at all.

The evidence provided to the players and their legal teams was loose, circumstantial and anonymous; an algebraic exercise involving person A supplying peptides to person B who injects them into an unwitting Cronulla player. The Cronulla players did not sign consent forms to be injected with peptides. The Deloitte search in 2013 found no documentation at the club to show Dank's program existed. ASADA seemed to be putting a lot of weight on the word of a discredited pharmacist. A summary of the evidence, known as document A, was provided to each player along with a transcript of their interview with ASADA and a pro-forma, 'show cause' notice. Richard Redman remembers reading the material in the chambers of barrister Andrew Coleman. It was past midnight on a Wednesday night and the lawyers were nursing open beers and a growing sense of disbelief.

'The evidence was laughable,' Redman says. 'It was like we were reading a script from *Seinfeld*. We were in side-splitting laughter at how bad it was. That is why our advice to all our clients was: if this is all they've got you will win.'[19]

The instinctive response from the players is that ASADA can shove it. They won't plead guilty to something that they don't know they've done. The lawyers are annoyed at the contrived nature of the deal and the short deadline. For an entire year they heard nothing from ASADA. Now they have less than two days to accept a plea bargain on a patchwork summary of evidence so that ASADA and the NRL can chalk off a few games' suspension at the end of a season and call it job done? The offer makes a mockery of what actually happened at Cronulla. The players, their lawyers and the ASADA and NRL investigators all know there are two distinct groups of footballers from Cronulla's 2011 season: those injected by Trent Elkin and Darren Hibbert in the away rooms at Shark Park, and those who continued to see Hibbert and Dank on the sly after the club doctor, coach and team manager ordered an end to the injections. Early in its investigation, ASADA promised that each case would be treated on its merits. In the end, it has thrown a blanket over the lot. The cookie-cutter sanction makes no distinction between players who will miss finals or, in Paul Gallen's case, national duties with the Kangaroos, and players who are already retired from the game. The players are advised by their lawyers that if they fight the case they will most likely win but it could take another two years to resolve and cost them $60,000 each in legal fees. Unlike Essendon, Cronulla can't afford to foot the legal bill and the Rugby League Players Association has already spent what money it has on the case.

Throughout Wednesday and most of Thursday, the players refused ASADA's terms. Day and night, the lawyers met with the players, their agents and their families. The scenes were raw. Parents of young footballers berated their sons for being so stupid: 'How could you do this,' they shouted. Girlfriends were reduced to tears. So were some players as they tried to explain that it was all approved by the doc, that the club told them it was all good. Late into Thursday night, the players debate it among themselves. In the end, twelve of the seventeen relent. They want it over. No sooner than they sign on the dotted line, they want to take it back, to undo the deal. They agree to sleep on it. In the morning, they stick with it. They just want it done. Even that morning, up to an hour before deadline, ASADA is providing the defence lawyers with more information about the case. Barrister Andrew Coleman says it was 'absolutely unconscionable' for ASADA and the NRL to force the hand of the players in a case that had dragged on so long. At the time of writing, the five players who didn't take the deal have received no word from ASADA on whether the case against them will proceed.

Richard Redman doesn't enjoy bad-mouthing ASADA. He was the anti-doping body's principal lawyer for four years. He liked working at ASADA and he respects people who work there still. Yet he is disappointed in how ASADA chose to resolve the Cronulla case.

'I think ASADA and the NRL thought the players would jump at the chance; they would be so happy and see it as a massive favour. We were like, "You're kidding aren't you mate?" The players are disgusted by this. They are disgusted by the whole thing. They are not taking this because they think this is a good deal, they are taking it because they are just over it and want to walk away.'[20]

When the Cronulla drugs scandal comes to an end, Damian Irvine is half a world away. He has taken a job as the commercial director at Notts County, one of England's oldest and most financially troubled football clubs. Despite the cold Midlands wind that blows off the River Trent in the winter months, Irvine is comfortable in his new life. He likes the passion that people of Nottingham have for their football team. He also likes the fact he and his family are a long way away from Shark Park and the bitter memories that place now holds for him. He feels betrayed by staff he trusted and let down by the ASADA investigation that produced a result but no resolution.

'There are certain facts that are undisputed, whoever you talk to,' he says. 'The players were administered needles. They can't tell you what was in them. Those facts alone shock and appal 99 per cent of the people you talk to. We have become desensitised to it because of all the other arguments. When you look at it on a measured scale, whatever happened is pretty wrong.' Irvine's comments apply equally to Essendon as they do Cronulla.

'The botching of the whole thing, from the government to ASADA, has totally overshadowed whether or not Australian sporting codes were doping. We have made our potential doping targets martyrs. They are all back working in the game. Because it was botched so badly there has been no answer, no solution. That to me is the really sad thing about it. We feel very let down by that. The sob stories about being hard done by? Spare me.'[21]

8
A VERY UNFORTUNATE MATTER

TANIA HIRD FEELS repulsed. She has known the tall, dark-haired man seated next to her since they studied together at university. He was a big man on campus back then, even bigger now that he is next in line to run the AFL. When he slides into the empty chair next to her in the AFL boardroom he means it as a conciliatory gesture; an acknowledgement that although the past two days and, indeed, much of the previous six months have been brutal, it is not personal. Gillon McLachlan doesn't realise that for Tania Hird, it is unavoidably personal. To her, the AFL deputy chief executive represents everything that is wrong with how the AFL does business.

'You are a disgrace and so is your organisation,' she says, her mouth tight with fury. McLachlan tries to explain that he is only doing his job, doing what he is told. It does nothing to placate her. 'You disgust me,' she says.

She has promised herself that whatever happens, they won't see her cry. It is not merely pride. She doesn't want her husband to think it is getting to her, that he should give up his fight for her sake. If anything, she wants him to fight more than he does. It is

27 August 2013, the second and final day of a specially convened meeting of the AFL Commission to decide Essendon's fate. When the Hirds arrive at AFL House that morning, they think it is a mere stepping stone to the Supreme Court. They don't trust the AFL to fairly deliberate their case and have no intention of accepting the settlement on offer—one that would force Essendon out of the finals series and James Hird out of football for a year. They accept Hird deserves some blame for what happened the previous year but don't understand why the senior coach is being judged most culpable for the failings of an entire football department. Their legal team has already lodged a Supreme Court writ to force the AFL Commission to back off and appoint an independent panel to hear the case. Yet after two days, two ridiculous, chaotic days of lawyers and AFL and club officials flitting between rooms inside AFL headquarters, haggling and cajoling, promising and threatening, Hird is about to accept the AFL's terms.

Hird is charged, along with Essendon football department manager Danny Corcoran, assistant coach Mark Thompson, club doctor Bruce Reid and the club, with bringing the game of football into disrepute. There is no accusation of doping. The AFL's principal allegation is serious nonetheless: that the club and its senior officials put the health and welfare of players at risk by not doing enough to stop Stephen Dank from injecting them with substances which may or may not be banned. It is a case primarily about failings of governance, management and responsibilities. Justice AFL-style is rough and swift. The Essendon officials received formal notification of their charges less than two weeks before the Commission hearing. The allegations against them are based on an estimated 65,000 pages of documentation, including ASADA's interim investigator's report and transcripts of interviews with 104 witnesses. Their lawyers have not been given a chance to question any of those witnesses or make submissions on behalf of their clients. There has been no hearing of the case, no deliberation of the evidence by the AFL Commission or anyone else. The entire two days has been about this moment, applying whatever leverage is necessary to get Essendon and its officials to accept a penalty and be done with it.

Julian Burnside QC, Hird's senior counsel during those two days at AFL House, doesn't know for sure which way the Essendon coach will go when he walks into the boardroom to face the commission. Throughout the entire two days, all but the last hour or so, Hird is resolute: he won't plead guilty to anything, he won't accept a year's suspension, he will take his chances before the Supreme Court. Then, abruptly, his resolve cracks. Nick Harrington, a commercial law barrister who, throughout the scandal, becomes one of the coach's trusted advisers, arrives at AFL House at about 6 p.m. after spending most of the day involved in another case before the Federal Court. When he learns what is on the table—no conviction and twelve months' suspension from the AFL and a coaching contract until the end of the 2016 season from Essendon—he urges Hird to take the deal. The previous night Harrington sat up late with Hird at the coach's house, talking things over. He knows this can't go on. Hird's solicitor Steve Amendola, who is advising the coach to take the AFL to court, is furious at Harrington's intervention.

'We went from being calm and under control, knowing what we were going to do, to a complete 180. I felt like punching him to be quite frank.'[1] Amendola now accepts that Harrington was right. Had Hird fought the AFL he might have won the case but he would have been cut loose by his own club. Paul Little has said as much.

As Hird sits before AFL chairman Mike Fitzpatrick and his fellow commissioners, Burnside passes him a sheet of paper. On it, the renowned human rights lawyer has written four words: 'Yes', 'No', 'Your Call'. Jeff Gleeson QC, the AFL's senior counsel, looks at Burnside and Burnside at Hird. The coach picks up a pen and circles the yes.

The AFL has gotten everything it wants. Nearly. Hird accepts a twelve-month suspension. Danny Corcoran, the Essendon football manager, agrees to a four-month ban. Mark Thompson, a former premiership captain and coach and Hird's high-profile assistant, accepts a $30,000 fine. None of them plead guilty or are found guilty of anything. Under the terms of the settlement reached, the AFL drops its charge against each club official in exchange for them accepting a penalty. The charge against Essendon stays; the club is found guilty of bringing the game into disrepute. Essendon is dumped from the finals series, stripped of draft picks and fined $2 million. In total, they are the most severe sanctions the AFL has ever imposed against one of its clubs. The only person who refuses to settle is Bruce Reid. For two days the club doctor has stared down the AFL. Reid isn't for turning. He will see them in court.

The three officials who come to terms with the AFL are each invited to address the commission. With a halting voice, Corcoran recounts the circumstances of his wife Maxine's illness and death. He doesn't intend it as an excuse but it goes a long way to explaining why he didn't notice things at the club he otherwise might have. Thompson has nothing to say. He sits with arms folded, glaring at the men and women who have judged him without asking his side of things. Hird speaks last. He speaks convincingly. He expresses genuine regret for what has happened. He takes responsibility. He says he trusted people that he shouldn't have. He is apologetic. Everyone in the room thinks it is over. Everyone hopes it is. There is a belief, widely though naively held, that now that Essendon and Hird have accepted punishment, ASADA won't pursue its case against the players. In the moment, Hird is relieved. In the days, weeks and months that follow, his decision sits uncomfortably, chafing his conscience, until his doubts are rubbed raw.

Tania Hird is composed. Without a further word to Gillon McLachlan she leaves the AFL boardroom with her husband and his legal team close behind. They walk down a corridor that leads towards the lift well. Then it hits her. She cries uncontrollably. She buries her face in the pinstripe suit of Steve Amendola and sobs. Looking on, Hird feels his own eyes welling. He puts an arm around his wife and guides her to the lift. He declines Harrington's offer of a lift home; they need some time alone. Later that night, the legal team of Amendola, Harrington and Burnside and public relations adviser Ian Hanke arrive at the Hirds' house. They find the couple sitting up with their three oldest kids in the lounge room. Tania is surrounded by her children. James is quiet. A bottle of red is opened. It tastes like ash. Tom Hird, twelve years old, wants to know why his Dad gave up.

When James Hird first reads the ASADA interim report he is convinced the fix is in. The report, made available to the AFL on 2 August 2013, is supposed to be an impartial summary of the evidence. In its explanation of the methodology behind the report, ASADA notes:

> The report does not include conclusions, findings or recommendations regarding potential anti-doping rule violations. Rather, it is intended to be [a] chronological summary of evidence received during the course of the investigation.[2]

Yet the report, in the weight it attaches to the evidence of some witnesses and not others, in the language it employs, asides it makes and, most critically, some of the information it omits, leaves the reader in no doubt where blame lies for the Essendon drugs scandal. Where convicted drug importer Shane Charter is presented as a reformed character and his motivation as 'altruistic, borne of a life almost lost due to the misuse of performance enhancing drugs,'[3] Hird's 'claims' are presented with scepticism. In instances where the evidence of dumped high-performance manager Dean Robinson clashes with that of experienced club doctor Bruce Reid, ASADA prefers the evidence of Robinson, a suspended employee contemplating legal action against Essendon. As Hird reads the report with growing dismay, he discovers allegations that ASADA has never put to him. The most glaring example is the belated recollections of AFL integrity services manager Brett Clothier about the peptide 'warning' he delivered to Hird in August 2011, before Stephen Dank joined the club.

Steve Amendola at first tries to calm his client. Then he reads the report for himself. With each page he gets angrier than Hird. It is a complete stitch-up. For nine hours he sat with Hird through his interview with ASADA. What he finds within the 434 pages of the ASADA report bears little resemblance to what he remembers his client telling the investigators in the interview room. The interim report raises damaging questions yet the Essendon coach is not given any opportunity to answer them.

'There are a whole lot of conclusions they draw on, all sorts of things from people they spoke to where they never called him back and asked him any questions,' the lawyer says. 'The peptide warning is one of them. Did ASADA call back Paul Hamilton? Did ASADA call back Danny Corcoran? Did ASADA call back James Hird when it decided to accept the evidence that was put forward by Brett Clothier, one of the investigators, of a note that happens to turn up two years after a meeting took place? Seriously? Before I got involved in this matter if I wanted to read a work of fiction I'd go down to Readings in Carlton. During this case if I want to read a work of fiction I generally read *The Age* sports writers or the interim report.'[4]

When Bruce Reid first reads ASADA's report he is furious, too. He has been interviewed twice by ASADA and the AFL. He concedes that some of his recollections are imperfect; that he confused dates and other aspects of the chronology. He is angry that on more substantive issues ASADA has either ignored or discounted what he told them. Although he approved AOD-9604 he never intended it for blanket use; his instructions were that it could be used on some players with sore joints or arthritis. He was comfortable with players being given intravenous vitamins at Paul Spano's Skinovate clinic over the road from Windy Hill because the treatment rooms were more sterile than the football club and there were qualified nurses who could administer the drips. His instructions were only to treat players who were showing signs of getting sick, not the whole team. As the key figure behind the cessation of all injections in January 2012 and the establishment of a protocol requiring medical approval for any new substances, the doctor cannot believe that ASADA credits Robinson with devising the protocol. The report puts him in meetings he didn't attend, gives his authority to things he didn't know about and fails to acknowledge the attempts he made, beyond his 15 January letter to football manager Paul Hamilton, to stop all injections at the club. He describes the report as a disgrace.[5]

There is an important caveat to these criticisms: it is only an interim report. The job of the ASADA investigators is incomplete, their investigation is still ongoing. When the investigations team submits its final report to ASADA chief executive Aurora Andruska in February 2014, their understanding of the Essendon drugs scandal has advanced considerably. A few days before ASADA makes the interim report available to the AFL, the anti-doping body is given new powers by the federal parliament to compel reluctant witnesses to attend interviews and produce documents. Armed with these powers, ASADA's investigators in late 2013 are able to question Nima Alavi, the compounding pharmacist doing a roaring trade along Peptide Alley. They are able to secure documents from the pharmacist that confirm some things that Shane Charter has told them. They also try, unsuccessfully, to secure testimony from Dank and his Sydney-based peptide business, the Medical Rejuvenation Clinic. In the second half of 2013 the focus of the investigation narrows in on the suspected use of Thymosin Beta 4, a banned peptide not on ASADA's radar when its work at Essendon began. At the very time that Essendon and the AFL believe the drugs scandal is abating, ASADA investigators are accelerating their work. The greatest flaw in ASADA's interim report is not the information it contains as of August 2013 but the purpose for which it is used.

On 1 August 2013, ASADA receives legal advice from the Australian Government Solicitors that the interim report, which includes highly confidential information, can only be provided to the AFL as part of an anti-doping investigation. ASADA's position after receiving this advice is that the report cannot be used to inform the AFL's disciplinary proceedings against Essendon and its officials. In a flurry of legal letters, the AFL makes clear to ASADA this is exactly what it plans to do. The report is distributed to the AFL commissioners who will decide the fate of Essendon, Hird and the other club officials. Parts of its text are cut and pasted into a 34-page charge sheet compiled against the club. Copies of the report are made available to Essendon and its lawyers. Once Hird, Danny Corcoran, Mark Thompson and Bruce Reid are charged, a copy is made available to them and a second one to their lawyers. When further copies are provided by the AFL to the AFL Players Association, the Australian Government Solicitors order the AFL to cease any further distribution of the report.

'Every man and their dog got that report,' says Amendola. 'How do you maintain confidentiality?'[6] They don't. By this stage, nearly all information contained in the interim report damaging to Essendon and Hird has been leaked anyway. The circumstantial case against the players for taking a banned peptide, Thymosin Beta 4, the mysterious 'Mexican' drug, ASADA's inflated guesstimate of how many injections were administered at Essendon—all have found a home on the front or back pages of the morning newspapers. When I read the interim report in full, I am staggered at how little of it hasn't been published.

Paul Little doesn't negotiate. Not in the normal meaning of the word. Where for most business people negotiation is the art of compromise, it is a blood sport for Little.

'He will always go into a negotiation saying he is going to win it,' says Ray Horsburgh, the man who encouraged Little to join the Essendon board. 'Sometimes to negotiate you have got to give ground to the other side. Paul's first stance is always never to give any ground.'[7] As the chairman of Toll Holdings when the logistics company laid siege to Patrick Corporation in 2005 and 2006, Horsburgh had a ringside view. For eight gruelling months it was the most hostile of takeovers. Paul Little, the chief executive who transformed Toll from a struggling, $1.5 million trucking company into a multibillion-dollar logistics leviathan, was pitted against Patrick's managing director Chris Corrigan, the bespectacled, bête noire of the maritime union, and chairman Peter Scanlon. It is hard to imagine three tougher hombres in Australian business and, in the end, Little was the one left standing.

'Paul was never going to negotiate, he was going to screw them,' says Horsburgh. 'There wasn't any compromise, it was a vicious takeover.'[8]

When Paul Little retired as Toll chief executive, Horsburgh suggested he should serve a stint on the board of the Essendon Football Club. Horsburgh was a past president of the club and knew that David Evans, the club's recently appointed chairman, was looking to add more business nous to his board. Little, apart from being one of the smartest businessmen Horsburgh knew, was a passionate Bombers supporter. With a vast personal fortune at his disposal and, suddenly, a lot of spare time on his hands, Little agreed. Horsburgh introduced Little to Evans and, at the end of 2010, Little joined the Essendon board in time for Hird's first season as senior coach. At the time, he imagined Evans would be chairman for many years to come. He had no interest in running the club.

'I was very happy with my once a month commitment,' he says.[9] David Evans had a five-year plan to revive the club from its commercial and on-field malaise of the post-Sheedy era. The Bombers hadn't won a finals match since 2004. Members weren't renewing, revenue was down and the club had grown out of its 1920s training base at Windy Hill. Evans and Hird were going to take the club into a new era. Little, for a change, was happy for others to lead the charge.

The morning after Evans collapses in the Essendon rooms after the Hawthorn match, he calls Paul Little.

'I can't do it anymore,' he tells his deputy chairman. Little is uncertain what he is being told. 'I want you to take over. I can't do it. From today. From now.'[10] Little agrees.

'From that Saturday morning, that phone call, it all changed.'[11] It is a critical time. The AFL is nearing its endgame. Within days, it will be armed with ASADA's interim report. The AFL already knows what's in the report; integrity services manager Brett Clothier spent two days reading it the previous week. AFL deputy chief executive Gillon McLachlan is confident it will give him what he needs to take the action necessary to protect the integrity of the competition: booting Essendon out of the finals series. Until now, Essendon has pursued a small target strategy: don't take on the AFL, don't say too much, be contrite, remorseful. It is a strategy that has frustrated Hird, Thompson and others at Essendon who want the club to do more to protect its own. Little agrees with Hird. He believes Essendon needs a new approach; that it has been too passive in its response to the drugs scandal and too trusting of the AFL. He is also in totally unfamiliar territory.

'I have been in some pretty hostile negotiations over the journey but this one was different. The facts were being leaked out either by journalists or the AFL or ASADA or occasionally James or someone else. I just felt that we needed to contain what it was that we were alleged to have done. To actually get on the front foot and fight back was not even part of the strategy.'[12]

The AFL doesn't negotiate either. Not in a way you might expect from sports administrators weighing decisions with career-defining implications for substantial figures in the game. First they are going to charge just James Hird. Then it is Hird and Danny Corcoran. Then it is Hird, Corcoran and Bruce Reid. Not sure about Mark Thompson. If Essendon sacks Corcoran and Reid, the AFL will only charge Hird. Or Reid could retire. How about Reid retires, Essendon sacks Corcoran and the AFL charges Hird? Thompson? Still not sure about Thompson. Yes, we'll charge him too. No we won't. Okay, now it is Hird, Corcoran and Reid. Maybe just Hird and Corcoran. Maybe just Hird. If Hird rolls over, we won't charge the others.

In his South Yarra office, Paul Little becomes dizzy with the nonsense of it all. For several days he has been on and off the phone with Gillon McLachlan, negotiating in circles. Sitting across from Little's desk is club lawyer Tony Hargreaves, steaming like a teapot with each AFL rethink. At the end of another phone line they've got Jack Rush QC, a former chairman of the Victorian Bar Council who is advising the club. Rush argued the test case for the Wittenoom miners against James Hardie, so he is well used to extracting information from difficult adversaries. Dealing with the AFL, however, is something else. With every phone call, there are different names in the dock. It's like they've opened a pack of Scanlens footy cards and can't decide which ones to swap.

It isn't fun for McLachlan either. Andrew Demetriou is thoroughly sick of this mess. He tells his deputy chief he has to sort it out before the finals. McLachlan is trying but he can't get Little where he wants him. On a morning when McLachlan thinks the AFL and Essendon are close to agreement, he can't even get him to answer his phone. Again and again he rings. Across town, Little sits in his office watching McLachlan's name pop up on the little screen and calmly ignores it. It is an old business trick—at a time when negotiations are at their most critical stage, let the other mob sweat. Finally McLachlan loses his nerve and drives over to Little's South Yarra office. The games that billionaires play. In the meantime, Little has other problems to deal with. Hird and his lawyers want to abandon negotiations with the AFL and head straight to the Supreme Court. They are convinced ASADA's entire joint investigation with the AFL was unlawful. They will hold that thought for another year.

By Friday, 9 August, it is clear that Essendon's most celebrated living player, James Hird, career administrator Danny Corcoran and the AFL's longest-serving club doctor Bruce Reid will be charged under the broad provisions of rule 1.6 for bringing the game of football into disrepute. When this is put to AFL chief executive Andrew Demetriou, he flatly denies that charges against any Essendon officials have been discussed.

'Our lawyers are speaking to Essendon about process but they are not in a position to talk about individuals or charges because

Andrew Dillon is yet to finalise his review of the ASADA report,' he says. 'It is wrong to say they have spoken to Essendon about charges or about individuals.'[13] It is a statement seemingly at odds with the events of the previous week.

Hird, Corcoran and Reid are duly charged four days later under player rule 1.6. Thompson, apparently as an afterthought, is later added to the AFL's lengthy rap sheet. Thompson remains bitterly disappointed at the episode.

'Paul Little rang me the night before the charges were released and said I wasn't going to be charged, it was only Reid, Corcoran and Hirdy. Then, within twenty-four hours, my name was thrown in and I was charged. I'm not sure why. Either you should be charged or you shouldn't be charged. You don't negotiate with people's lives.'[14]

Shortly before the AFL issues its charges against the four Essendon officials, it makes one last offer to Paul Little to pass on to Bruce Reid: if the doctor agrees to retire he won't be charged. The doc's response: 'You tell them to fuck off.'[15]

Essendon makes its stand on 21 August at a press conference hastily arranged in a penthouse suite of The Olsen, a plush boutique South Yarra hotel, which, by coincidence, sits smack in the middle of Peptide Alley. Earlier in the day, the AFL published a 34-page document that accuses Essendon, in devastating detail, of implementing a scientifically pioneering program in which footballers were injected with 'exotic, mysterious and unfamiliar compounds' without proper regard to their health and the World Anti-Doping Code. The document, titled a 'Statement of Grounds', is the AFL's Big Bertha, its heaviest artillery. For the past week it has been trained on the Essendon Football Club and the four club officials implicated in the drugs scandal, with the AFL making clear its preparedness to pull the trigger on its release.

AFL chief executive Andrew Demetriou refers to the Statement of Grounds as the charges against Essendon but its contents, now published in full on the AFL website, go well beyond the particulars of any alleged offence. The material is drawn almost entirely from testimony and documents provided to ASADA and AFL investigators on the proviso of strict confidentiality. It includes text messages and emails sent between club officials, communications between Stephen Dank and drug importer Shane Charter, and the contested allegation that the senior coach was injected with the vanity agent Melanotan II. Bruce Reid's letter is reproduced in full. Essendon has already seen the Statement of Grounds. It has spent the past week negotiating with the AFL to ensure it never sees the light of day. As a result of those negotiations, the document has been heavily revised. Publishing the original draft has a tactical purpose: to weaken the club's negotiating position by further damaging Essendon and Hird's public standing. It is also seen by Essendon as an act of retribution.

The decision to release the Statement of Grounds is taken less than twenty-four hours after Dr Andrew Garnham, a sports medico who served on the AFL anti-doping tribunal before becoming an adviser to Essendon, reveals in a television interview that he was told by ASADA at the start of the drug scandal that AOD-9604 was not a banned substance. The advice Garnham received in February 2013 echoes the advice ASADA provided to the Australian Crime Commission when it was preparing its blackest day report. The advice is twofold. ASADA's position, according to Garnham, was that AOD-9604 was not banned under the World Anti-Doping Code's S2 category of substances, which covers human growth hormone, growth hormone releasing peptides and other growth factors. ASADA further advised that because AOD-9604 was assessed under S2, the broad S0 category, which covers substances not approved for therapeutic use, does not apply.[16] The classification arguments around AOD-9604 are complex and nuanced. For Essendon, Garnham's revelation confirms a greater sin: that ASADA and the AFL stood mute on the sidelines as Jobe Watson was publicly roasted for his AOD-9604 admission when they both knew he had no case to answer. Hird's fury at the AFL is now shared by Little, Essendon's new chairman and an accomplished corporate pugilist. In the penthouse suite of The Olsen, first Little and then Hird read from prepared statements loaded with simmering grievances.

With reading glasses balanced on the end of his nose, Little grasps the prepared statement in both hands, rarely looking up or wavering from the text. He accuses the AFL of releasing the charge sheet as a reprisal for Garnham's interview and for 'reprehensible' conduct in failing to publicly clarify the status of AOD-9604. He describes some of the allegations contained in the Statement of Grounds as without foundation. He reveals that the club and the league negotiated substantial changes to the Statement of Grounds and accuses the AFL of breaking its word by releasing the original charge sheet, a document 'designed to do little more than score media headlines and ultimately intimidate us.' He says Essendon wants the scandal resolved but won't accept being treated as a drug cheat. He declares he has lost confidence in the AFL executive team of Andrew Demetriou and Gillon McLachlan and calls on commission chairman Mike Fitzpatrick to personally intervene.[17] Hird is no less strident in his attack on the AFL, accusing it of abuse of process and trial by media. In a direct challenge to the AFL's authority to deal with the doping scandal, he calls for the AFL boss and its commission to recuse itself from the case and appoint an independent arbiter to hear the charges against Essendon and its officials.[18]

Little says the press conference was instinctive and reflexive.

'In hindsight I don't know if it was a good or bad thing. I just felt events were moving far too quickly. We had people calling for James' head in the paper every second day of the week. He was the coach of our side. I just couldn't sit back and let those sort of criticisms and those sort of wild allegations go. We didn't have any facts to fight back with so we simply said, "Look, get off our back. We'll fight you if we have to, enough is enough. We will draw the line in the sand here." That was all rhetoric. We had no facts. And to this day, arguably we still have very few.'[19] It is a compelling performance nonetheless. Listening to Little and Hird on the top floor of The Olsen that afternoon, I do not doubt that a high stakes, courtroom showdown is looming between the AFL and one of its most powerful clubs. This is a rarity in football. The last one was thirteen years earlier, when Carlton president John Elliott took the AFL to court over a disputed claim on broadcast rights at his club's home ground. Hird's lawyers appear to confirm as much the next morning when they make the short walk from their William Street office to the Supreme Court's prothonotary's office and lodge a ten-page writ that strikes at the integrity of the league's most senior officials. It reprises the tip-off allegation against Demetriou and makes a similar one against McLachlan. It also accuses the AFL of providing copies of ASADA's interim report and other confidential information from the anti-doping investigation to journalists. The allegations, denied by the AFL, deeply offend Demetriou. Bad blood now courses between Essendon, Hird and the league. Pretensions at civility are abandoned. It is an open, ugly, public feud, with a billionaire businessman and a big name footy star prepared to call out the AFL for its bullying, manipulating ways. Or so it seems. The very night of Little and Hird's press conference, the fixer steps in.

If you want to know how the big end of Melbourne really works, talk to John Wylie. A Rhodes Scholar, investment banker, sports lover and philanthropist, Wylie is impeccably connected in business, sport, politics and the arts. When it comes to big asset sales, acquisitions, mergers and other sticky deals he is the go-to adviser for state and federal governments and corporate Australia. He isn't from Melbourne—he was born in Brisbane and started his working life in New York—but he understands how the city works and has the ear of everyone who runs it. Wylie advised the Kennett Government on its radical break-up and sale of the State Electricity

Commission and the Howard Government on how best to flog off Telstra and Medibank Private. In 2015, he has helped Victoria's Labor Government extricate itself from an unwanted $5.3 billion road and tunnel project. Wylie's former corporate clients include BHP Billiton, Coles, Telstra, Qantas and Bluescope Steel, and his sporting CV is topped with his 2012 appointment as chairman of the Australian Sports Commission, the federal government's peak sporting body. Before that, he spent fifteen years chairing the Melbourne Cricket Ground Trust, the government-appointed board that administers the city's most important sporting asset, the MCG. His most remarkable achievement in that role was securing, through negotiation, a small but valuable slice of AFL broadcast revenue for thirty years. As John Elliott found out in his failed court bid, the AFL would rather give up its firstborn child than TV money. If Wylie hasn't written the book on making deals in modern Melbourne he knows where to find one—he is also board president of the State Library of Victoria.

On the night of 21 August 2013, with the AFL and Essendon seemingly locked in a mutually destructive spiral, John Wylie steps in to help Paul Little. It is not the first time. Throughout his aggressive expansion of Toll Holdings, Little consulted Wylie at every step. When it appeared as though Toll's attempted takeover of Patrick would be thwarted by the corporate regulator and Chris Corrigan's resistance, it was Wylie who advised Little on how to complete the $6.2 billion kill. Little says there is no one in business he trusts more than Wylie. He also considers him a friend. The two men have walked the Kokoda Track together.

'John had my ear,' Little says. 'John is creative, he is clever, he is committed and he is a mate.'[20] Wylie is also a mate of AFL chairman Mike Fitzpatrick. They are fellow Rhodes Scholars and investment bankers, and their careers, family lives and sporting passions have been enmeshed for thirty years. When Wylie was a twenty-something Oxford masters graduate, it was Fitzpatrick, then working in the New York offices of Credit Suisse First Boston, who gave the fellow expat his first job in merchant banking. They have remained firm friends ever since. If anyone can bridge the bitter divide between Fitzpatrick and Little and the AFL and Essendon, it is John Wylie.

'It was a genuine offer of help from John to try and create a settlement package that I could sign off on, to all intents and purposes from the club and Hird's point of view, and Fitzy could sign off on, to all intents and purposes from the AFL's point of view,' Little says. 'Whether John wants to be remembered for that I don't know. Whether Fitzy would agree to it I don't know. But that is what happened. It was quite helpful.'[21] Yes, Little and Fitzy are mates too.

Wylie's intervention in the drugs scandal, albeit a cameo role, was contentious. As the chairman of the Australian Sports Commission, Wylie was the nation's most senior government-appointed sports official. Although his intentions were sound—he was convinced the AFL's primary motive was to protect the integrity of its finals series and competition—the boss of the ASC could not be seen to be meddling in an affair subject to an ongoing anti-doping investigation. In his desire to help two old mates, to solve a problem, to be the fixer, Wylie did not see his conflict at the time. He was not the only one.

AFL chairman Mike Fitzpatrick is not supposed to be involved in the day-to-day management of the drugs scandal. According to paper wall divisions within AFL House, the entire AFL Commission is meant to stay above the fray so that when the time comes it can judge any charges against Essendon and club officials fairly and impartially. This is why, throughout the scandal, Andrew Demetriou, a member of the commission, presents himself as being at arm's length from the AFL and ASADA investigations into Essendon and defers negotiations with Essendon to his deputy chief executive, Gillon McLachlan. Until this point, Fitzpatrick has been careful not to be drawn into the morass. The moment he starts constructing a settlement offer with Wylie and Little, he is knee deep in it.

Hird's legal advisers see Wylie as an AFL emissary who has come to sweeten the deal for the Essendon coach. Hird sees him as someone genuinely trying to help. What they don't appreciate is Wylie's effect on Little. Little doesn't always agree with Wylie but he does listen to him. Through the course of negotiations, it is Wylie who persuades Little that Hird, as the senior coach, should accept a one-year ban for the good of the club. Little fears that if the dispute bleeds into 2014, the club could lose premiership points, with sponsors, members and players to abandon Essendon. From open conflict with the AFL, Little is drafted to the league's principal cause: finding a speedy, all-in resolution that avoids court action. Less than a month after taking control of the Essendon board from David Evans, Paul Little is prepared to pressure Hird in a way Evans never was.

Over the next three days, the AFL chairman and Essendon president negotiate a proposed settlement to the drugs scandal through their mutual friend. The negotiations are highly secretive. Even within AFL House, few people know they are going on. With a two-day AFL commission meeting scheduled the following week to hear the charges against Essendon and its officials, Fitzpatrick and Little don't negotiate directly. Instead, all their discussions are channelled through Wylie, as Little explains, 'A couple of times I said to Wylie, "I can't deliver that, just forget it mate", and then Wylie would come back and say, "Look, I've spoken to Fitzy, maybe we can do that and do that." John was certainly trying as hard as he could.'[22] It is a quintessentially Melbourne, old boys' approach—why leave it to a commission hearing or the Supreme Court when school chums and business colleagues can quietly sort it out? As Essendon football manager Danny Corcoran puts it, 'The big end of town, Paul, Fitzpatrick, Wylie, mobbed up to get a result.'

The negotiations produce a settlement package that is acceptable to the AFL and Essendon and tempting to Hird. It also contains proposed sanctions against the three other Essendon officials facing disciplinary action by the commission. A draft is sent from Wylie to Little and from Little to Hird on Friday, 23 August. Its terms are strikingly similar to those contained in the settlement accepted by Essendon and its officials a few days later in the boardroom of AFL House.

Essendon Club
- Charge reduced to governance one viz failure of supervision and conduct of a safe workplace
- Deducted 12 premiership points so as to miss finals
- $1.5 million fine
- No player sanctions
- Draft picks remain an open point—AFL 2 each for 2014 and 2015; club position zero—club already sanctioned by elimination from 2013 finals series, substantial financial penalty and sanctions against the individuals

Key individuals
Hird
- Charge reduced to a governance one viz failure of supervision and conduct of a safe workplace
- Charge of bringing game into disrepute dropped
- 12 months suspension starting now. Efforts will be made to find an outstanding career development opportunity for him during time away from the game
- Acknowledgement by AFL as a legend of the game
- Remains in the AFL Hall of Fame
- Can remain on Essendon payroll while suspended
- Withdraws all legal action immediately

Reid/Corcoran
- 6 month suspension of which 2 months is suspended sentence. Could be reduced in further discussion with the AFL, cannot be increased or mix changed adversely

Thompson
- $40k fine
- Can coach in 2014

Commitments by AFL
- Acknowledge that club and key individuals are not drug cheats and do not support such culture
- No disparagement or triumphalism about club or key individuals on or off the record (ie that AFL "won" or Essendon "rolled over")
- No double jeopardy—this is the end of the matter

Commitments by Essendon
- Will abide by WADA, ASADA, AFL and AIS codes of conduct/best practice in future regarding SSM
- No disparagement of AFL or AFL executives on or off the record.[23]

What is this outstanding career development opportunity referred to in the document? The original idea conceived by Fitzpatrick and Wylie was for Hird to spend his year away from coaching studying at their alma mater, Oxford University. There is no doubt that between them they can help make this happen. Wylie, among other honorary roles, is a trustee of the Global Rhodes Scholarship Trust. The AFL's biggest concession to Hird is a commitment to drop the charge against him and limit the allegations to poor governance and management, rather than anything suggesting cheating or doping. He can also be paid during his year of suspension. His team won't play finals this season but as the document makes clear, this is the end of the matter; they won't have anything further to fear from anti-doping investigators.

The terms are accompanied by a proposed form of words, emailed from Wylie to Little, to be adopted by the AFL and Essendon. The club and coach will concede that the supplements program was inadequately vetted and controlled and put at risk the health of the players. Hird will take responsibility as senior coach for failures of governance and oversight. The AFL will not find Hird guilty of bringing the game into disrepute, and Hird will accept a one-year suspension from coaching.[24] Little raises with

Hird the possibility of a two-year contract extension to ensure his eventual return to the club. He tells the coach the AFL offer is as good as it is going to get.

The following night, the Bombers take on Carlton at the MCG. Played in the shadows of the commission hearing, the match produces another epic. After trailing by seventeen points at three-quarter time, the Bombers run down the Blues, with David Zaharakis, the player who famously said no to Stephen Dank's needles, kicking the winning goal with less than a minute to play. In the winners' rooms, Essendon players refuse to sing the team song without their coach. Football manager Danny Corcoran fetches Hird from the coaches' room. He joins Paul Little in a circle of sweat-drenched footballers and belts out a jubilant chorus. It is a powerful and genuine show of unity from the club, coach and president. In the press conference that follows, Hird dismisses reports of divisions at Windy Hill.

'It has brought us closer together despite what people want to say about the fractures at the club, the fact that players don't want to be here, the fact that people don't want to be at our club. That is just not true. If you saw the rooms tonight, if you saw our training sessions, if you saw the way we act around each other ... we are a very tight group.'[25] Hird believes this, as does Paul Little. Little also believes he has an agreement from Hird to end the drugs scandal. He doesn't.

It is within the comfortable surrounds of Gillon McLachlan's stylish Prahran house that James Hird faces his accusers for the first time. It is late Sunday morning, the day after the Carlton game. Hird doesn't know it yet but he won't coach another game for eighteen months. After repeated requests by Hird to put his case directly to either Andrew Demetriou or his deputy McLachlan, Little has arranged the meeting. There are four people in attendance: Hird, his lawyer Steve Amendola, McLachlan and the AFL's general counsel, Andrew Dillon. The meeting runs for four hours.

The AFL officials are conciliatory towards the coach but their purpose is clear: Hird must accept the sanction being offered to him so the league can put the drugs scandal behind it in time for the finals series. Hird presses them on why his penalty must be twelve months and not six. McLachlan says, 'It is about the optics'—that anything less than twelve months won't look right. Dillon says the scandal 'needs a face'. Both men tell Hird that the decision is his alone, that the AFL already has an agreement with Essendon, that the Bombers will be dealt with regardless of what the coach does. The AFL, however, is not an organisation that likes loose ends.

Hird is still inside McLachlan's house when an angry text message from his club president appears on his phone:

> James AFL telling me you are trying to change the negotiated deal. I can't help you any further James as Fitzpatrick has the shits and the Total deal now has the wobbles up. I will have to cut you loose. I thought you & I had an agreement. I need to know this afternoon what your decision is. Paul.[26]

While Hird and his lawyer have been talking to the AFL officials, Paul Little has been receiving updates from the AFL. As soon as the meeting ends, Hird receives a blistering phone call from Little, accusing him of backsliding on what they'd agreed. Hird digs in. He tells Little that his position hasn't changed, that he just wants a fair hearing of the allegations against him. Shortly after the call, another text message arrives, this one more explicit than the last:

> James AFL have said they will not do EFC deal unless we stand you down. Your decision not to take 12 months is going to impact the total club. This dispute is about to get very messy because you won't take another 6 months, ie a total of 12. If you really want to do what's in the best interest of the club & its players take 12 months. Anything else will be selfish. Paul.[27]

Later that night, the Essendon chairman plays his last remaining card. He calls Hird at home and tells him that Mike Fitzpatrick, the AFL chairman, is adamant that Hird must either accept the twelve-month suspension or be sacked as Essendon coach. Little gives Hird a deadline of 9 a.m. Monday, the morning of the commission meeting.

Paul Little says he had no intention of sacking James Hird.

'I just told him I couldn't protect him anymore. You have got to do what is in the best interests of the club now, it is a package.'[28] When the Essendon coach comes to the businessman's South Yarra offices first thing the next morning, Little is apologetic. The Essendon chairman has been in tougher negotiations throughout his career but never something like this. Little has not dealt with the AFL before. When various threats are made to strip the club of 2014 premiership points, dump it from the traditional ANZAC Day match against Collingwood, and deregister the club altogether, he has no way of knowing what they are serious about and what is bluster. Like most people at Essendon, Little wants Hird to survive the drugs scandal and thrive as a long-term senior coach. This does not mean, however, that Little is entirely in Hird's corner. John Wylie has convinced him that the best chance Hird has to continue his career is to bury his grievances with the AFL and accept the penalty on offer. Little essentially wants what the AFL wants: an immediate resolution to the drugs scandal that has torn his club apart. The task before him is unchanged; he must persuade Hird to take the deal.

The two-day commission meeting at AFL House is best understood by what it isn't rather than what it is. It isn't a hearing of disciplinary charges against Essendon, James Hird, Mark Thompson, Danny Corcoran and Bruce Reid. It isn't a hearing of any kind. No case is presented. No evidence is led. No witnesses are called. No submissions are put. The most redundant figures in the process are the commissioners themselves. For the best part of two days they sit, idle at their own meeting, swiping their tablets and fiddling with their phones, while lawyers representing

Essendon and the four club officials charged with bringing the game into disrepute and lawyers representing the AFL negotiate settlement terms.

The absurdity of this is illustrated by who the AFL commissioners are. Mike Fitzpatrick, Rhodes Scholar, champion footballer, successful funds manager and company director. Linda Dessau, a retired justice of the Family Court. Richard Goyder, managing director of Wesfarmers, one of Australia's largest retail groups. Paul Bassat, a co-founder of the online jobs search juggernaut Seek. Chris Lynch, the chief financial officer of mining giant Rio Tinto. Sam Mostyn, an experience company director and a human resources and corporate culture expert. Chris Langford, a 300-game, Hall of Fame Hawthorn champion and company director. These are highly capable, considered people. It is hard to imagine a better-equipped jury of peers to judge what went on at Essendon. They are never given the chance.

The show begins at 2 p.m. The commissioners file in. A Pinteresque silence fills the AFL boardroom. AFL chairman Mike Fitzpatrick reaches for his most serious, judicial voice: 'I will open the hearing of what is a very unfortunate matter.' Fitzpatrick immediately throws to the AFL's senior counsel, Jeff Gleeson QC, who asks for an adjournment so the real business of the day can begin: negotiations. They get off to a rough start when the four accused officials discover that the charge against them is still in place. Under the in-principle agreement negotiated between Essendon chairman Paul Little, AFL chairman Mike Fitzpatrick and John Wylie, the charges are supposed to be dropped. Little is livid and so is Mark Thompson. The assistant coach is adamant there are two things he won't do: plead guilty and accept any penalty that suggests he was involved in cheating. The AFL lawyers insist the charges are non-negotiable, then immediately start negotiating their removal. It is a sign of things to come.

At the outset, everyone is put in the same room. When it is pointed out that the lawyers need to consult privately with clients, the Essendon delegation and each of the accused are scattered throughout AFL House, with Gleeson tasked to shuttle mediate between the respective legal teams. Before the AFL lawyers approach Hird, Little pays a visit. The Essendon chairman, renowned for his composure in the heat of a multibillion-dollar takeover, is flustered. He also has a football. He gives the ball to James Hird, then he gives him the hard word: he must take the deal for the good of the club. When Hird tells his chairman he can't accept what is on offer, Little takes the ball back and marches out of the room.

At about 4 p.m., the parties are called back to the boardroom. Hird's counsel Julian Burnside QC says he wants to make his application to disqualify the commission from hearing the case against his client; instead Gleeson asks to adjourn for another hour and a half. They file back out. An AFL delegation knocks on Hird's door. Hird is urged to accept the AFL's terms: a guilty plea to bringing the game into disrepute and a twelve-month ban. Corcoran has almost settled, Hird is told, as has Thompson. You'll soon be on your own. A quick call from Hird to Corcoran and Thompson reveals neither thinks they are close to settling. Burnside urges the coach, football manager and assistant coach to all work together so they can't be picked off by the AFL, one by one. Within AFL House, a knot of resistance is formed. Little again presses Hird to accept the deal. Hird refuses.

At 5.30 p.m., Hird and his legal team walk into the AFL boardroom to find it deserted. It seems the unfortunate matter has been adjourned sine die. Through the window, they can see camera crews still camped on the footpath below, waiting for news that won't be coming tonight. Bruce Reid and his legal team are calling it a day, albeit one entirely wasted. Reid's only purpose in coming to the meeting is to formally request the commission acknowledge its own bias and refer his case to an independent, qualified person to hear it. First at 2 p.m. and again at 4 p.m., Reid's counsel Ross Gillies QC tells the commissioners he wants to make a submission. Neither time is he given a chance to speak. Aside from a cursory check to see if Reid had any interest in accepting his penalty, the AFL lawyers have otherwise ignored the club doctor.

For everyone inside AFL House, it is an exhausting, all-consuming, mind-numbing ordeal. Paul Little's day began early in the morning across town at the chambers of Hird's lawyer. As the parties head home after dark from the Docklands, Little asks one of the Essendon lawyers to drive him to where he had parked his wife's car. When they reach the corner of Lonsdale and William streets, the centre of Melbourne's law precinct, Little realises he has no earthly idea where he parked. Beneath the city lights, they drive block after aimless block. Finally, Little gives up, too tired to look any longer. He joins the city commuters on a train. At this time of day, the billionaire can at least find an empty seat. Later in the night, at about 10.30 p.m., the commissioners return to the empty boardroom. Apparently, they are now ready to resume their hearing. By this time, even the last of the news crews have gone home. The accused are either snug in their beds or well into a second bottle of wine.

A new day brings more of the same. The commissioners file into the boardroom—minus those who've been unable to juggle work commitments to spend another full day at AFL House—and another adjournment is granted. Burnside realises, if he hasn't already, that the AFL Commission is not planning on hearing the case against his client, Hird.

'At the start I thought, "How on earth does the AFL propose to hold this hearing they are talking about?" It became very quickly apparent that they didn't want a hearing at all. What they wanted was a negotiated settlement and the more time that passed, the weaker they looked. Although Essendon was quite enthusiastic to get rid of the thing we were ready to stand up and fight the allegation.'[29]

Once the negotiations resume, the dynamics are clear. Essendon, other than haggling over what draft picks it will lose, is willing to accept the AFL's terms. The AFL and Essendon want Hird as part of the settlement. For Corcoran and Thompson, there is less pressure from the AFL or Essendon but they still face a devil's choice. Corcoran is closest to reaching settlement. He believes they are all at fault, to varying degrees, for what happened at Windy

Hill throughout 2012. He wants to take responsibility for his part. Thompson is less accepting. He never expected to be charged, he didn't expect to be here. It isn't the penalty on offer from the AFL that troubles him, it's the principle. Hird is set. The events of the past few days have convinced him that he cannot trust his fate to the AFL. He has a date later that week before the Supreme Court. He won't be bullied into a settlement by either the AFL or his own club. Hird's solicitor Steve Amendola says the game plan was agreed.

'When we walked in there it was going to be Reid and us, then the rest.'[30] Little says Hird simply won't budge.

'James is a very hard guy to negotiate with because he is so stubborn. It is probably part of what makes him such a good sportsman; he is so single minded and so stubborn. The negotiation with James was incredibly hard and was still going on, minute to minute, for the two days we spent in the commission.'[31]

As for Bruce Reid, he is still waiting to make his application. When the commission returns to the boardroom, his counsel Ross Gillies asks pointedly whether anyone from the AFL is planning to approach his client with an offer.

'Do you want to be?' Mike Fitzpatrick asks the barrister.

'We have made our position quite clear; acquittal is the only result we will deal with,' Gillies responds.

'It might be a lonely day,' says Fitzpatrick.[32]

Essendon is the first party to settle. It will plead guilty to bringing the game into disrepute. It will take no part in the finals series. It will pay the AFL $2 million. It will cough up two years of early draft picks. It is a heavy penalty, but not excessive. The entire AFL Commission has read ASADA's report and Ziggy Switkowski's report. They condemn what happened at Essendon.

'This can't happen again in our game,' says AFL chairman Fitzpatrick as he confirms the sanctions. 'We can't let—no matter how clever they were in disguising what they were doing—we can't ever let a group of people take hold of a player group in the way that this group did. That must never happen again. The penalties that have been assigned today, arguably, are the greatest penalties that the AFL/VFL have ever handed out. But frankly, what happened there is probably the worst thing that has happened in a footy club.'[33]

Danny Corcoran, career sports administrator and Essendon football manager, is the next domino to fall. His negotiations with the AFL have been productive. The league has abandoned its starting position that he must plead guilty to a charge of bringing the game into disrepute. The charge is dropped. In exchange, Corcoran accepts a six-month ban from the game, with two months of his penalty suspended. Within four months, he can resume his career at Essendon. He doesn't want to. The past two years have been the worst of his life. He has watched his wife die. He has watched friends turn against one another. While serving his suspension from football, he again seeks solace in travel. He goes to Senegal in West Africa, where he volunteers for a children's charity and puts his French to good use. When he returns, he tells Paul Little he doesn't want his old job back. He stays involved in football by taking over the presidency of his local VFL club, Sandringham. He makes a living selling real estate. He tries not to spend all his time thinking about what happened at Windy Hill.

Mark 'Bomber' Thompson also comes to terms. Like Corcoran, he doesn't plead guilty. The same sleight of hand applies: so long as he cops a penalty the charge against him will disappear. At the end of negotiations, his fine is a paltry $30,000, less than what his legal team has cost the club. At the time, it appears as though Thompson has got off lightly. More than two years later, the settlement remains a heavy weight.

'We are accepting guilt,' he says. 'We are accepting we had a hand in it and we are guilty of intentionally doping players. They can write it up how they want but in the end I have been charged and fined $30,000 for my involvement in a supplementation program that possibly or possibly did not involve performance-enhancing drugs.'[34] As soon as Thompson settles his case, he heads outside for some fresh air, trailed by a tangle of camera crews and jostling microphones. In Hird's absence he will coach Essendon the next season, another season engulfed by scandal. Like Corcoran, he too will eventually leave the club. There is a part of him that wishes that he'd never walked back inside Windy Hill.

'I left on reasonably good terms but I look back on my four years and I probably could have done something a lot better somewhere else and been happier.'[35]

With Corcoran and Thompson in the bag, Gleeson makes one last pass at Bruce Reid. His final offer is three months: a three-month suspension, no guilty plea. Take the deal and the doc can be back at the club before Christmas. Reid is unmoved. The AFL won't be settling its case with Reid. Gleeson should not take it personally. The next morning, Essendon chairman Paul Little tries his arm with no more luck. Reid is called to Little's office where the Essendon president, club director Paul Brasher and stand-in chief executive Ray Gunston are waiting.

'It's best for the club, just to finish it all, that you take the hit,' they tell him.[36] Reid says he will resign but he won't plead guilty to anything.

'I've got five kids, I've got nine grand kids, in fifteen years I might be dead and I am not going to be remembered as part of cheating. They said you might have to step aside. I said give me a pen and I'll resign.'[37] Little says he doesn't want the doc to quit. If he is determined to take on the AFL, the club will support him. Three weeks later, the AFL abandons its case against the Essendon club doctor.

All that is left is James Hird. In this case, however, the negotiations with the Essendon coach are being led by Little, not the AFL lawyers. It is the culmination of a bargaining process that began six days earlier, shortly after the defiant press conference in the penthouse suite of The Olsen. The offer before Hird from his club, an offer the AFL is willing to acquiesce to, would sorely tempt anyone. If Hird accepts a twelve-month ban from coaching and agrees to abandon his Supreme Court challenge, the AFL will drop the charge against him. It will enter into a non-disparagement agreement that will legally restrain its officials from fuelling the public relations campaign against him. If he accepts these terms Essendon will extend his contract for a further two years, until the end of the 2016 season. The club will pay him close to $1 million for each of those two seasons. It will also pay him during his year of suspension. Hird has decided he doesn't want to go to Oxford University, as the two Rhodes Scholars Mike Fitzpatrick and John Wylie proposed, but he is interested in further study. The club can help him with that too. If he takes his punishment the club will look after him in return.

The contract extension is not an empty promise. Its terms are negotiated within the walls of AFL House. In a bizarre scene, Little sits down in a room with the coach he threatened to cut loose four days earlier and their respective lawyers. Tania Hird, chosen as the party with the neatest handwriting, puts it all down in longhand. If Hird cops twelve months, if he provides a face to the scandal, his future at Essendon is assured. The alternative is bleak. Little tells his coach that if he does not settle with the AFL he is on his own. The club won't pay for the cost of his Supreme Court action and wherever that leads. Little won't sack Hird but he would expect him to stand down from coaching while he remains in dispute with the AFL. If Hird doesn't settle, there will be no contract extension, no 'outstanding career development opportunity' and no cease-fire from the AFL. They will keep hunting him. The AFL could strip his team of premiership points next season or stand down the club altogether. Even if they don't, Essendon will be forced to start another season with the drugs scandal unresolved. It will hurt sponsorship, it will hurt membership and it will hurt Essendon's players. Even if he takes on the AFL in court and wins, he might not coach again.

It is this last point that gnaws at Hird. His solicitor Steve Amendola wants him to fight on. Tania wants him to fight on. Burnside thinks he should go to court. When barrister Nick Harrington walks into AFL House, looks at what is on offer and urges him to take the deal, Hird realises this is what he really wants.

More than anything, he wants to coach Essendon. What is the point of winning against the AFL if, ultimately, he loses? In the AFL boardroom, with the air still thick from Tania's tirade, Danny Corcoran's loss and Mark Thompson's silent fury, Hird circles yes. He says he did so under 'great duress, threats and inducement',[38] but he circles it.

The next morning and many mornings after that, James Hird will wake angry at the choice he makes. Julian Burnside says the AFL process was shambolic and unjust. For Steve Amendola, the bitterness from those two days still lingers.

'As an outsider to the AFL before acting for James Hird, what most struck me about the AFL was that it behaved like it could do what it wanted, just because. It was like a manifestation of Tom Wolfe's masters of the universe from *The Bonfire of the Vanities*. Its default position quickly reached is to bully and threaten and when challenged, to ignore you until you are overwhelmed or capitulate. It is constantly horse-trading and constantly changing its position, a form of deliberate chaos to try and wear you down. As Elen Perdikogiannis from ASADA said of negotiating with the AFL, "Seriously, seven-year-old girls are more reliable negotiating parties." In its proceedings against Essendon Football Club, Hird, Thompson, Reid and Corcoran, it was clear that it had no intention of proceeding to hearing and would not have been in a position of prosecuting a hearing. That proceeding was a farce.'[39]

9
A FAUSTIAN COMPACT

AS THE BOSS of a sporting organisation that almost always wins, Andrew Demetriou should be better at it. Essendon and James Hird's acceptance of AFL judgement represents a spectacular capitulation from the position claimed at The Olsen less than a week earlier by club and coach. Essendon is out of the finals, Hird is out of football for a year, and the AFL is firmly in control. However rough its methods, the AFL has achieved its ends. Within the league's Docklands headquarters, there is a belief that the anti-doping investigation into Essendon will go nowhere, that with a finals series about to start, everyone can get back to watching the footy. Yet Demetriou is not a man who easily lets things go. Although he has dealt with Hird he has not forgiven the tip-off allegation levelled against him by the Essendon coach nor the journalists who reported it in the face of his denials. The AFL boss considers himself a man of integrity. He expects to be taken at his word.

'I don't tell lies,' he says. 'I just don't do it.'[1] In the wake of the two-day commission meeting, he repeatedly says things that are wrong. He misrepresents the AFL's position towards Essendon club doctor Bruce Reid. He misrepresents the sanctions accepted by Hird. He ensures that football's most damaging drug scandal cannot rest.

Hird is tormented by his decision to take the deal. He is indignant at his treatment at the hands of the AFL. He is convinced that ASADA acted unlawfully throughout the joint investigation. Yet he knows his opportunity to do something about it was the Supreme Court case he abandoned. His year in exile is consumed by regret, a yearning to have that moment in the AFL boardroom back. This regret, along with an acute sense of injustice, takes him to the Federal Court, an appeal hearing before its full bench, and to the brink of losing something he fought so doggedly throughout 2013 to keep: his coaching job at Essendon. He hires one of Australia's best commercial silks and, by the end of it, sinks $800,000 in legal costs to pursue what is, ultimately, a losing cause. Yet through these actions, he exposes the high-level scheming that shaped the AFL, ASADA and the federal government's approach to the drugs scandal and the emptiness of Demetriou's claim that on the night of Hird's fortieth birthday, he didn't know which club was under investigation. He ensures, too, the drug scandal cannot rest.

Squeezed between these two primal forces, Bruce Reid is the mouse who roars. The club doctor is the only Essendon official who refuses the AFL deal. The day after the commission meeting, Reid returns to AFL House with his legal team in tow. This time, only three commissioners are in attendance: chairman Mike Fitzpatrick, retired Family Court judge Linda Dessau and dot com businessman Paul Bassat. Despite Essendon, Hird, Corcoran and Thompson all coming to terms with the AFL for their failings throughout the 2012 season, Reid's position has not changed. His counsel, Ross Gillies QC, formally asks the commission to refer the Essendon doctor's case to an independent arbiter. The AFL refuses; Reid prepares for court. A week later, Victorian Supreme Court Justice David Beach makes his views clear.

'What's in it for your client not to farm it out to someone independent?' he asks AFL counsel Jeff Gleeson. 'I would invite your client to rethink the position.'[2] Justice Beach sets a hearing date for 19 September 2013. It won't get that far.

AFL chairman Mike Fitzpatrick does not want to spend the entire 2013 finals series in dispute with Bruce Reid. To the AFL, the Essendon doctor was a peripheral target. He has thirty years of credit from his work in football, he is well liked and admired by other AFL club doctors and the old bugger is now dug in for a fight, with a very good legal team paid for by his medical indemnity insurance. The AFL misunderstands Reid. It thinks his reluctance to settle is because any admission of guilt could trigger action by the state's Medical Practitioners Board and cause problems for Reid in his day job. When Demetriou muses about this during a radio interview,[3] the doctor is further offended. The reason Reid won't admit guilt is he believes he is innocent of the AFL's charge. His practising certificate has nothing to do with it. The AFL doesn't have leverage over Reid in the way it does Hird. Fitzpatrick knows, through his discussions with Essendon chairman Paul Little, that the club doctor is willing to be sacked before he accepts a deal. While the footy mad public are engrossed with the first week of the finals series, Fitzpatrick, Little and Reid's lawyers continue to discuss how to extricate the club and competition from the last remaining dispute from the drug scandal. By 12 September, the arrangements are all but complete. The AFL will drop the charge against Reid. Reid will face no sanction. All that remains is for everyone to agree on the wording of a joint press release.

The negotiations are conducted without the knowledge of Demetriou. When the AFL boss reads on the front page of the next morning's *The Australian* that his organisation is poised to abandon its case against Reid,[4] he is contemptuous of the story and me, its author, in a bizarre radio interview.

> Neil Mitchell: 'It is reported in *The Australian* today that you are looking at dropping charges against Dr Bruce Reid at Essendon. Is that correct?'

Demetriou: 'Neil, that is just another piece of garbage written by Chip "Homer" Le Grand who didn't bother to ring us up yesterday to even get a comment from us. I'll tell you one thing he is, he is consistently wrong. I have got to give him credit for being consistent. He has misreported the whole Essendon saga. He has been on this case, been wrong, he is wrong again and what he should do as a journalist Neil is pick up the phone and ring someone at the AFL to get a comment rather than writing garbage.'

Mitchell: 'So no settlement offer has been put to Essendon?'

Demetriou: 'Absolutely garbage. Not correct.'

Mitchell: 'So the AFL pursues Dr Reid as before?'

Demetriou: 'Absolutely and please, please, if you are listening Homer, pick up the phone …'

Mitchell: 'Why is he called Homer?'

Demetriou: 'That is his real name Neil, Homer.'[5]

Demetriou gets the name right but the rest dreadfully wrong.

On 18 September, the day before the parties are due back in court, the case is dropped. A joint press release issued by the AFL and Reid's lawyers says: 'The AFL accepts Dr Reid's position and withdraws all charges against him, without penalty.'[6] The timing is telling. Two days before settlement, the AFL's manager of integrity services Brett Clothier lodged an affidavit in the Victorian Supreme Court's prothonotary's office. The contents of the affidavit are unremarkable but, once filed, it means Clothier can be cross-examined if the case proceeds to a hearing. Within a day of Clothier lodging the affidavit, Reid's lawyers filed an application to do just that. Brett Clothier, the AFL's point man in the joint investigation with

ASADA, is the last person the AFL wants on the stand. Within hours of the application, the AFL's case against Reid is dropped.

Demetriou's comments to broadcaster Neil Mitchell are instructive in two ways. The first is that Demetriou is out of the loop on an important, publicly sensitive AFL decision; something that once would have been unthinkable. A recurring criticism of Demetriou by his fellow commissioners during this period is that he is not across the details of the drugs saga. At a time when the AFL most needs a strong, effective chief executive, Demetriou delegates too much to his deputy Gillon McLachlan and pays insufficient attention to events as they unfold. There is a clear conflict in Demetriou's dual position as the AFL's most senior executive and a member of its commission. When the AFL takes disciplinary action against Essendon, it is the executive that prosecutes the case and the commission that sits in judgement. Demetriou publicly accepts he cannot do both. His solution is to remain in both roles but to claim an arm's length distance between the daily management of the scandal and his office. This is neither credible nor workable. Although it is McLachlan who acts as the AFL's negotiator-in-chief in its dealings with Essendon, Demetriou is still running the AFL. This becomes a frustration for Paul Little, who is told to deal with McLachlan but is used to negotiating with the person in charge.

'Gill was reasonable enough but if I backed Gill into a corner he'd say I can't agree to that because Andrew will never agree. I said, "Well, bring Andrew into the room".'[7] This situation becomes ludicrous during the August commission meeting, when Demetriou spends both days inside his own office while AFL underlings run messages to and from negotiations. Demetriou is the AFL's best negotiator. He should be in the thick of it. Had he followed Bill Kelty's lead and recused himself from commission deliberations on Essendon and done his day job, the doping scandal may have been handled far better by the AFL.

The second revealing aspect of the Mitchell interview is the petty nature of Demetriou's attack. Friends and admirers of the AFL boss later remark it is one of his worst moments in the entire scandal. Demetriou's slagging off of a journalist, on the face of it, is insignificant. Most listeners to Mitchell's program would enjoy the sport. To Demetriou's peers, it is a sign that all is not well with the AFL chief. In a subsequent interview with ABC sports broadcaster Gerard Whateley, Demetriou provides an insight into why he reacted to the Reid settlement story with such hostility.

'There have been two or three journalists, including that so-called journalist, who have been inferring for quite a while that myself and Gillon McLachlan were party to providing information to David Evans, a consequence of which would have seen us in jail. Despite the fact that we denied it, despite the fact that also David Evans denied it, the ACC clarified that it was not true and so did ASADA. So, Gerard, if you think that having your reputation impugned, a consequence of which is going to jail, goes just past the wicket keeper, you are mistaken. And if you think it was a response to that, absolutely. Make no mistake.'[8] The tip-off story still rankled.

Demetriou describes himself during his playing career as a good ordinary footballer. By his own self-deprecating assessment, he was never much of a kick but he was blessed with one attribute: sure hands. When the promising young winger was recruited by league club North Melbourne from Pascoe Vale, he soon caught the eye of Ray 'Slug' Jordan, the Kangaroos' U19s coach.

'You don't fumble son,' Jordan remarked.[9] When the *Herald Sun* and *The Australian* reveal the secret negotiations between Mike Fitzpatrick, Paul Little and Australian Sports Commission boss John Wylie that preceded the two-day AFL Commission meeting,[10] Demetriou fumbles badly.

The published stories do not implicate the AFL chief executive. As they make clear, the settlement package was negotiated between three old friends, John Wylie, Mike Fitzpatrick and Paul Little, without the involvement of the AFL chief executive. When Demetriou walks into Mitchell's radio studio, he makes himself the story. Demetriou is a very good communicator. More than a decade in a senior executive position has not infected his speech with managerial jargon. His language remains simple, earthy, and powerful. Give him a radio microphone and there is rarely a problem he cannot fix, a fissure he can't smooth over. Not this time. As Demetriou settles into Mitchell's broadcast booth early on a Wednesday morning, he is poorly briefed, unprepared and brimming with misplaced confidence that he can discredit the stories. Both newspapers report Hird is receiving his full salary while on suspension, in line with the settlement terms negotiated between Fitzpatrick, Wylie and Little. Demetriou is adamant this is wrong. One fact out of place is all he needs. If they've got this wrong, why believe anything else they've written? Demetriou hammers this point in the interview that follows.

'Neil, I want to make it very clear. The sanction to James Hird is twelve months suspension is suspension without pay. So it is incorrect that he is being paid by the Essendon Football Club … I can categorically tell you that part of the sanction from the AFL is that he is suspended without pay from the Essendon Football Club … Let's be very clear. The AFL is not paying anybody, including James Hird, any money. Neil, that is one thing I will go to my grave on: I know 100 per cent the AFL is not paying and I know that Essendon is not paying Neil.'[11]

During the interview, Demetriou admits he was not privy to the negotiations between Fitzpatrick, Wylie and Little. He cannot say what was discussed. His explanation of what went on at Gillon McLachlan's house the day before the commission meeting is similarly vague. Mitchell is an experienced journalist and broadcaster who has regularly interviewed Demetriou throughout his time as AFL chief executive. He cannot recall the AFL boss ever being less convincing.

On his point of attack, a point on which he vows to go to his grave, Demetriou is dead wrong. James Hird is being paid by Essendon. There is nothing in the settlement reached between the AFL and Essendon and the AFL and James Hird that precludes Hird from receiving his usual salary from Essendon during his year in exile. His pay arrangements have not changed since the commission meeting ten weeks earlier. The AFL could have easily checked this. The clubs outsource their payroll functions to the AFL. Whatever information Demetriou needs about Hird's pay is accessible from inside league headquarters. Failing this, a phone call to Essendon chairman Paul Little or chief executive Ray Gunston would have cleared up the matter. Instead, it takes dozens of phone calls over many days and another mini-crisis for Essendon, the AFL and Hird to crunch together a contrived arrangement that enables Hird to keep his money and Demetriou to save face. In the end Essendon agrees to pay Hird's entire 2014 salary by New Year's Eve so that in strict accounting terms, Hird is not paid during his calendar year of suspension. Hird's penance arrives as a whopping lump sum before Christmas. Andrew Demetriou blames Essendon, the Hirds and so-called journalists for his humiliation.[12]

Demetriou believes the club has been sneaky in its dealings with the league, that Little has tried to slide one past the AFL Commission. This is humbug. To unravel the mystery of Hird's pay arrangements, you need to go back to the final hour of the AFL Commission meeting on 27 August 2013. Hird was close to agreeing to terms with the AFL and accepting a year's suspension. The deeds of settlement between the AFL, Hird and Essendon had been examined and approved by the AFL Commission. The crisis was nearly at an end. There was just one outstanding issue. The AFL Commission wouldn't accept Hird being suspended with pay. This would be the wrong look. The AFL knew it could not prevent Hird from earning money from other means. If someone connected to Essendon with deep pockets decided to pay Hird a figure close to his coaching salary for doing other work, the commission and AFL administration would turn a blind eye. Yet, officially, Hird had to be suspended without pay. This was what the AFL wanted. It is not what Essendon and Hird agreed to. It is not what was written into the settlement agreement drafted by the AFL lawyers that Hird signed.

When Paul Little was waiting with the club lawyers to appear before the commissioners one last time, there was a knock on his door. McLachlan, the AFL deputy chief executive who led negotiations with the club, asked for a word with Little. The pair moved out of the room to speak in private. McLachlan said Hird couldn't be paid, the AFL Commission wouldn't agree to it. They already have, Little replied. The deal was done. The settlement had been ratified. McLachlan said it was a problem. Demetriou wouldn't wear it. It had to be changed. Little told him it is too late to change things now. McLachlan disappeared to talk to Demetriou again. When he returns, McLachlan says Demetriou was insistent: Hird can't be paid. Little knew this was a potential deal breaker. He wouldn't re-open negotiations with his coach. Hird would be paid, he told McLachlan. The deal was done.

McLachlan was merely a messenger. He knew Essendon wouldn't shift and neither would his boss. Little was right; the deal was done. McLachlan was right as well; it was not the deal the AFL Commission believes it had endorsed. If McLachlan went back to Demetriou and told him Essendon was intending to pay Hird, the entire settlement agreement could have collapsed. If that happened, the days locked in negotiations, the hours spent with Hird and his lawyers the Sunday before, the weeks of persuading and cajoling and shaping and assembling a solution to this mess in time for the finals would have been for nothing. McLachlan had one other choice: eat the message. If Demetriou and his fellow commissioners believed Hird was not being paid, everyone could leave AFL House thinking they'd got what they wanted. What did he do? If you were in McLachlan's shoes, what would you do?

In the days that followed the commission hearing, McLachlan tried to defuse the bomb ticking away within Hird's settlement. He approached Paul Little again to see if other pay arrangements could be made. Andrew Dillon, the AFL's general counsel, made a similar approach to Essendon's stand-in chief executive Ray Gunston. Their efforts were fruitless. Essendon was determined to stick by the letter of its agreement with the AFL. The club didn't even raise the issue with its coach. When the generous terms associated with Hird's punishment were made public, the hypocrisy at the heart of the AFL's handling of the doping scandal was exposed. The day of Demetriou's radio inverview with Neil Mitchell, Hird had just returned from Fontainebleau, an exclusive university campus surrounded by an oak and pine forest south of Paris, where he was studying an MBA. This is the outstanding professional development opportunity referred to in the Wylie-negotiated settlement. About half of Hird's $120,000 tuition and expenses are being met by the club, which is also paying his $1 million-plus salary while he is suspended. His extended coaching contract gives him financial security until the end of 2016. It is a punishment most people would dream of.

There is also a 'no disparagement' clause attached to the settlement agreement. This means that Hird cannot say what he thinks about Demetriou's comments on radio. There is no such restriction on Tania Hird. As the pay dispute flares into a second week, Tania Hird is greeted one morning in her driveway by Ashley Argoon, a young reporter from the *Herald Sun*. The paper's news desk has sent Argoon to the Hirds' house every day to ask the same question since the story broke. Her luck is about to change.

'Tania, is your husband being paid by Essendon?'

'Well look, of course he is getting paid. That was the deal. Andrew Demetriou knew it, the AFL knew it. We wouldn't have taken a sanction without pay. James took a twelve-month suspension because he was threatened. The club was threatened, he was threatened. In the end the club said it is in the best interests of the club, we need to move on, which is what we did. We would have taken the AFL to the Supreme Court and they knew that. Demetriou knew that. In my opinion it is time for the AFL to stop threatening my husband, it is time for them to stop threatening the club and it is time for them to stop distorting the truth.'[13]

The next morning, when Andrew Demetriou pulls into his priority parking spot beneath the Docklands stadium, he is greeted by a camera crew and questions about what he knew about Hird's pay arrangements. The AFL boss, his jaw clenched, does not say a word as the back door to AFL headquarters slams shut behind him.

As one door closes at AFL House, another is opening for ASADA. Nima Alavi, the proprietor of the Como Compounding Pharmacy, had up until now been an elusive figure in the doping scandal. On legal advice, he has steadfastly declined to talk to anti-doping investigators for the best part of a year. As his lawyers see it, he has everything to lose and nothing to gain by opening the books on his Toorak pharmacy and his dealings with Stephen Dank, Shane Charter and the rest of the colourful cast of Peptide Alley. Best that he keep his head down until the whole thing blows over. Besides, he has plenty of work to do; peptide sales have boomed since the blackest day in Australian sport. Within ASADA, however, there is a belief that Alavi can still be persuaded to talk. Law changes passed by federal parliament before the 2013 winter recess—one of the last acts of the Gillard Government—have given the anti-doping body new tools to work with. Instead of relying on its powers of begging and pleading, ASADA can coerce witnesses to produce documents and attend interviews. It still can't compel anyone to answer questions at the risk of self-incrimination. Greens Senator Richard Di Natale, a doctor and former league footballer, ensured that idea was left on the cutting room floor of the Upper House. Yet ASADA had what it needed to get Alavi into a room. Lead investigator John Nolan is confident that once they do, Alavi will want to tell his story.

Nolan is in familiar surrounds—at the centre of a contentious, high-profile, complex investigation. An experienced police detective, he was one of the first investigators to join Victoria's Office of Police Integrity (OPI), a police watchdog established by the Victorian Government amid growing evidence that corrupt police were willing combatants in Melbourne's gangland war. Victoria's powerful Police Association hated the OPI from its inception, arguing that police should not be subjected to coercions that don't apply to any other profession. The relatively brief history of the OPI is dominated by two politically charged operations: the ill-fated pursuit of police assistant commissioner Noel Ashby and long-serving Police Association secretary Paul Mullett, and an investigation into spurious corruption claims against deputy commissioner Ken Jones, which ultimately contributed to Simon Overland quitting his post as Victoria Police chief commissioner. As a central figure in both these operations, Nolan attracted the ire of powerful, high-profile critics. None of them doubt his abilities as an investigator. At the end of 2012, when the soon-to-be-abolished OPI was fast shedding staff and ASADA needed experienced investigators to run Operation Cobia, Nolan accepted a twelve-month contract with the anti-doping body. He brought with him Sharon Kerrison and Aaron Walker, fellow OPI detectives also looking for new work. The three of them ran the investigation into Essendon.

On 19 November 2013, Nolan and Walker sit down with Nima Alavi for the first time. Over the next three weeks they conduct a further three interviews with the pharmacist, who also provides ASADA with documents related to his dealings with Essendon sports scientist Stephen Dank. It is a time of intense activity for ASADA's Melbourne-based investigations team. Kerrison has decided to return home to the United Kingdom and Nolan's twelve-month contract is coming to an end. ASADA's investigations budget was doubled in 2013 to cope with the extra workload of the doping scandal but both the previous sports minister Kate Lundy and her Abbott Government successor Peter Dutton made it clear the extra money is a one-year deal. If ASADA is going to crack the Essendon case it needs to happen before the New Year.

What Alavi tells ASADA's investigators helps and hurts their case. Documents he provides hold a mirror to what drug importer Shane Charter has already told them—that Charter arranged the importation of peptides from Shanghai to Alavi's Toorak pharmacy, and that Alavi supplied these to Stephen Dank. Yet the gaps in the chain of custody are still plain for anyone to see. Yes, Alavi supplied a Thymosin peptide to Dank in early 2012 and, yes, he believes that, more than likely, it was Thymosin Beta 4, a substance banned by WADA. But without having tested it, he can't be sure. As for what Dank did with the peptides, Alavi has no idea. Taken at its strongest, Alavi's evidence puts Thymosin Beta 4 in Dank's hands in January 2012 when the sports scientist was employed at Essendon. It doesn't put the banned peptide at Windy Hill. It certainly doesn't put it under the skin of Essendon players.

'That is why this case is not going to go anywhere,' Alavi says. 'All they have got is that one batch I gave Dank. There is where it ends. How are you going to prove that those vials were injected at Essendon?'[14]

John Nolan and his team are convinced that Dank administered Thymosin Beta 4 to Essendon players. They believe that Charter imported it, Alavi compounded it and Dank injected it into the bellies of unwitting footballers. They suspect he probably gave them Hexarelin as well. The stuff was in identical, clear vials, distinguished only by handwritten labels. They also accept that for practical reasons, it is not a case that ASADA can prove. Of the entire 2012 Essendon squad, only two footballers recall being injected with something from clear vials. Only one of those was told it was Thymosin. As for anything injected from an amber vial, the investigators conclude there are 'near insurmountable obstacles'[15] to ever knowing what was in the needles. In the investigator's final report, lead author Aaron Walker recommends against charging the players. Aside from the difficulty in proving the case, he questions the public interest in pursuing a bunch of footballers who were lied to about what they were injected with.[16]

The strongest case that ASADA has against any AFL player for taking a banned substance has nothing to do with Essendon. In a separate report submitted to ASADA management in October 2013, the investigators conclude that Gold Coast Suns defender Nathan Bock has a case to answer for using the banned peptide CJC-1295. The ASADA lawyers refuse to take action against Bock. The explanation they give at the time is that for reasons of procedural fairness, the case against Dank should be heard first. Over the next year, as ASADA dithers, the allegations against Bock are left to die on the vine. At the end of the 2014 season, while Bock announces his retirement from AFL football, ASADA launches thirty-four prosecutions it won't win and ignores the one it might. This is convenient for the AFL, as it owns the Gold Coast Suns, a loss-making expansion club trying to establish a following in a strategically important sporting market. At least ASADA has a watertight case against Dank. In this much, Nolan leaves the anti-doping body on 31 December 2013 knowing he has got his man.

ASADA chief executive Aurora Andruska takes a different view to her investigations team. She accepts the report but not the recommendation to drop the case against the Essendon players. Andruska acknowledges that Nolan and his team are experienced investigators but as she points out, they are not anti-doping experts. Paul Simonsson and Nolan only started work at ASADA a few weeks before Senator Kate Lundy and Justice Minister Jason Clare stood up at that press conference in Canberra. Aaron Walker spent his first day in his new job sitting in on interviews with Essendon president David Evans and chief executive Ian Robson. Andruska believes ASADA's lawyers should take up where the investigations team has left off. They are given the entire brief of evidence and told to make it work.

'In my mind, we were never not proceeding,' Andruska says.[17]

Within ASADA's Fyshwick office, a siege mentality has developed. The new Sports Minister Peter Dutton, a straight-talking former Queensland cop, believes the biggest investigation in ASADA's history is a shambles. He doesn't blame ASADA entirely for this—as he sees it, the fiasco surrounding the release of the Australian Crime Commission report set up the anti-doping body to fail. But he has no confidence in Aurora Andruska, who is nearly at the end of her contract at ASADA. She wants another year to see through the Essendon and Cronulla cases; the government won't offer her one. When Dutton commissions retired Federal Court Justice Garry Downes to conduct an independent review of Operation Cobia, Andruska fears the worst.

'My contract was coming to an end and I was thinking, I hope they haven't brought in this bloke just to shut things down.

Probably more, I was thinking, they are probably hoping that this guy will think there is not enough evidence.'[18]

Garry Downes isn't there to shut things down. He is there to assess whether, after a year-long investigation, ASADA is on a mad folly or a winnable cause. While Downes reviews the work ASADA has done, Andruska seeks her own advice. Richard Young, one of the world's most accomplished sports and anti-doping law experts, flies in to Canberra from Colorado Springs. Young led the US Anti-Doping Agency's successful prosecution of Marion Jones and other athletes implicated in the BALCO doping scandal, Tour de France winner Floyd Landis and the biggest doping cheat of them all, Lance Armstrong. Since March 2013, he has been advising ASADA on its pursuit of doping allegations at Essendon and Cronulla. After evaluating the evidence gathered against the Essendon players, Young's advice to Andruska is she has a case worth running. Young's assessment, along with that of ASADA counsel Malcolm Holmes QC and Downes' green light, are the reassurances that Andruska needs. Her only regret is that she won't be the one to send out the infraction notices to Essendon players. She decides this task is best left to her replacement, Ben McDevitt. When ASADA's new chief executive walks into his Fyshwick office to start work on 10 May 2014, he finds in his in-tray the biggest anti-doping case Australia has ever seen. On 12 June, McDevitt pulls the trigger against thirty-four current and former Essendon players.

If there is any place in the world that James Hird can cleanse his soul of the doping scandal it is springtime in Fontainebleau. Sumantra Ghoshal, the late management guru who taught for eight years at INSEAD's prestigious business school south of Paris, says it's 'the smell of the place', a clean, pine-scented air that fills your senses and lifts your spirits.

'I genuinely challenge you to go to the forest of Fontainebleau in spring,' he would say to his students. 'Go with a firm desire to have a leisurely walk and you can't. The moment you enter the forest there is something about the crispness of the air, there is something about the smell of the trees in spring, you'd want to jump, you'd want to jog, you'd want to catch a branch, run, do something.'[19] In May 2014 Fontainebleau is a dappled landscape of young pine needles and brilliant, broken light. The inspiration of Renoir and Monet, it is one of the prettiest places in all of Europe. Apart from the forest, Fontainebleau is dominated by a twelfth-century chateau. The castle was the traditional summer palace of French monarchs and Napoleon Bonaparte's home before his abdication and exile: 'The real abode of Kings, the house of ages' is how Napoleon described it.[20] Between business classes, Essendon's exiled king takes regular walks through the forest. Whether it is the crispness of the air, the smell of the trees or the advice of his lawyers back home, he is compelled to do something. He will take on ASADA in the Federal Court.

Hird does not decide this on a whim. The legality of ASADA's joint investigation with the AFL is something nearly every lawyer who has come into contact with the doping scandal has questioned. Chris Pollard, a solicitor appointed by the AFL Coaches' Association to represent Essendon staff, flagged it as an issue early in the investigation and Hird's barrister, Tony Nolan QC, echoed those concerns at the start of his client's interview with ASADA and the AFL. Had Hird continued with his Supreme Court challenge to the AFL's jurisdiction over his case, the legality of the joint investigation and the interim report would have been two central issues at trial. Had the AFL not abandoned its case against Essendon club doctor Bruce Reid, the legality of ASADA's conduct would have been challenged by Reid's legal team. ASADA's own lawyers even questioned the legality of the AFL being inside the ASADA tent. ASADA's director of legal services, Darren Mullaly, queried the proposed arrangements on 8 February, one day after the blackest day in Australian sport.[21]

The argument, at its simplest, is about power and confidentiality. ASADA is a statutory body. What it can and can't do is set out by the ASADA Act and regulations. There is no provision within the ASADA Act to conduct a joint investigation with a sporting body. There is no provision for ASADA to use coercive powers held by another organisation to compel witnesses to answer questions in an anti-doping investigation. There is no provision for ASADA to share information with another organisation for a purpose other than an anti-doping investigation. ASADA does all these things in its joint investigation into Essendon. Has it acted beyond its powers? By March 2014, when the first breath of spring is rustling Fontainebleau Forest, Hird's legal team is armed with a legal opinion from Peter Hanks QC, one of Australia's leading constitutional and administrative law experts, that the joint investigation is unlawful. James Hird is ready to go. He wants to have the fight he believes he shouldn't have walked away from that night at AFL headquarters. He just doesn't want to go it alone.

As rumours spread of impending 'show cause' notices against Essendon players, Hird and his legal advisers are in the ear of Paul Little and Essendon's new chief executive, Xavier Campbell, urging them to lead a pre-emptive strike against ASADA. Hird has good reason to get in early. He knows the moment ASADA initiates anti-doping proceedings against any current or former Essendon players there will be further calls for his head. It is as certain as the change of seasons at Fontainebleau. Besides, he has grown weary of Essendon reacting to every shift in the doping scandal. This is a chance to drive one. As Hird's lawyer Steve Amendola puts it, 'I wanted ASADA to be the hunted rather than the hunter.'

Little and Essendon are not convinced. Essendon's lawyer Tony Hargreaves also doubts the legality of ASADA's actions, in particular the decision to provide the AFL with an interim report. Three days before ASADA provided the report to the AFL, Hargreaves wrote to both organisations warning against such a move. Yet Hargreaves is loath to go to court unless Essendon has to. The club can take Federal Court action if and when the 'show cause' notices ever arrive. On the day they do, Essendon is caught flat-footed when Hargreaves is immediately seconded to the players' legal team, leaving Essendon unadvised. Luckily for the club, or perhaps unluckily, Hird's legal team has drawn up the necessary papers for Essendon to initiate proceedings—a pre-cooked, ready-to-eat litigation that just requires the signature of a solicitor. By agreement, Essendon files first and Hird follows.

Essendon and ASADA trading blows in the Federal Court is the last thing the AFL wants. Not in the middle of a football season. The day after the notices are issued, the AFL's recently installed chief executive Gillon McLachlan calls Little and suggests he meets with ASADA's Ben McDevitt to negotiate an outcome for the players. The moment McLachlan calls, Little is pulling into the front gates of Essendon's Tullamarine headquarters. There are television vans on the side of the road, photographers swarming the entrance to the drive.

'I'll tell you what, Gill,' he says to the AFL's new boss, 'you can tell McDevitt three things. You can tell him to get fucked; you can tell him we don't do deals; you can tell him I'll see him in court.'

It is a big day when footy goes to court. The public gallery fills quickly. The Essendon saga, a slow-moving, cumbersome vessel, has collected all manner of barnacles. Would-be anti-doping experts and quasi-legal bloggers, Hird-o-philes and Hird haters, jumper-wearing fans and countless others who have donned the sash or stood by Hird or rallied to a hashtag in a groundswell of support for their footy club and coach; all find a seat next to sportswriters and court reporters and back-page columnists, courtroom groupies and lawyers in between other cases who have dropped in to see the day's popcorn trial. At the order of Federal Court Justice John Middleton, a media-friendly judge who prefers his proceedings open and to the point, television cameras are allowed in court to broadcast live what passes for action across the arid expanse of federal administrative law. Club officials wear red and black-striped ties and dour expressions. Essendon chairman Paul Little has fought many a legal battle throughout his business career but has never spent three consecutive days sitting in a courtroom, listening to how lawyers earn his money. James and Tania Hird arrive to a sweep of photographers. A newspaper fashion column is dedicated to her choice of trench coats. Would-be jurors sit in lounge rooms and city offices, casting judgement on how the coach performs in the witness box.

There are two cases to be decided. At the front of the courtroom it is about the law: Essendon and Hird's claim that ASADA's partnership with the AFL was a 'Faustian compact'[22] that breached the anti-doping agency's statutory obligations to operate independently of the sports it investigates and guard the information it obtains; and ASADA's withering 'nonsense on stilts' response that such co-operation is wholly consistent with ASADA's overriding purpose to prevent and detect doping.[23] At the back of the room, it is about Hird's one-man war against ASADA and the AFL. This is Hird's chance to show a full courtroom and live television audience that the fix was in from the start.

It is a fine line that Hird and his legal team must tread. Pre-trial discovery has reaped a bountiful harvest of internal ASADA communications. Like all good public servants, the women and men who run the anti-doping body are diligent note takers. The spiral bound notebooks filled by Aurora Andruska's hand provide a dot point, as-it-happened account of how the investigation took shape, the tensions that emerged between the AFL and ASADA, the unexplained attendance of departmental and public relations officials at sensitive meetings, and the pressure on ASADA to bring its investigation to an end before the twin deadlines of a September federal election and a finals series. The mutterings throughout 2013 about the AFL being prepared to flog the club and its staff in order to spare the players, about the blackest day in Australian sport turning blacker still for the Gillard Government, about Essendon's 'self reporting' being a sham, about ASADA and the AFL nearly ending up in court over the interim report; it is all there in the notebooks and emails and other discovered material. It is all true. Yet much of it has little to no bearing on the issues Justice Middleton has been asked to decide.

When James Albert Hird is called to the witness box, he gets his licks in—the tip-off allegation against AFL chief exectutive Andrew Demetriou, his allegation that David Evans asked him to lie about what was said the night of his fortieth birthday party—he testifies to them all on the record, all under oath. He opens a window to the damaging split that emerged between club, coach and president over the handling of the drug scandal, he makes clear that his settlement with the AFL was induced and contrived, that taking full responsibility at that first press conference at AFL House for what happened at Essendon was never his idea. His testimony is measured, assured and revealing. Does it help his and Essendon's case, the one being judged on the law? Not a jot.

While Hird has his day in court, Andruska is growing increasingly nervous about hers. During a lengthy cross examination of the Essendon coach, the ASADA chief executive spends her afternoon listening to meditation tapes, trying to prepare herself for the most brutal public examination of her career. At the end of the day's hearing, she receives a phone call from one of the ASADA lawyers. Hird is taking longer on the stand than they anticipated and Andruska won't get on until midway through the next morning. Andruska is warned what to expect: 'They are going to make you look confused, like you weren't in control, that you were incompetent. They may be showing you material that you haven't seen. But don't worry. We are going to win this on the law.'[24]

Andruska puts down the phone. She feels sick. Is that why they've flown her to Melbourne, to be a punching bag for fancy suits hired by Essendon and James Hird? If ASADA is going to win the case anyway, why does she need to subject herself to that?

'If the other side is going to do all this stuff to me, where my reputation is absolutely smashed, what opportunity will I ever get to rehabilitate myself? James has still got an opportunity. He really does. But at my age, and the end of my career, what opportunity would I have? Isn't it enough what my kids have read for eighteen months? I rang him back and said, "I don't know if I'm going to be the right witness for you. You say you are going to win anyway, I don't think you need me." I think enough is enough.'[25]

ASADA needs Andruska to take the stand. After the Commonwealth Law Courts building in Melbourne empties for the day, the ASADA legal team gently goes to work on its star witness, convincing her to testify. They arrange for John Andruska, Aurora's husband, to fly to Melbourne early the next morning so he can be in court to support her. John Andruska has seen the impact the doping saga has had on his wife, the damage it has caused. He wants her to be able to leave behind this entire, awful episode. If standing up and testifying will help her do that, he believes it is worth doing. The examination of Aurora Andruska that unfolds over the next six hours is painstaking and, at times, excoriating. Although Andruska was ASADA chief executive throughout its joint investigation with the AFL, her job was not all about Essendon. There was the Cronulla investigation to worry about, there was ASADA's usual tasks of conducting drug tests and educating athletes about doping. She delegated to her senior staff key decisions about how the Essendon investigation should be run and where the boundaries should lie between ASADA and the AFL. Once under oath in the Federal Court, she can't say when the ground rules were agreed to and how they were decided. Her insistence that the joint investigation was based on well-established practice is greeted with scorn by her main questioner, Essendon counsel Neil Young QC.

'Ms Andruska, until this investigation, ASADA had never conducted a joint investigation with any person other than another Commonwealth body; that's the case is it not?'[26] He accuses her of being non-responsive, evasive.

From the back of the room, the former ASADA boss looks to be in trouble. Her habit of offering lengthy silences before she answers a question prompts derision in the cheap seats. Yet at the front of the court, where Justice John Middleton sits, Andruska is credible and convincing. Rather than a witness trying to conceal, she is the one trying to peel back the silly bits of pink paper that someone from ASADA has used to redact her own notes, so she can clear up what was actually said at a particular meeting. Once the paper is removed, damaging observations from a meeting on 4 June with Gillon McLachlan, David Evans and Richard Eccles turn out to be things said by ASADA's own public relations adviser a day earlier. She hands her notes back to Neil Young with a little thrill of triumph.

There are some questions that Andruska doesn't need to answer to make clear what was going on. Why was Richard Eccles, a senior federal government bureaucrat, sitting in on a teleconference on 1 February 2013 when the details of how ASADA might work with the AFL on a highly sensitive anti-doping investigation were first discussed?

'I guess that's a question for Mr Eccles,' she says. Were you under political pressure to complete the investigation into Essendon?

'I ignored all political pressure.'[27]

After more than a year of claim and counterclaim and bluster and bulldust, Andruska confirms that the AFL's Andrew Demetriou, Gillon McLachlan and Brett Clothier all knew a week before the blackest day in Australian sport that Essendon was a club of interest in the Australian Crime Commission probe.[28]

Essendon and Hird leave the Federal Court thinking they've have had a good day. Andruska is uncertain how she's gone until she walks into a little room in the court building where ASADA's senior counsel Tom Howe is beaming and barrister Sue McNicol gives her a warm hug. On the day that Justice Middleton dismisses the application by Essendon and Hird against ASADA, Howe calls Andruska, who has just returned to port after sailing around the Whitsunday Islands.

'You have been vindicated to the nation,' he tells her.[29]

Judgement day is preliminary final day. It is Sydney against North Melbourne for a place in the big one. Buddy Franklin, Sydney's million-dollar recruit, should be the talk of football. Instead, all the action is taking place inside a packed courtroom in Melbourne, where sports scientist Stephen Dank has just walked in to take a seat. Dank is as welcome as an uninvited ex-boyfriend at a wedding. He has refused to help the ASADA investigation; he has done nothing to assist Essendon's cause. He is the reason that, in September 2014, everyone is still talking about substances injected into Bombers players more than two years earlier instead of that night's game. He has come to court, as Essendon and Hird's legal team and many observers have, expecting to hear Justice Middleton declare ASADA and the AFL's joint investigation unlawful. It soon becomes clear the judge will do nothing of the sort.

Justice Middleton reads a summary of his judgement to the court and TV cameras. Although he is too judicious to say so, it is evident he agrees with Tom Howe's description of Essendon and Hird's case as nonsense on stilts. He finds that ASADA acted lawfully at all times—that the investigation was lawful, that the use of the AFL's compulsive powers to compel Essendon footballers and staff to answer questions was lawful, that the provision of the interim report to the AFL was lawful. The way the judge sees it, ASADA and the AFL rightly co-operated in the investigation for separate but related purposes: ASADA to determine whether anyone had broken anti-doping rules, the AFL to sanction Essendon, Hird and other club staff for the failings in governance and management, which put the players at risk of doping. Although the ASADA Act doesn't explicitly provide for a joint investigation, the judge finds there is nothing in the conduct of that investigation that contravened the Act. The application is denied, costs are awarded against club and coach.

Justice Middleton goes further. Even if the investigation was unlawful, he wouldn't have given Essendon and Hird what they were after—the removal of interview transcripts and other material gathered by the joint investigation from ASADA's brief of evidence against the thirty-four players accused of doping. To do so would be pointless, Justice Middleton reasons, as ASADA could simply reacquire the information from the AFL. As for Andruska, Justice Middleton provides a glowing review.

'The only witness whose credit was impugned was Ms Andruska. It was submitted by Essendon and Mr Hird that Ms Andruska was non-responsive, evasive and partisan. It was observed, as was the fact, that there were long pauses between the questioning of Ms Andruska and her responses. I do not consider these criticisms, to the extent they impact on her veracity, can be sustained. Ms Andruska was a truthful witness.'[30]

For the Essendon Football Club and James Hird, it is a crushing judgement. While a wall of TV cameras assembles outside the revolving door of the court building, the high-priced lawyers who didn't see this coming study the judgement. They believe Justice Middleton has got it wrong, that club and coach have been robbed. Every lawyer loses cases but Neil Young QC, one of the smoothest silks in commercial law, rarely does. He reads the judgement in bewilderment. He urges Essendon, in unequivocal terms, to appeal. The club is torn. It wasn't expecting this outcome. It wasn't prepared for it. Essendon chief executive Xavier Campbell says that, for the players and staff, it is one of the lowest moments of the entire scandal.

'It really sucked the life out of everyone,' he says.[31] The senior players meet and make their view clear. They want the doping charges against them heard and decided. They don't want the club to do anything that will further delay an already protracted process. Paul Little, one of the richest men in Australia, is not inclined to throw good money after bad. He thought Essendon had a good case. He was told Essendon had a good case. He also knows when he's beat.

'We got completely done over in a legal sense,' he says. 'You have to accept it and I did.'[32]

Hird on the other hand, is determined to double up. The final line of Young's written advice to the club about the prospect of an appeal reads less like a legal opinion than a call to arms: 'I strongly recommend that you appeal and you will succeed.' Hird cannot help but charge in, to risk all against ASADA once more.

Of all the reasons Paul Little has had to sack James Hird, the coach's decision to appeal Justice Middleton's judgement is the most tenuous. The Essendon chairman knows this side of Hird by now, this stubbornness in the face of reason, threats, pressure, fear. Yet it frustrates Little that Hird won't let it go, can't let go of his quest to prove that ASADA acted unlawfully. It is no longer a matter of Hird wanting to cruel ASADA's case against the Essendon players—ASADA is pushing ahead with its case against the players regardless. It has become a matter of higher principle for Hird. It has moved beyond self-interest to something far less predictable. Winning this case against ASADA means more to Hird than protecting his job at Essendon. He makes this clear enough on the morning of 2 October 2014. At 9.50 a.m., he is preparing to lodge his appeal application before the Federal Court when Little rings. The Essendon president cannot be more clear: if Hird submits the paperwork, he will be sacked. Ten minutes later Hird lodges his appeal application. He makes his choice.

Little is furious. Hird is not the only headstrong coach he is dealing with. The previous night, at the club's best and fairest count, he tries and fails to discern Mark Thompson's intentions for the next season. After Thompson goes on stage to make a speech that is widely interpreted as an application for Hird's job, Little and club chief executive Xavier Campbell buttonhole Thompson in a kitchen behind the Palladium function room at Melbourne's Crown Casino.

'If James isn't there, would you be interested in the role?' they ask him.[33] It is the culmination of several weeks of uneasy negotiations between Thompson and the club. They have talked about him staying on as a technical director or an ambassador or another role. Thompson's problem is he has fallen back in love with coaching. He wants Hird to come back and coach but there is a part of him that wants to keep doing the job himself. To complicate matters, Essendon thinks he is being courted by the Gold Coast. Thompson says his speech was misunderstood. He says that far from a job application, it was his farewell to Essendon.[34] Ultimately, when the day to leave Essendon comes, Thompson is bitterly disappointed to be going.

After carefully considering its legal advice, Essendon keeps Hird on as coach. The full bench of the Federal Court is less forgiving. For two days the arguments are run. For two and a half months, the three appeal judges carefully weigh the competing submissions. Their decision when it arrives is unanimous and once again, emphatic. Justice Middleton is upheld on every point. It is now 4–0 against James Hird. The High Court is still an option but even an offer by barrister Neil Young to do the application pro-bono can't convince Hird to carry on his lonely cause. Besides, a more urgent battle is already underway.

A block down William Street from where the appeal judgement is handed down, sports scientist Stephen Dank and thirty-four current and former Essendon players are on trial for doping. An AFL tribunal, chaired by retired Victorian County Court Judge David Jones, has been hearing the case in a closed courtroom since before Christmas. There are no TV cameras or journalists in the courtroom and no one in the public gallery. It is only lawyers, a handful of witnesses, three panel members and a blizzard of paper from which ASADA is endeavouring to extract enough circumstantial evidence to show that Essendon footballers were given a banned peptide called Thymosin Beta 4. For Stephen Dank, a generation of Bombers players, ASADA and Essendon coach James Hird, the reckoning has begun.

10

ENTHUSIASTIC AMATEURS

FOR A FORMER police detective like Luke O'Connor, it looks an easy enough assignment. The biggest doping case in Australian history is away. The AFL[1] has sent infraction notices to thirty-four footballers, their lawyers and sports scientist Stephen Dank. A tribunal hearing will convene in a matter of weeks to hear the case. The brief of evidence is nearly complete. All that is missing is the sworn statements of ASADA's two star witnesses, drug importer Shane Charter and pharmacist Nima Alavi. O'Connor hasn't met either of these two characters. Since joining ASADA in September 2013 after a decorated career with Queensland Police, he has worked on the NRL side of Operation Cobia. In November 2014, with the Cronulla case largely settled and ASADA understaffed in Melbourne, O'Connor has been asked to fly down from Canberra to help his fellow investigator, Aaron Walker, tidy things up. At ASADA's Fyshwick headquarters, he is given a plane ticket to Melbourne and copies of prepared statements with spaces left blank for Alavi and Charter to sign. Both witnesses have been co-operating with the investigation for more than a year. All they need to do is swear up to what they've already said. How hard can it be?

O'Connor is real police. At Oxley CIB, they still talk about a homicide he solved with his partner Jack Maddock back in 2006 after the body of a local man was found beaten, strangled and dumped in bushes west of Brisbane. The poor fellow, a 59-year-old devout Muslim, had been out walking in a park late at night when he was set upon by two assailants. They wanted his mobile phone and wallet. After a savage beating they took his life as well. Traditional police work led the two detectives to the killer. A scene straight out of CSI nailed his accomplice. The usual DNA testing had drawn a blank but in the crime scene photos the detectives noticed the victim's shirt sleeve was crumpled at the cuff, as if someone had either pinned him down or dragged him by the arms. With the help of forensic scientists and pathologists, they reconstructed the crime and figured out where the second assailant might have dug his thumb into the victim's arm. Then, using a new form of DNA testing, they pulled a single, dead skin cell from inside the man's wrist. The DNA matched a sample recovered from another crime. The accomplice, once confronted, made a full admission and got nine years for manslaughter. O'Connor got his sergeant's stripes and a nice write up in the *Police Bulletin*.[2]

O'Connor and Walker have arranged to meet Charter at a Melbourne cafe. Nothing flash but, for a frugal government agency like ASADA, free lunches are as rare as hen's teeth. With O'Connor and Walker is a lawyer from the Australian Government Solicitor's office. For the first hour or so, things look to be progressing well. Charter is on time. For a convicted drug importer, Charter seems a likeable sort of bloke. Well dressed and neatly groomed, he is articulate and insightful. He has obviously spent plenty of time talking to cops—he knows the lingo and understands what they want. He reads through his statement, suggesting where some things could be changed. It's minor stuff mostly. There are no deal-breakers as far as anyone can tell. At this rate, they'll have it sorted before coffee. Then, without warning, Charter gets up from the table and says he needs to be someplace else. He hasn't signed the statement but promises he'll finish it the next day. Arrangements are hastily made, and then he is gone. ASADA is left with the bill; O'Connor with empty hands.

For the next ten days, Charter frustrates the anti-doping authority. The promise to meet on Wednesday becomes the first of several no-shows. Charter says he is too busy to meet with investigators between visiting his sick father-in-law and picking up the kids from school[3] but he finds time to do a TV interview that afternoon with Channel Seven. An arrangement to meet on Thursday is cancelled by a telephone call from Charter's wife Donna, who says her husband is feeling anxious about his statement and giving evidence at a tribunal hearing. By Friday it is O'Connor who is starting to feel anxious after Charter again fails to show up at a meeting and can't be reached by telephone. First thing Monday morning, O'Connor drops by Charter's work unannounced. The two men talk at length, with Charter raising new issues with every breath: his family pressuring him not to appear as a witness; Donna urging for them to take an overseas holiday; the media circus that will descend on the AFL tribunal if he agrees to give evidence. The news from Alavi isn't much better. The pharmacist has called Walker to say that because of an illness in the family he won't be able to meet the investigators that day. Or Thursday. Or Friday. There must be a pestilence sweeping down Peptide Alley.

O'Connor doesn't need to be a forensic whizz to detect the bullshit. Nonetheless, he can't go back to Canberra without the sworn statements. Walker is going on leave the next day. If ASADA doesn't have admissible evidence from Charter and Alavi it doesn't have a case. For the next three days, O'Connor divides his time in Melbourne between getting stuffed around by a drug importer and being stonewalled by a pharmacist. At the end of the week he finally receives an email and text message that confirm his Melbourne mission has been a complete waste of time. The email is from Paul Marsh, a solicitor who has been engaged by Alavi. It reads:

> My client has decided not to sign the witness statements, not to appear at the hearing of the AFL tribunal to give evidence. It is

our position that he cannot be compelled to do so. He has fully complied with his obligation to ASADA.[4]

The text message is from Donna Charter. It arrives the morning after Charter has failed to show up at another meeting with O'Connor: 'Hello Luke this is Donna. I have taken Shane away for 4 days for our wedding anniversary. So he is out of contact until Tuesday.'[5] With the ASADA investigation doomed, O'Connor boards a flight back to Canberra. As his plane takes off, it probably banks over a semi-rural property on the edge of Melbourne where Shane Charter might be heard laughing into the night.

ASADA does not easily give up on Charter and Alavi's testimony. ASADA cannot compel anyone to give evidence and, even if it could, an AFL tribunal cannot compel anyone to answer questions. Yet, inside ASADA's Fyshwick headquarters, a plan takes shape to use a provision within the Commercial Arbitration Act to force the drug importer and the pharmacist to take the witness box. It is an ingenuous notion. Under the Act, the Victorian Supreme Court can issue a subpoena compelling a witness to attend an arbitration hearing and produce documents. If ASADA's plan works, it can not only compel Alavi and Charter to front the AFL tribunal, it can compel Dank's fellow directors of the Medical Rejuvenation Clinic to hand over documents about their trade in peptides. It is also a long shot. There is no precedent for anyone using the provision to compel a witness in an anti-doping case before an AFL tribunal. The reason for this is because few people think such a case is a commercial arbitration, least of all Australia's foremost expert on the Commercial Arbitration Act and the judge who will decide ASADA's application, Victorian Supreme Court Justice Clyde Croft.

On the first day of hearing, Charter, the drug importer so worried about creating a media circus, comes to the Supreme Court with his own documentary film crew in tow. He sits in the middle of the public gallery, a pink shirt unbuttoned to reveal his expansive chest, while lawyers for ASADA explain to Justice Croft the difficulties they've had in tracking him down. By the time anyone from the bar table is alerted to his presence the peptide Pimpernel has skedaddled from the court. ASADA's legal team spends the next three days in futile argument, trying to hammer a square peg into a round hole. In the meantime, a bitter divide has emerged within the ranks of the anti-doping agency over how it ever came to this.

To understand how ASADA dropped the ball so badly, go back to when the game started. On the morning of the blackest day in Australian sport, ASADA was an investigations body still assembling an investigations team. Paul Simonsson, the former NSW detective who will lead Operation Cobia, had started work at ASADA two weeks earlier. John Nolan, the lead investigator in Melbourne, joined ASADA just before Simonsson. ASADA's three most senior managers, Aurora Andruska, Trevor Burgess and Elen Perdikogiannis—a social policy expert, an accountant and a lawyer—have all come to the anti-doping body from Centrelink. The investigators are learning on the job about anti-doping law and ASADA's leadership has no experience managing investigations. Thrown together in the high-pressure environment of a national doping scandal, this untested coalition of cops and career bureaucrats is asked to solve a mystery involving unfamiliar substances, unreliable witnesses and shoddy documentation, all while being pressed by an electorally unpopular government and a controlling AFL. It should surprise no one that mistakes were made. Among these, three are potentially fatal to the case.

The first is a structural flaw in how the case against Essendon was investigated and assembled. In a police investigation, detectives interview witnesses, take sworn statements and gather other supporting material and prepare a brief of evidence that prosecutors will rely on when they present the case in court. ASADA's investigators have all worked as police detectives and want to run the anti-doping probes into Essendon and Cronulla with the same rigour applied to a criminal investigation. ASADA management decides this is unnecessary. The investigators are told to conduct interviews but not to bother with sworn witness statements—if needed, they can be taken at a later date. The task of preparing the brief of evidence is given to ASADA's in-house legal team of Perdikogiannis and Darren Mullaly. This means the investigators, who have spent time with the witnesses and secured all the documents, are sidelined from the most critical phase of Operation Cobia. When ASADA's brief of evidence is shown to the lawyers representing the players, the weakness at the heart of the case is exposed: there is a mountain of information but a paucity of evidence. There are no statements from Alavi, from Charter, from anyone who had anything to do with the supplements program at Essendon.

It is a bizarre departure from accepted investigative practice. Rather than take a statement from Charter when he is interviewed by investigators in May 2013, or from Alavi when he finally agrees to be interviewed six months later, this crucial task is deferred until November 2014, when O'Connor boards his plane to nowhere. By this stage, the investigations team that first persuaded Charter to cooperate has been dismantled. O'Connor tries to win Charter's confidence but it is way too late. Charter has never met him and has no reason to help him. He is also concerned at discrepancies in the statement he is being asked to sign and what he remembers telling investigators eighteen months earlier during his interview. According to the statement drafted by ASADA, the drug importer claims never to have sourced Thymosin Alpha, a permitted form of Thymosin peptide, for Stephen Dank. This is a crucial element of the ASADA case, as it adds weight to the central allegation that the Thymosin sourced by Charter and delivered to Alavi was Thymosin Beta 4, the banned form of the peptide. Charter says this is wrong and that both forms of Thymosin were requested by Dank.

'Thymosin Alpha was on the shopping list,' he says.[6]

It is a similar story with Alavi. The statement ASADA wants him to sign is laced with references to Thymosin Beta 4. Alavi does not know what kind of Thymosin he compounded. He told them this, over and over, in his five interviews. Someone back in Fyshwick appears to have taken a whisk to the pharmacist's transcripts and produced a soufflé. Alavi says he won't put his name to what he sees as a beat-up.

'Once I sign this I have to back it up. It has to be 100 per cent accurate. So I went through it and started reading it and it wasn't accurate. There were bits missing. You know how you can cut and paste to make the whole thing sound different? There was a bit of that going on. It wasn't a true reflection of what I thought.'[7]

This is what happens when statements are taken after a lengthy delay, when they are prepared by lawyers 600 kilometres away rather than investigators sitting in a room with the witness as they tell their story for the first time. A statement should reflect what the witness says, not what ASADA, in this case, needs the witness to say. Ron Iddles, a retired Victoria Police detective who worked on homicides for twenty-five years and was involved in more than 320 murder investigations, now lectures young police on investigative techniques. His area of expertise is witness statements. His guiding rule is simple: commit your witness to a story.

'If you are talking to someone and you believe they have evidence in relation to the matter you are investigating take a written statement then and there,' Iddles says. 'If you do it on transcript you still need to take a statement to say this is what I've said, this is the truth and this is the evidence I'm prepared to give. You have got to commit them to a story.'[8] Police agencies are full of sorrowful tales of young detectives who leave statements to the next morning, or the next week, only to find their witness has decided not to co-operate. The ASADA lawyers left it for eighteen months.

Charter and Alavi, the twin pillars on which the ASADA case rests, never commit to a story. Greg Davies, Iddles' predecessor as secretary of the Police Association of Victoria and a policeman with thirty-eight years' experience, says it is 'investigator 101 stuff'. The best way for bureaucrats and lawyers to manage any investigation is to let qualified, experienced investigators do their job, Davies says—'God preserve us from enthusiastic amateurs.'[9]

It is indicative of a cultural divide within ASADA between a management staffed with public service careerists and the hired help—ex-police investigators brought it on short-term contracts to do the grunt work. The room inside the Fyshwick office where Perdikogiannis and Mullaly assembled the case against the Essendon players is dubbed 'the bunker'. Butcher's paper is taped on all windows, obscuring the view both inside and out. It is a fitting metaphor for ASADA's myopic approach. ASADA's investigators who come to the bunker with concerns about the case are met with a standard response: 'We'll be the judge of that.' ASADA's investigators and lawyers are at odds over how witnesses should be treated and how the brief of evidence should be prepared. They are spectacularly at odds over whether the AFL should be able to use the interim investigator's report in its disciplinary proceedings against Essendon. They are at odds over whether ASADA should pursue doping charges against Essendon footballers. The lawyers don't accept that ASADA must build individual cases against current and former Essendon and Cronulla players. They approach them as job lots. Two days before Ben McDevitt issued 'show cause' notices to initiate proceedings in the Essendon case, Walker received a call from a confused ASADA lawyer who doesn't understand why the colour of the vials that Dank used at Windy Hill is an important detail.

When McDevitt issued 'show cause' notices against the Essendon thirty-four he was either unaware of or did not heed the warnings contained within the investigators' final report. None of the investigators had the ear of the ASADA chief. He was listening to the lawyers, who were telling him what he wanted to hear; that ASADA had a strong, compelling case. It is only six months later, after the AFL tribunal hearing has begun, that McDevitt learns what a dog's breakfast it really is. Paul Simonsson, the former police detective who oversaw ASADA's investigation into Essendon and Cronulla, has left the anti-doping body. He calls McDevitt and tells the ASADA boss what the lawyers should have said long ago. McDevitt feels queasy as he listens. There is nothing he can do now.

At a glance, the ASADA case was compelling. On closer consideration it was hollow at its core. This is why, when it was heard before an AFL tribunal chaired by retired Victorian County Court Judge David Jones, ASADA's senior counsel Malcolm Holmes QC spent six days outlining the case. It is not an opening; it *is* the case. An outline was all ASADA had. A week-long opening, a closing submission of 363 pages and no material witnesses in between. It was left to the hapless members of the tribunal to join the dots between disparate emails, text messages and quotes from transcripts and fill in the gaps with supposition and inference. It is little wonder they describe their task as formidable.[10]

ASADA has not adequately explained its unorthodox management of the Essendon case. Andruska says she doesn't know why statements were not taken but defends ASADA's approach.

'There was a view that best practice, and I think it is best practice, [is] investigators do their work and then it gets handed over to the lawyers. The lawyers were not going to just take the investigator's report. That provided pointers for them to go back into the transcribed interviews, other material.'[11] McDevitt says ASADA performed extraordinary work in assembling a 'very complex and comprehensive brief'. He accepts no blame for ASADA's failure to present its two most important witnesses at hearing, lamenting instead the lack of power to compel witnesses held by ASADA and the AFL tribunal. According to Charter, O'Connor was more candid, describing ASADA's witness management as a stuff up.[12] O'Connor has since left the anti-doping agency as part of the post-Cobia exodus with Simonsson, Nolan and Kerrison.

If Australian sport woke up to another black day tomorrow, ASADA would be no better resourced to handle it than it was in February 2013. Did ASADA believe it could prove its case on the strength of interview transcripts? After all, most anti-doping cases are carried on a positive test and single interview. Justice Garry

Downes, the retired Federal Court judge commissioned by then Sports Minister Peter Dutton to review ASADA's work, seemed to think so. He concluded that the Essendon case was stronger than the Cronulla case and was untroubled by the missing links in the chain of custody from Charter to Alavi to Dank to Essendon and the absence of witness statements. ASADA took assurance from Downes' view that it was on the right track. The limitation of the Downes' review is that it appears to merely reflect the view from the ASADA bunker. If Downes read the final report of ASADA's investigators, he wasn't troubled by their concerns about the case. Throughout his review, he did not meet or discuss the case with anyone from the investigations team. Like McDevitt, he talked to the lawyers, who without realising it, had become advocates for a doomed cause.

Another explanation is ASADA didn't believe it would ever have to prove its case at hearing. When ASADA initiated proceedings against the AFL players in June 2014, it offered them a six-month ban in exchange for a guilty plea. In the same way that ASADA was able to dispense with the case against a dozen current and former Cronulla footballers with token suspensions, it might have expected scandal-weary Essendon players to jump at the chance to admit to what they took, write off the remainder of the 2014 season and gratefully begin pre-season training. The brief of evidence gathered against the Cronulla players had the same hollowness as the case presented against the Essendon. The difference is that unlike the Cronulla players, the Essendon footballers had no financial imperative to settle. The club and the AFL Players Association would provide a well-resourced defence team for as long as they needed one.

The AFL tribunal allowed the transcripts of Charter and Alavi's interviews to be admitted into evidence. As it explained in its reasons, the tribunal was not a court of law, it was not bound by strict laws of evidence. It allowed ASADA to rely on the transcripts, Dank's comments to Fairfax journalist Nick McKenzie,[13] on other media reports and hearsay evidence. It conceded the players aren't able to cross-examine ASADA's most important witnesses but said the players, through their submissions to the tribunal, could attack the credibility of those witnesses and anything they say. It also made this telling point: 'The admission of hearsay evidence is an entirely separate issue to the question of the assessment of weight to be given to hearsay evidence. The weight to be given to the contentious evidence will be decided separately in the Tribunal's decision on the question of whether there has been a violation of the AFL Code.'[14] The tribunal judgement, handed down on 31 March 2015, two days before the start of a new football season, was an emphatic rejection of ASADA's case.[15]

The second potentially fatal flaw within ASADA's approach was its failure to go to China. From early in the investigation, it became clear that the biggest challenge for ASADA was establishing a chain of custody between the peptides that Charter sourced in China, the peptides that Alavi compounded in Toorak and the peptides that Dank injected into Essendon players. Once Charter told ASADA where the peptides were manufactured, an obvious place for investigators to make inquiries would be the GL Biochem factory, south of Shanghai. When the travel request was made within ASADA, it was knocked back on budget grounds. ASADA's investigation could impact on the professional futures of a generation of Essendon players, yet Fyshwick headquarters wouldn't fork out the cost of a plane ticket to China.

It was a remarkably short-sighted decision. There were two potentially important sources of information about the case in Shanghai. One is the offices of GL Biochem, where Vincent Xu, the company's global sales manager, dealt with Charter in November 2011. The other is the Shanghai branch office of Austgrow, the fabric manufacturing company run by Charter's associate Cedric Anthony. Charter did his best to shield Anthony from the drug scandal.

'Seriously, the guy wouldn't know the difference between poo and peptides,' he quips. 'He makes clothing.'[16] Yet it is Anthony who stitched up the delivery of peptides to Alavi. It is Anthony who removed the original labels, batch numbers and certificates of analysis from the peptide shipment that arrives at the Como Compounding Pharmacy on 28 December 2011. This was the shipment that contained 0.25 grams of Thymosin, which Alavi compounded into clear vials and gave to Dank. This is the crux of ASADA's case. Charter says he asked Anthony to keep the batch number and certificate of analysis on file for future orders.[17] If any documentation about that shipment still exists it is most likely at Austgrow's Shanghai office. If found, it will go a long way to confirming whether the shipment to Alavi contained Thymosin Beta 4. In the absence of any such documentation, the AFL tribunal is not satisfied it did.

GL Biochem is not a black-market operation. It is a large biochemical manufacturer that supplies peptides to universities, research institutes and pharmaceutical and biotechnology companies around the world. When I first made contact with Vincent Xu in October 2014, the sales manager was reluctant to talk about the specifics of Charter's order:

> Mr. Shane drop by to our company when he was in Shanghai in the middle of 2011, and he claims that he has a pharmaceutical company, and was interested in our product peptides. So I provide him some sample, after he come back to Australia, he order some peptides at the end of that year. We really do not know he would get involved in the anti-doping issue, and he commit that the raw-material we provide won't be used to human, and even though he signed a statement, just like we declare again and again, our product is only for lab research use only. It's been a long time that this is what I can recall now. Thank you for your understanding![18]

After further prodding, Xu agreed to search his files for any records he had about his business with Charter. The only document he sends through is the pro forma agreement signed by Charter, assuring the company that the peptides were for research purposes only and not for human use. The document confirms the deceit at the origins of the drug scandal: the peptides were provided to Charter on the false claim that he owned a pharmaceutical company and on a false assurance that they wouldn't be injected into anyone. Xu does not provide any records of the peptides he supplied to Charter. When asked about a Thymosin peptide quoted by the company in a December 2011 email from GL Biochem to Charter, Xu says the only Thymosin synthesised by GL Biochem is Thymosin Beta 4.[19]

After Xu's comments are published in *The Australian* newspaper, ASADA made contact with the Shanghai-based sales rep for the first time. An investigator spoke to Vincent Xu on 8 November 2014, twenty-one months after the blackest day in Australian sport. Xu told the investigator that he has provided all the documents he has about his dealings with Charter to the Australian journalist.[20] ASADA accepted this at face value. No proper investigations were made of GL Biochem. Infraction notices were issued to the thirty-four players just six days later.

The third flaw is ASADA's decision to stake the credibility of its case on a mysterious second batch of peptides that Alavi says he received from China in February 2012. When Nolan and Walker interview Alavi over four days in November and December 2013, their questions are sharply focused on the initial batch of peptides that Alavi received from Shanghai. The ASADA case hinges on twenty-six clear vials of Thymosin prepared by Alavi and provided to Dank. ASADA says these vials are prepared from the initial batch and contain the Thymosin Beta 4, which Dank takes to Essendon and injects into Essendon footballers. Alavi hasn't told them anything about a second batch. The records he is compelled to provide ASADA don't record a second batch. It is not until 14 April 2014, when Walker interviews Alavi for a fifth and final time, that the pharmacist mentions the possibility of a second batch.

The evidence that ASADA presented supporting the existence of this batch of peptides was flimsy, certainly doctored and possibly fabricated. The only record within the Como Compounding

Pharmacy of a second shipment arriving from Shanghai was a handwritten note entered in a diary by Alavi's lab assistant, Vania Giordani, for 18 February 2012. Charter had no involvement in this shipment. According to what Alavi told ASADA, the shipment was arranged by Anthony, Charter's Shanghai-based associate. Alavi's belief is that the peptides came from the same source as the initial batch but he doesn't know. He tells Walker that the peptides, like the first batch, arrived without any documentation. When Alavi questioned Anthony about this, Anthony emailed him certificates of analysis and HPLC reports.[21] Alavi tells Walker he has discovered certificates of analysis for Thymosin and Hexarelin in a box in a storage container. Is this ASADA's Eureka moment? After more than a year, does the anti-doping authority finally have documented evidence of Alavi receiving Thymosin Beta 4 from China? It is fool's gold.

Like so much of the documentation ASADA found along the treacherous path that runs between Peptide Alley and Windy Hill, the certificates of analysis belatedly produced by Alavi were incomplete, inexact and unreliable. They were undated and had no company stamp or other identifying features that traced them back to GL Biochem or another manufacturer. There was no reference to a batch number, nor to whoever performed the chemical analysis. The molecular weight recorded on the certificate was close but not quite right for Thymosin Beta 4. Alavi says the documents were probably altered in Shanghai to conceal Charter's source. There were other problems with the second batch story. Alavi had no invoices, no proof of payment, text messages or emails confirming the delivery. He says it was ASADA that kept 'banging on' about a second batch of peptides and he merely gave them whatever scraps of documentation he had. Alavi says the certificates of analysis from Shanghai couldn't be trusted and a handwritten note from his lab assistant doesn't prove a thing.

'If I had given Essendon a second batch I would have invoiced them for it. There is no invoice for it. It didn't come from me. I have found some dodgy handwriting and said, "Could it be this?" They have photocopied it and said, "We'll take, we'll take this." They are trying to construct another batch that never actually existed.'[22]

ASADA needed a second batch of peptides for two reasons. The first was that 0.25 grams of Thymosin powder, the initial amount received by Alavi on 28 December 2011, wasn't enough to account for all the Thymosin Beta 4 that ASADA says Dank used at Essendon. The second was that ASADA needed to explain the bronze-coloured vials that Essendon staff and players recall Dank using. The initial batch of Thymosin was compounded into clear vials but only one Essendon player out of the entire thirty-four remembers being injected with something called Thymosin from a clear vial. In its growing desperation, ASADA had begun looking at its own case through amber-coloured glasses. David Jones and his fellow panel members remained clear-eyed. As far as the AFL tribunal was concerned, there was no second batch of peptides.

For the same reasons that Essendon's players lost faith in Stephen Dank, for the same reasons that Ziggy Switkowski savaged the club's management and governance failures, for the same reasons the AFL Commission cited when it dumped Essendon from the 2013 finals series for bringing the game into disrepute, ASADA cannot establish with any certainty what went on in the basement office of the club's sports scientist. The AFL tribunal describes Essendon's attempts at record keeping as deplorable and Dank's own conduct as inept.[23] ASADA chief executive Ben McDevitt says what happened at Essendon in 2012 was 'absolutely and utterly disgraceful.'[24] He'll get no argument from Essendon club doctor Bruce Reid, who used the same phrase to me that night in his Hawthorn house. Yet when it comes to trying to prove a doping case, Dank and Essendon's failure to document his work provides the players with an alibi. Throughout the hearing, the most scathing assessment of what took place at Essendon comes not from ASADA nor a member of the tribunal but the legal team representing two former Essendon players, Stewart Crameri and Brent Prismall. In their closing submission, the lawyers for the pair conclude:

> The Tribunal is being asked to perform the almost impossible task of reconstructing a series of events which were on any view ill conceived, little understood and poorly regulated. Not only does the absence of records reveal a scandalous breach of the duty of care owed to the players, it places insurmountable obstacles in the path of ASADA. Furthermore those responsible have been shown to be lacking in appropriate expertise, to be ignorant about the nature of the so called supplements and to have acted with a reckless disregard for the welfare of the players. The evidence that has been submitted relies to a considerable degree on people who are demonstrably unreliable and dishonest. In the result the Tribunal is left with limited and unreliable evidence from which it is effectively being asked to make quantum leaps of reason rather than drawing properly available inferences.[25]

In the end, the tribunal's task is not as difficult as first appears. To prove its case, ASADA must establish three things: that Shane Charter arranged for a shipment of peptides, including Thymosin Beta 4, to be sent to Nima Alavi; that Alavi compounded Thymosin Beta 4 and provided it to Stephen Dank in his role as Essendon sports scientist; that Dank took Thymosin Beta 4 to Essendon and injected it into thirty-four players. ASADA does not satisfy the tribunal that the shipment of peptides arranged by Charter contained Thymosin Beta 4. ASADA does not satisfy the tribunal that Alavi compounded Thymosin Beta 4, nor that he provided whatever he did compound to Dank in his role as Essendon sports scientist. The ASADA case does not establish that Thymosin Beta 4 ever left Shanghai, let alone made it all the way to Windy Hill. Having failed in the early rounds, ASADA doesn't earn a shot at the jackpot. The tribunal has no basis to consider whether Thymosin Beta 4 is given to a single Essendon player, much less thirty-three of his teammates.

The question that has plagued Essendon, the AFL, Australian sport and ASADA for more than two years is left unanswered.

Everyone at ASADA—the investigators who worked on the case, the lawyers who prepared the brief of evidence, the successive chief executives who made the call to prosecute the players, the pinch-hitting lawyers like Richard Young and Malcolm Holmes who assessed the strength of the evidence—they all believe Essendon footballers were injected with banned substances by Stephen Dank. As investigator Aaron Walker writes in the final report submitted by the investigations team: 'there can be little doubt this investigation has established that prohibited substances were used by Essendon players as part of their 2012 Essendon supplementation program.'[26] Yet ASADA cannot say with any certainty what substance the players were given. Thymosin Beta 4? Hexarelin? Something else? It simply does not know for sure. It also cannot disprove the alternate hypothesis that Dank has long maintained: that Essendon players were injected with a permitted form of Thymosin.

When Charter goes to Shanghai, GL Biochem is not the only peptide manufacturer he visits. He is impressed with the company's facilities but they don't have everything he needs. As Xu confirms, they only sell Thymosin Beta 4, not Thymosin Alpha. Charter has both on his shopping list. He travels just south of the city centre, to a smaller biochemical supplier named RD Peptide. On 28 November 2011, he buys another $16,000 worth of human growth hormone, SARMs, a testosterone-boosting peptide called HCG and 10 grams of Thymosin, which Charter says is Thymosin Alpha.[27] Charter says he takes a single gram vial of Thymosin back with him to Melbourne and gives it to Alavi at his Toorak pharmacy. The other nine vials are given the usual treatment by Cedric Anthony—the labels are ripped off, certificates of analysis kept on file and the peptides are stored in a fridge in Austgrow's Shanghai office until they are required. Within this fridge there is a shelf set aside for Thymosin. The nine vials with little blue caps are stored next to a single, black-capped 0.25-gram vial of Thymosin Beta 4 supplied about three weeks later by GL Biochem.

On 9 December 2014, three years after his Shanghai trip, Charter produces a copy of his RD Peptide transaction to Tony Hargreaves, a solicitor representing thirty-two of the current and former Essendon players. The invoice is not original but either a photoshopped copy of a genuine invoice or, as ASADA contends, a forgery. If it is a forgery then Charter, who is on a family holiday to the Gold Coast when he sends the document to Hargreaves, is going to a lot of trouble to demolish what remains of ASADA's case. In truth, the invoice is no more or less reliable than many of the documents ASADA has built its two-year investigation upon. As with Alavi's suggestion of a second batch of peptides from China, the AFL tribunal does not accept Charter's claims about his second supplier. Charter's trip to RD Peptides, if indeed he ever went, has no bearing on the outcome of the doping case against the Essendon players. Yet if Charter is telling the truth on this, it means it is likely the players were not doped at all.

For a moment, put yourself in the Italian loafers of Cedric Anthony, the fabric manufacturer who in late 2011 found himself running Charter's peptide mini-warehouse in Shanghai. In a corner of the office is a fridge full of peptides. A few days before Christmas, when a courier comes to pick up an air-freight delivery for the Como Compounding Pharmacy, you put together an Esky according to Charter's instructions. You go to the fridge and pull out a couple of vials of GHRP-6, a vial of CJC-1295, a vial of Melanotan II and a vial of Mechano Growth Factor. All that is left is the Thymosin Beta 4. There is a shelf in the fridge marked Thymosin and on the shelf there are ten vials, each identified by a handwritten label Thymosin. Do you grab any one of these vials or do you look for the one with the black cap? Do you know about the different coloured caps? Do you even know there are different kinds of Thymosin? After all, you're the bloke who doesn't know peptides from poo. Charter says he doesn't know, nor does he much care, what was delivered to Alavi.

'Fact is, I got paid. What do I care? Seriously.'[28] The odds are it wasn't Thymosin Beta 4.

There is a fundamental problem with ASADA's story. If Dank is intent on cheating, why does he run the anti-doping gauntlet with substances that have not been proven to boost performance? After ten years of clinical trials, no one knows whether AOD-9604 actually does anything. If Thymosin Beta 4 helps players recover faster—and there is no hard evidence it does—it is at the margin of what can be construed as performance enhancing. This is why Alavi believes that for all that Dank did wrong he didn't set out to dope.

'If they wanted to dope the players there is 1001 things they could have done. They could have asked me to make up bio-identical testosterone, which is undetectable. They could have asked me to make up growth hormone, which they didn't.'[29] The AFL tribunal takes a similar view. It is not convinced that Dank cheated at Essendon, nor that he intended to. In its judgement, Dank is a world removed from the evil genius of Michele Ferrari, the blood-boosting doctor who meticulously designed to within a single haematocrit Lance Armstrong's assaults on the Tour de France.

'The tribunal's view is that he was out of his depth, over-confident and irresponsible. He was endeavouring to implement a program that was beyond his capability.' In the words of the tribunal, Dank's work was characterised by incompetence rather than malevolence.[30] The same can be said of much of the great doping scandal.

The ASADA investigators now doubt that the contentious peptide AOD-9604, which turned out not to be prohibited in 2012, was even used at the club. Dank told the players that he was injecting them with the peptide and Essendon doctor Bruce Reid wrote his letter declaring his concerns about it, but it was not until August 2012, when the Essendon season was in its death throes and Dank had nearly left the club, that Alavi first supplied him with AOD-9604. Throughout its entire investigation, ASADA was unable to find an earlier source of the peptide to either Dank or his Medical Rejuvenation Clinic. The fans at Subiaco Oval who heckled Watson during the West Coast game, the columnists who called for him to be stripped of his Brownlow, the protracted hand-wringing within ASADA and WADA over the status of AOD-9604: it was all done in the absence of any proof—beyond the word of Stephen Dank—that Essendon players were actually injected with it. None of this provides comfort to Watson or his teammates. The obvious next question is, if not AOD-9604, then what? This too, remains unanswered.

Dank's incompetence not only provides an alibi for Essendon players, it means that many of the charges against the sports scientist are also unable to be proved. The day the three members of the tribunal handed down their judgement against Stephen Dank, I spoke to him shortly before the decision was published. He was angry and defensive. He made his usual threats of Federal Court action against ASADA, of defamation suits against journalists. He had not been represented in the hearing. He had not offered a word of explanation for what he did. He maintained that everyone was wrong, that only Stephen Dank was right. The judgement clears Dank of the most serious anti-doping allegations, that he administered banned substances to Essendon players and that he was involved in providing a banned substance to Nathan Bock. Although the tribunal was satisfied that Dank supplied what he thought was CJC-1295 to the Gold Coast defender, his lack of credibility and the lack of documentation meant the tribunal couldn't be satisfied that it was actually CJC-1295 in the vials. Throughout the entire doping saga, Dank was not found guilty of giving a banned substance to any athlete.

The tribunal judgement is damning, nonetheless. The tribunal was satisfied that Dank attempted to supply banned peptides to three coaches at Essendon and to Bock at the Gold Coast. He was found guilty of providing banned substances to Carlton tackling coach John Donehue and to baseball coach John Deeble. In total, ten trafficking or associated charges were upheld against him. Two counts of trafficking attract a life ban from all WADA-compliant sports. Dank won't work with athletes in mainstream sport again. On one reading, it feels as though ASADA had got Dank on a technicality. In truth, it is a judgement that captured Dank's fundamental failing:

an inability to separate his fascination and commercial interest in peptides and growth hormones and other banned substances from his work with footballers covered by the World Anti-Doping Code.

When Dank was employed for three months by the Gold Coast Suns, when he was contracted for a year by Essendon, he had no business dealing in banned drugs. Essendon had no business hiring someone whose principal business was peptides. When Dank, while working for Gold Coast, gave Dean Robinson a styrofoam box full of CJC-1295, when Dank, while on staff at Essendon, provided Hexarelin to Suki Hobson and Sue Anderson and Paul Turk and gave banned peptide creams to John Deeble and an assortment of banned substances to John Donehue, he was in breach of the WADA code. It doesn't matter that Deeble didn't actually use the creams or Donehue was trying to fix a bung shoulder or Sue Anderson just wanted to lose a few kilos. Each time Dank, while on staff at Essendon, supplied a banned substance to clients of the Medical Rejuvenation Clinic, he was in breach of anti-doping rules. None of these infringements equate to cheating. Yet they are hardly victimless crimes. Not when you consider what Essendon footballers and Cronulla footballers and others have had to endure.

Whatever becomes of Dank, searching questions must still be asked of ASADA. The day after the AFL tribunal hands down its decision in the case against the players, Ben McDevitt declares that ASADA is not the enemy, that Australia needs to remain at the forefront of anti-doping, that athletes have the right to compete in drug-free sport.

'Some may find this hard to believe but these allegations had to go before a sports tribunal,' he says.[31] Australia also needs an anti-doping agency that is well resourced, well managed and judicious. Pursuing a doomed case against the Essendon players to its inevitable conclusion did nothing to further the interests of clean athletes. Neglecting to prosecute an alleged doping breach by a star player at the AFL's expansion club did nothing to build confidence in ASADA. The only thing standing between ASADA and a complete overhaul of anti-doping arrangements in Australia is Canberra's desire to forget this lamentable episode.

The moment that doping allegations are lifted from a generation of Essendon players, Jobe Watson is the only footballer to shout for joy. Most of the thirty-four are gathered before a big television screen in the lounge bar of a suburban pub in Melbourne's Albert Park. Watson is one of the few who has followed the case daily. He has read the transcripts of the seventeen days of hearing. He has read the voluminous opening and closing submissions. He understands the evidence. He understands what the case is all about. He understands that when retired Victorian County Court judge David Jones says he is not comfortably satisfied, it is a good thing. Not one doping charge against 34 current and former footballers is upheld. Throughout the pub, the players hug one another. Some shed a tear. They don't feel elated. They don't know quite how to feel. They are consumed by an overwhelming sense of anti-climax. For two years, they have lived, played and slept under the constant threat of career-destroying bans. It had become the new normal.

'I've almost forgotten what it's like to be an AFL player without having this hanging over our heads,' Watson says on the day. 'When you live through something for twenty-six months it becomes a part of you.' On the other side of town, James Hird is on the brink of tears. He doesn't feel vindicated. He doesn't feel like he's won. He knows what winning feels like and this ain't it. Bruce Reid is happy for the players but that night, when the club gathers to celebrate, his heart isn't in it. More than anything he is just tired.

For everyone at Essendon, relief is short. In the early hours of 12 May 2015, the World Anti-Doping Agency announces it will seek a rehearing of the case before the International Court of Arbitration for Sport. Watson's constant companion is back after a mere six-week break. Where ASADA failed dismally, WADA will try to succeed with much the same evidence, arguments and shortcomings. It is a scandal that will not relent. On a late summer's morning at Mark Thompson's house, I ask the former Bombers' coach what is worse: what happened at Essendon in 2012 or what has happened since. He doesn't hesitate.

'What's happened since. It is almost like it is too big to control, everybody needs to win, everybody's arse is at stake. And the truth has been hidden because no one wants to talk about it. A lot of untruths have been told. That got brought out in the Federal Court. But they don't get acted upon. Nothing really matters. What matters is everyone is trying to win for themselves.'

Thompson and Hird have rarely spoken since the end of the 2014 season. Their friendship, like so many, is collateral damage to this saga. Yet despite this, Thompson's admiration for Hird has grown.

'He has been resolute, he has been a champ. I don't know how anyone could go through this and be so strong. I have supported him and I have respected him. They went early on him and called it early on him without finding out and asking him what happened. That shouldn't happen and that is the reason I supported him. It is a perfect storm. I think a lot of people are responsible and he has got some responsibility. There is no doubt. So has Steve Dank, so has Dean Robinson, so has Paul Hamilton, so has Mark Thompson, so has Ian Robson. I'm not sure we all should have lost our jobs because of it. I don't think there should have been as much carnage as there has been.'[32]

That James Hird survives this carnage to coach Essendon again is an extraordinary outcome, one that confounds the AFL. Late in 2014, when Hird was waging his solo campaign against ASADA, he was invited to meet Mike Fitzpatrick at the AFL chairman's South Yarra home. The meeting had been arranged by Paul Little in the hope of encouraging Hird to abandon Federal Court litigation. Fitzpatrick, a retired ruckman and premiership captain for Carlton and a highly successful investment and funds manager, is a man of formidable intellect and limited patience for lesser beings. Once Hird is seated in his house, he looks at the Essendon coach as though he is a stain on the carpet.

'Why haven't you stood down?' he asks, genuinely perplexed that Hird is still in the game.

'Because we haven't cheated,' Hird replies.

Throughout the drugs scandal, Hird's personal responsibility for what happened at Windy Hill has been exaggerated, conflated and wilfully misunderstood. He was not in charge of the Essendon football department. He was not Stephen Dank's boss. Dank's work was at the far edges of Hird's concerns as a senior coach trying to win the next weekend's football game. Towards the end of a nine-hour interrogation conducted by ASADA investigators John Nolan and Aaron Walker, an exhausted Hird is asked the question that will forever plague him: how could you not know that this was happening?

'Because I had a job to do, which was coach a football team. My day and my weeks and my months and my years are spent head down, bum up, coaching a team, getting the best strategy, talking to players, trying to coach opposition games, opposition analysis. The supplementation in my life in 2012 took up such a small part of my time and even my thought process … and I presumed that we had people in place, that Bruce was being told everything, that Paul Hamilton was receiving was what going on. Short of putting a security guard next to Steve Dank, I don't believe that—you know, this bloke has just, and Dean Robinson, who was meant to be supervising him—these guys have just run amok.'[33] There is an important rider on this.

Robinson and Dank believed, or at the very least convinced themselves, that they had Hird's support for what they were doing. Nothing carried more weight at Essendon in 2012 than the imprimatur of the senior coach. The Essendon revolution, the rush to build a bigger, stronger football team through more aggressive training techniques and advanced sports science, was carried out in Hird's name. Like all senior coaches at the start of their careers, Hird in 2012 is impatient. He understands that his standing and achievements as an Essendon player—the premierships, the best and fairest awards, the Brownlow—will buy him a finite amount of time. He need only look to Michael Voss, the Brisbane champion he tied with in the 1996 Brownlow, to see what becomes of great players with ordinary coaching records. At the end of the 2012 season, Hird tours the headquarters of the Spanish football giant Real Madrid with an Essendon delegation. When he asks Jose Mourinho his secret for surviving so long as a coach, the legendary manager offers the following advice: 'Win quick.'

Hird's response to the drug scandal, his refusal to yield to the AFL, his front-on challenge to the legality of ASADA's investigation, his preparedness to turn against foes and friends when they threaten his interests, has exposed to everyone his sharp, ruthless edge. It is a quality that can make Hird difficult to deal with. It is also a quality found in every successful coach.

'He is complex, he is driven, he is stubborn and he is talented,' says Little. Is he ethical?

'I think he is. He can be selfish. I have accused him of that. But he is ethical. I would never expect James to do the wrong thing. Fundamentally, I believe him. I just don't agree with how he has gone about trying to prove his case. You can't help but get the feeling that if you stood in the way of the Hirds you wouldn't be sidestepped around. It wouldn't matter who you were. They are fiercely focused on what they believe in. There are not too many shades of grey for James or Tania.'[34]

Aurora Andruska is retired from the public service. Her house in Canberra overlooks a thickly wooded nature reserve, where she and her husband John can walk and breathe in the eucalypts and the biting morning air of the capital; their own Fontainebleau. She feels a connection to Hird, an empathy. Late one morning, when the sun is shining into her kitchen, she imagines a dinner party with everyone who has been damaged by the drug scandal.

'Wouldn't it be interesting?' she muses. 'Not that they'd ever come. You'd have James at the table, you'd have David Evans, you'd have Ian Robson at the table, you'd have Aurora Andruska at the table, you'd have Stephen Dank.'[35] If it did happen it would need to be a banquet. You'd also want to invite Kate Lundy and

Jason Clare, Andrew Demetriou, Danny Corcoran, Bruce Reid and Mark Thompson, Paul Hamilton, Suki Hobson and Simon Goodwin, and thirty-four current and former Essendon footballers: Tom Bellchambers, Alex Browne, Jake Carlisle, Travis Colyer, Stewart Crameri, Alwyn Davey, Luke Davis, Cory Dell'Olio, Ricky Dyson, Dustin Fletcher, Scott Gumbleton, Kyle Hardingham, Dyson Heppell, Michael Hibberd, David Hille, Heath Hocking, Cale Hooker, Ben Howlett, Michael Hurley, Leroy Jetta, Brendan Lee, Sam Lonergan, Nathan Lovett-Murray, Mark McVeigh, Jake Melksham, Angus Monfries, David Myers, Tayte Pears, Brent Prismall, Patrick Ryder, Henry Slattery, Brent Stanton, Ariel Steinberg and their captain, Jobe Watson.

The Essendon Football Club, for all its failings in 2012 and some since, is a resilient institution. Since 4 February 2013, the night when James Hird's birthday dinner was interrupted by a panicked phone call from David Evans, Essendon has not lost a sponsor. During the 2014 season, more than 60,000 people signed up as club members, setting a club record. In the two years engulfed by scandal, Essendon has won enough games to qualify for finals.

'I don't know how it didn't fall apart to be honest,' says Thompson.[36] What took place at Essendon in 2012 was appalling. On this, nearly everyone but Dank agrees. No one oversaw Dank's work. No one was in charge of the football department that hired him. Too much power and influence resided in an ambitious, inexperienced senior coach. The back door to Windy Hill located outside Dank's basement office was left open to abuse. Yet what happened at Essendon in 2012 could easily have happened at another AFL club. To think otherwise is to misunderstand the relentless competitive forces that drive football clubs, coaches and players.

When the biggest scandal in Australian sport breaks, Stephen Dank has already moved on. At the Melbourne Football Club, the oldest in Australia, Dank is looking to introduce new methods. Thymomodulin for increased immunity. Tribulus to boost testosterone levels. AOD-9604 cream for nagging injuries. For five months he courts the Demons. He is never on staff but he is sometimes at training and only ever a text message away. He meets with the club's football manager, Neil Craig, and high-performance boss David Misson. He pitches his ideas to club doctor Dan Bates. He knows Bates already, having met with him earlier in the year to spruik AOD-9604. Bates is a young, bright doctor, young enough to be Bruce Reid's son. He is open to new ideas, interested in pioneering treatments involving platelet-rich plasma and stem cells. Dank takes him to Como Compounding Pharmacy and introduces him to Nima Alavi. Emerging Demons star Jack Trengove meets Alavi when he is sent to Peptide Alley to pick up some AOD-9604 cream for his sore ankle. Bates doesn't approve Dank's program but he accepts his recommendation on where to send Melbourne players for off-site injections at a good price. It is only vitamins at this stage, something Melbourne has been doing for a few years. Dank is courting Melbourne, winning the trust of the club, its players, its doctor.

If not for the Essendon scandal, what happened at Windy Hill will repeat at Melbourne. If not, then at another club—your club. Stephen Dank will never work in the AFL or NRL again but what he offers, what he promises, remains irresistible in professional sport. It is the secret other clubs don't have, the hidden advantage. It is what they all want.

ACKNOWLEDGEMENTS

Newspapers by nature are not patient. Most stories are turned around in a day. Spend a week on a yarn and we call it a special investigation. This was a special case indeed; for two years my editors urged me to chase the story of the great doping scandal for as long and hard as it would run.

To *The Australian*'s editor-in-chief Chris Mitchell, editor Clive Mathieson, sports editor Wally Mason, my bosses here in Melbourne, Patricia Karvelas and John Ferguson, and colleague Patrick Smith, thanks for your support and enthusiasm for a story that was, at times, bewildering in its complexity and chemistry.

I am also grateful to journalists at a rival publication. In October 2013, after Essendon was booted out of the AFL finals series, I started re-examining what had gone on. At a certain point, I found myself pursuing the same leads as two reporters from the *Herald Sun*, Michael Warner and Mark Robinson.

Between the three of us, we convinced first ourselves, then our respective editors, that collaboration rather than competition was the way to get to the bottom of things. For six weeks we worked as an investigations team and produced a series of award winning articles. That collaboration provided the origins of *The Straight Dope*.

It has been a pleasure to witness the skilled handling of this project by Sally Heath and the team at Melbourne University Publishing. A special thanks to copy editor Joanne Holliman, who worked, quite literally, through the night. To Louise Adler, I made a rookie mistake by accepting terms over our first coffee at The European. Next time I'll sting you for at least a sandwich.

This story has been painful in the telling for many good people. Unavoidably, publication of this book will open some old wounds and create new ones. I am indebted to everyone who shared their time, thoughts and reflections.

To Nicole, Max, Amelie and Jasper, I apologise for spending so much time delving into the affairs of a football club we don't even like. We can now get back to what really matters; waiting for St Kilda's next premiership.

NOTES

Chapter 1 Is it Essendon? Say no more
1 The quotes attributed to David Evans are taken from James Hird's interview with ASADA and AFL investigators on 16 April 2013. The account is supported by two other witnesses present at Evans' house that night, Danny Corcoran and Bruce Reid, in their interviews with the author. David Evans declined to be interviewed for the book.
2 James Hird, interview with ASADA and the AFL, 16 April 2013.
3 Danny Corcoran, interview with author, 8 January 2015.
4 This account of David Evans' conversation with Bruce Reid was provided by Reid during an interview with the author on 22 December 2014. The account is consistent with what Evans told ASADA and AFL investigators during an interview on 15 February 2013, and what Reid told investigators in his interview three days later.
5 James Hird, interview with ASADA and the AFL, 16 April 2013.
6 Bruce Reid addressed his letter of 17 January 2012 to James Hird and Paul Hamilton but didn't give a copy to the coach. Although Hird knew Reid was intending to write a letter setting out his concerns about the club's supplements regime and encouraged him to do so, he only became aware of its contents more than a year later, on the night of his fortieth birthday.
7 David Evans, interview with ASADA and the AFL, 15 February 2013.

8 The idea that vitamin and other dietary supplements should be injected rather than taken in pill or liquid form was strongly advocated by Essendon's former high-performance manager Dean Robinson during his time with the Bombers. Although it is true that intravenous vitamin treatments are not uncommon in elite sport, Essendon players told ASADA and AFL investigators the scale and frequency of injections administered during the 2012 season went well beyond what they had previously experienced.
9 Mark Thompson, interview with author, 20 January 2015.
10 David Givney's recollection of his conversation with Paul Bloomfield is contained within the 'Kavanagh Report', a club-commissioned investigation conducted by Court of Arbitration for Sport arbitrator Tricia Kavanagh into substance use by Cronulla players during the 2011 season. Givney no longer works for Cronulla. Bloomfield has since left Manly and been appointed chief medical officer of the NRL.
11 Hird's recollections of the 5 February 2013 boardroom meeting are contained in his interview with ASADA and the AFL on 16 April 2013, his Supreme Court writ filed against the AFL on 21 August 2013, and a transcript of his evidence to the Federal Court on 11 August 2014.
12 James Hird, interview with ASADA and the AFL, 16 April 2013.
13 Transcript of Hird's evidence to the Federal Court, VID 327 of 2014, 11 August 2014, p. 84.
14 David Evans, interview with ASADA and the AFL, 17 April 2014.
15 Danny Corcoran, interview with author, 8 January 2015.
16 Transcript of Federal Court proceedings, VID 327 of 2014, 12 August 2014, pp. 37 and 44.
17 ibid., p 44.
18 Andrew Demetriou, interview with Radio 3AW broadcaster Neil Mitchell, 25 July 2013.
19 John Lawler, 'AFL Alleged Disclosure to Essendon FC', ACC media release, 26 July 2013, cited at https://crimecommission.gov.au/media-centre/release/australian-crime-commission-media-statement/alleged-afl-disclosure-essendon-fc.
20 Chip Le Grand, 'Gillon McLachlan Completes His Rise in the AFL', The Australian, 1 May 2014, cited at www.theaustralian.com.au/news/features/gillon-mclachlan-completes-his-rise-in-afl/story-e6frg6z6-1226901402250.
21 Mark Thompson, interview with author, 20 January 2015.
22 Aurora Andruska affidavit affirmed on 22 July 2014 in preparation for Federal Court proceedings, VID 327 of 2014, and tendered as evidence 12 August 2014.

Chapter 2   Grey cardigans, blackest day

1   Aurora Andruska, interview with author, 23 January 2015.
2   ibid.
3   ibid.
4   James Hird, interview with ASADA and the AFL, 16 April 2013.
5   Aurora Andruska, interview with author, 23 January 2015.
6   ibid.
7   The Honourable Robert Anderson QC, 'Second Stage Report to the Australian Sports Commission and to Cycling Australia', 27 October 2004, p. 62.
8   Kevin Andrews, House of Representatives, Australian Sports Anti-Doping Bill, Second Reading Speech, 7 December 2005, p. 8.
9   Aurora Andruska, interview with author, 23 January 2015.
10   Senate and Regional Affairs and Transport Legislation Committee, Answers to Questions on Notice, Australian Sports Anti-Doping Authority, Additional Estimates, 12 February 2012, question 183.
11   Transcript of 7 February 2013 press conference, cited at www.jasonclare.com.au/media/transcripts/1897-press-conference-canberra.
12   Aurora Andruska, interview with author, 23 January 2015.
13   ibid.
14   ibid.
15   Kate Lundy, interview with author, 29 January 2015.
16   ibid.
17   Former ASADA chief executive Richard Ings coined this phrase, which became the catchline for the doping scandal. He first used it in a television interview with *Fox Sports* shortly after the 7 February 2013 press conference where the ACC released its report, 'Organised Crime and Drugs in Sport'. 'This is not a black day in Australian sport, this is the blackest day in Australian sport.'
18   Graham Ashton, interview with author, 29 January 2015.
19   Essendon counsel Neil Young QC during his cross-examination of Aurora Andruska in the Federal Court on 12 August 2014 asked about Richard Eccles, an experienced federal bureaucrat who was then serving Sports Minister Kate Lundy as a deputy secretary within the Department of Regional Australia, Local Government, Arts and Sport. Young: 'Now, Mr Eccles is someone who had a persisting involvement in relation to the investigation that unfolded, is he not?' Andruska: 'Yes.' Transcript, VID 327 of 2014, p. 144.
20   The 9 February 2013 exchange between Richard Eccles and Gillon McLachlan is reconstructed from notes of the meeting taken by Aurora Andruska and Paul Simonsson and the transcript of Andruska's

testimony to the Federal Court on 12 August 2014, VID 327 of 2014, p. 170.
21   Aurora Andruska, interview with author, 23 January 2015.
22   ibid.
23   The no fault or negligence provision the AFL wanted ASADA to consider for Essendon footballers is contained within Article 10.5.1 of the 2009 World Anti-Doping Code. The explanatory notes within the code make clear why the provision is rarely, if ever applied: 'To illustrate the operation of Article 10.5.1, an example where No Fault or Negligence would result in the total elimination of a sanction is where an Athlete could prove that, despite all due care, he or she was sabotaged by a competitor. Conversely, a sanction could not be completely eliminated on the basis of No Fault or Negligence in the following circumstances: (a) a positive test resulting from a mislabeled or contaminated vitamin or nutritional supplement (Athletes are responsible for what they ingest (Article 2.1.1) and have been warned against the possibility of supplement contamination); (b) the administration of a Prohibited Substance by the Athlete's personal physician or trainer without disclosure to the Athlete (Athletes are responsible for their choice of medical personnel and for advising medical personnel that they cannot be given any Prohibited Substance); and (c) sabotage of the Athlete's food or drink by a spouse, coach or other Person within the Athlete's circle of associates (Athletes are responsible for what they ingest and for the conduct of those Persons to whom they entrust access to their food and drink).'
24   Paul Simonsson email to Brett Clothier, 13 February 2013, contained in Essendon and James Hird's outline of opening submissions to the Federal Court, VID Nos 327 and 328 of 2014, filed 4 August 2014, p. 12.
25   Richard Eccles email to Elen Perdikogiannis, 13 February 2013, contained in Essendon and James Hird's outline of opening submissions to the Federal Court, VID Nos 327 and 328 of 2014, filed 4 August 2014, p. 12.
26   Elen Perdikogiannis email to Darren Mullaly, 18 February 2013, contained in Essendon and James Hird's outline of opening submissions to the Federal Court, VID Nos 327 and 328 of 2014, filed 4 August 2014, p. 13.
27   ASADA Statement of 20 February 2013, 'Australian Sport Anti-Doping Investigation Into Activities at Essendon FC'.
28   Aurora Andruska, interview with author, 23 January 2015.
29   Richard Redman, interview with author, 9 January 2015.

30 ibid.
31 John Marshall's comments to the meeting are recounted by Richard Redman in his interview with the author on 9 January 2015. Marshall declined to comment on any advice he provided while acting for ASADA.
32 ibid.
33 Roy Masters, 'Bombers' Secret Deal Exposed', *Sydney Morning Herald*, 28 March 2013.
34 ASADA's replacement statement was attached to a 7 March 2013 email from Elen Perdikogiannis to the AFL. The statement is undated, unsigned and carries the utilitarian title: 'Australian Sports Anti-Doping Authority Investigation following on from Australian Crime Commission report into Organised Crime and Drugs in Sport (ACC report)'. Although the AFL never agrees to its terms and pretends ASADA's original statement still applies to the Essendon case, the replacement statement is included in the 'show cause' pack issued on 12 June 2014 to thirty-four current and former Essendon players accused of doping.
35 Kate Lundy, interview with author, 29 January 2015.
36 Andrew Clennell, 'The Price the NSW Government Paid to Get Rid of Chris Eccles, the Wolf of Macquarie St', *The Daily Telegraph*, 11 August 2013, cited at www.dailytelegraph.com.au/news/nsw/the-price-the-nsw-government-paid-to-get-rid-of-chris-eccles-the-wolf-of-macquarie-st/story-fni0cx12-1227019835130.
37 Affidavit of Aurora Andruska, sworn 22 July 2014, VID No. 327 of 2014.
38 As a serving public servant, Richard Eccles was unable to be interviewed for the book. His involvement in the doping scandal polarised opinion. Sports Minister Kate Lundy spoke highly of his abilities and professionalism, telling the author, 'Richard is a phenomenal bureaucrat.' This assessment was supported by other senior federal bureaucrats who worked with Eccles. Some sports chiefs and ASADA officials were less flattering, portraying Eccles as a bureaucrat out of control.
39 Glenys Beauchamp's comments to Aurora Andruska about the internal Labor Party pressure on Senator Kate Lundy to resolve the doping scandal are contained in diary notes taken by Elen Perdikogiannis of a meeting on 4 June 2013. The notes are contained in James Hird's opening submissions to the Federal Court, VID No. 327 of 2014.
40 Aurora Andruska, interview with author, 23 January 2015.
41 Trevor Burgess diary notes from his 13 June 2013 conversation with Richard Eccles were tendered to the Federal Court on 13 August 2014, VID No. 327 of 2014.

42 During the trial of Essendon and James Hird's Federal Court challenge to the legality of ASADA and the AFL's joint investigation, Trevor Burgess was asked whether 'G' was a reference to AFL chief executive Gillon McLachlan. Burgess replied that he couldn't remember. Transcript of VID 327 of 2014, 13 August 2014, p. 276.
43 Brett Clothier email to Darren Mullaly, 18 April 2013, contained within James Hird's opening submissions to the Federal Court, VID No. 327 of 2014.
44 Aurora Andruska affidavit, sworn 22 July 2014 and tendered to the Federal Court on 12 August 2014, VID No. 327 of 2014.
45 Transcript of VID No. 327 of 2014, 12 August 2014, p. 192.
46 Aurora Andruska, interview with author, 23 January 2015.
47 Aurora Andruska, affidavit sworn 22 July 2014.
48 Trevor Burgess letter to Gillon McLachlan, 4 July 2013, tendered to the Federal Court on 13 August 2014, VID No. 327 of 2014.
49 Trevor Burgess affidavit sworn or affirmed 23 July 2014 and tendered to the Federal Court on 13 August 2014, VID No. 327 of 2014, p. 6.
50 ibid, p. 7.
51 ibid, p. 9.
52 Aurora Andruska, interview with author, 23 January 2015.
53 Stathi Paxinos, 'No Back-Room Deals: Demetriou', *The Age*, 9 August 2013.
54 Craig Rawson letter to Andrew Dillon, 20 August 2013: 'It is in these circumstances, we do not presently see any reason for ASADA's Interim Report (or any part of it) to be used at the hearing on 26 August 2013 or any adjourned hearing for: a. proving the charges; or b. determining any appropriate sanctions; or c. exercising any other powers under the AFL Rules unconnected with the NAD scheme.'
55 Aurora Andruska, interview with author, 23 January 2015.
56 ibid.
57 Agreed Protocol between AFL and ASADA Regarding ASADA's Interim Report, signed by Aurora Andruska, 29 August 2013, VID no. 327 of 2014.

Chapter 3   There's plenty of Danksy juice getting around

1 Mark Thompson, interview with author, 20 January 2015.
2 Mark Robinson, 'Former Bombers Fitness Adviser Stu Cormack Says All Clear On His Watch at Windy Hill', *Herald Sun*, 23 April 2013, cited at www.heraldsun.com.au/sport/afl/former-bombers-fitness-advisor-stu-cormack-says-all-clear-on-his-watch-at-windy-hill/story-e6frf9l6-1226626207004.

3   Paul Hamilton, interview with ASADA and the AFL, 13 February 2013.
4   Mark Thompson, interview with author, 20 January 2015.
5   Danny Corcoran, interview with author, 8 January 2015.
6   Bruce Reid, interview with author, 22 December 2014.
7   Kevin Norton, interview with author, 16 February 2015.
8   Ben McDevitt made his 'snake oil' comment to the Senate Community Affairs Legislation Committee, 17 October 2014, while arguing for the need for amendments to the ASDA Act to include a new category of 'prohibited association', intended to prevent athletes from working with support staff previously involved in doping. 'The reality here, in my view, is that this is a protective mechanism for athletes. We have many athletes who are naive and do not understand the reality that there are across the globe some sports scientists and sport support personnel who move around sports, plying their trade and their snake oil and so on. This is an opportunity to protect those athletes by notifying them about such persons and ensuring that they protect themselves.' Had this provision been in place in 2011, it would not have prevented Stephen Dank, who had not previously been found guilty of a doping offence, from working with either Cronulla or Essendon footballers.
9   Cynthia Graber, 'Snake Oil Salesmen Were on to Something', *Scientific American*, 1 November 2007, cited at www.scientificamerican.com/article/snake-oil-salesmen-knew-something.
10 Danny Corcoran, interview with author, 3 February 2015.
11 Danny Corcoran, interview with ASADA and the AFL, 26 April 2013.
12 Bruce Reid, interview with author, 22 December 2014.
13 James Hird, interview with ASADA and the AFL, 16 April 2013.
14 Dean Robinson, interview with ASADA and the AFL, 19 March 2013.
15 The prohibitions against possession and trafficking and banned substance that applied to Stephen Dank during his time at Gold Coast and Essendon are contained within articles 2.6 and 2.7 of the 2009 World Anti-Doping Code. Both provisions feature heavily in ASADA's case against Dank, which includes charges of possessing Thymosin Beta 4 and a Selective Androgen Receptor Modulator at Essendon; trafficking Thymosin Beta 4, Hexarelin and Humanofort, a product containing banned substances, at Essendon; trafficking one of Human Growth Hormone, SARMs, Hexarelin, Mechano Growth Factor and CJC-1295 at the Carlton Football Club and trafficking CJC-1295 at the Gold Coast Suns.
16 Danny Corcoran, interview with author, 3 February 2015.
17 ibid.
18 Mark Thompson, interview with author, 20 January 2015.

19 Bruce Reid, interview with author, 22 December 2014.
20 ibid.
21 ibid.
22 ibid.
23 Bruce Reid, interview with ASADA and the AFL, 18 February 2013.
24 Bruce Reid, interview with author, 22 December 2015.
25 James Hird and Peter Wilmoth, *Reading the Play*, Macmillan Australia, 2007, p. 66.
26 James Hird, interview with ASADA and the AFL, 16 April 2013.
27 Bruce Reid, interview with author, 22 December 2014.
28 ibid.
29 Caro Meldrum-Hanna, 'Essendon Coach Deeply Involved in Supplement Program', ABC's *7.30*, 11 April 2013, cited at www.abc.net.au/7.30/content/2013/s3735256.htm.
30 Danny Corcoran, interview with author, 4 February 2015.
31 Mark Thompson, interview with author, 20 January 2015.
32 Suki Hobson, interview with ASADA and the AFL, 21 April 2013.
33 Paul Turk, interview with ASADA and the AFL, 5 March 2013.
34 Paul Turk, interview with ASADA and the AFL, 15 April 2013.
35 Simon Goodwin, interview with ASADA and the AFL, 14 March 2013.
36 Caro Meldrum-Hanna, 'Essendon Coach Deeply Involved in Supplement Program', ABC's *7.30*, 11 April 2013, cited at www.abc.net.au/7.30/content/2013/s3735256.htm.
37 Nick McKenzie, 'Hird Injected Banned Boosters: Dank', *The Age*, 11 April 2013.
38 James Hird, interview with ASADA and the AFL, 16 April 2013.

Chapter 4 What's in that bloody drug?

1 Mark Thompson, interview with author, 20 January 2015.
2 James Hird, email to Dean Robinson, 15 January 2012.
3 Bruce Reid, letter to Paul Hamilton and James Hird, 17 January 2012.
4 High-performance manager Stuart Cormack.
5 Mark Thompson, interview with author, 20 January 2015.
6 Dr Ziggy Switkowski, review of Essendon Football Club governance, publicly released summary, 6 May 2013.
7 Paul Hamilton, interview with ASADA and the AFL, 13 February 2013.
8 Ian Robson, interview with ASADA, 15 February 2013.
9 Ian Robson and Paul Hamilton declined repeated requests for interviews. At the time of writing, Robson was chief executive of Melbourne

Victory, a professional football team within Australia's domestic A-League competition, and Hamilton remained in the AFL industry as the league's general manager for central Victoria.

10 Luke West, 'Hamilton Declares Conscience is Clear as Essendon Investigation Rolls On', *Bendigo Advertiser*, 10 May 2013.
11 Ian Robson statement, 23 May 2015, cited at www.essendonfc.com.au/news/2013-05-23/ian-robson-resigns.
12 Danny Corcoran, interview with author, 7 February 2015.
13 Mark McVeigh's comments during the meeting of the player leadership group are recalled by Jobe Watson in his interview with ASADA on 6 May 2013 and contained in the 'Decision of the AFL Anti-Doping Tribunal in the Matter of an Alleged Violation of the AFL Anti-Doping Code By [34 current and former Essendon players]', handed down 31 March 2015, p. 87.
14 David Jones, John Nixon and Wayne Henwood, 'Decision of the AFL Anti-Doping Tribunal in the Matter of an Alleged Violation of the AFL Anti-Doping Code By [34 current and former Essendon players]', handed down 31 March 2015, pp. 75–76.
15 Mandy Crameri, interview with author, 1 April 2015.
16 David Jones, John Nixon and Wayne Henwood, 'Decision of the AFL Anti-Doping Tribunal in the Matter of an Alleged Violation of the AFL Anti-Doping Code By [34 current and former Essendon players]', handed down 31 March 2015, p. 90.
17 Chip Le Grand, 'No Proof Drug Lifts Game of Athletes', *The Australian*, 4 May 2013.
18 David Kenley, interview with author, 8 February 2015.
19 Caro Meldrum-Hanna, 'Email Exchange Reveals Drugs in Sport Twist', ABC's *7.30*, 2 May 2013.
20 Stephen Dank, email to Irene Mazzoni, 2 February 2012.
21 WADA's S0 classification for non-approved substances has been included in the World Anti-Doping Code's prohibited list since 1 January 2011. At the time Stephen Dank is working at Essendon, S0 is defined as: 'Any pharmacological substance which is not addressed by any of the subsequent sections of the List and with no current approval by any governmental regulatory health authority for human therapeutic use (i.e. drugs under pre-clinical or clinical development or discontinued).' Athletes are prohibited from using substances covered by S0 in and out of competition times. WADA, 'The 2011 Prohibited List International Standard', cited at https://wada-main-prod.s3.amazonaws.com/resources/files/WADA_Prohibited_List_2011_EN.pdf.
22 Irene Mazzoni, email to Stephen Dank, 7 February 2012.

23 Stephen Dank's email in reply to Irene Mazzoni's 7 February email is dated 6 February 2012 due to the time difference between Melbourne and Montreal.
24 Irene Mazzoni, email to Stephen Dank, 7 February 2012.
25 Jobe Watson, interview with ASADA and the AFL, 6 May 2013.
26 Bruce Reid, interview with author, 22 December 2014.
27 Brendan De Morton, interview with ASADA and the AFL, 19 February 2013.
28 Dean Robinson, interview with ASADA and the AFL, 19 March 2013.
29 James Hird, interview with ASADA and the AFL, 16 April 2013.
30 Mal Hooper, interview with ASADA and the AFL, 26 February 2013.
31 The Chiropractic Board of Australia cancelled Mal Hooper's registration for two years after the Victorian Civil and Administrative Tribunal upheld an earlier finding against him for multiple counts of unprofessional conduct and professional misconduct in his treatment of a cerebral palsy patient. Chiropractic Board of Australia v Hooper (Review and Regulation) VCAT 1346 of 2013, 2 August 2013.
32 Paul Spano, interview with ASADA and the AFL, 19 July 2013.
33 Bruce Reid, interview with ASADA and the AFL, 26 March 2013.
34 Aurora Andruska, interview with author, 23 January 2015.
35 Paul Little, interview with author, 19 March 2015.
36 Bruce Reid, interview with ASADA and the AFL, 18 February 2013.
37 Mark Thompson, interview with ASADA and the AFL, 3 July 2013.
38 Luke Darcy, 'Dean Robinson—The Inside Man', Seven Network, 31 July 2013.
39 Bruce Reid, interview with author, 22 December 2014.
40 Bruce Reid, interview with ASADA and the AFL, 26 March 2013.
41 Bruce Reid, interview with ASADA and the AFL, 18 February 2013.
42 Bruce Reid, interview with author, 22 December 2014.
43 Danny Corcoran, interview with author, 7 February 2015.
44 Essendon's 2012 injury tally and missed matches from soft tissue injuries are documented in the club's defence to Dean Robinson's breach of contract claim. Essendon Football Club defence, SCI 05289 of 2013, filed 20 November 2013, p. 7. The case was settled nearly a year later, with Robinson receiving an undisclosed payment understood to be in excess of $1 million. Had the case gone to trial it is likely that Robinson would have disputed the injury figures.
45 Football journalist Mike Sheahan asked Jobe Watson his opinion about Stephen Dank during an interview with Fox Sports Australia's 'On the Couch' program on 24 June 2013. Sheahan: 'Stephen Dank is the evil chemist as it were, is seen to be that. What was your view when he was

at Essendon?' Watson: 'My view was that he was very knowledgeable in his field, that he had an extensive background in professional sport in Australia and that he had a great understanding of the supplement field. In my talking with him that is the impression that I got.' Cited at www.youtube.com/watch?v=Z6d24fng-v0.
46 Jobe Watson, interview with ASADA and the AFL, 6 May 2013.
47 Bruce Reid, interview with ASADA and the AFL, 18 February 2013.
48 Bruce Reid, interview with author, 22 December 2014.

Chapter 5 Peptide Alley

1 Robin Willcourt, interview with author, 4 February 2015.
2 The circumstances of Shane Charter's illegal importation of pseudoephedrine are taken from the transcript of The Queen v Shane Geoffrey Charter, his 30 January 2007 plea hearing before Victorian County Court Justice John Smallwood and his 2 February 2007 sentencing.
3 Justice John Smallwood, Victorian County Court, The Queen v Shane Geoffrey Charter, sentencing of Shane Geoffrey Charter, 2 February 2007.
4 Robin Willcourt, interview with author, 4 February 2015.
5 ibid.
6 ibid.
7 ibid.
8 Shane Charter, interview with ASADA, 8 May 2013.
9 Nima Alavi, interview with author, 18 June 2014.
10 George Williams, interview with author, 20 February 2015.
11 Cedric Anthony, interview with author, 7 November 2014.
12 Signed undertaking by Shane Charter, 8 December 2011, provided to the author by GL Biochem, Shanghai.
13 Stephen Dank, interview with author, 2 June 2014.
14 Transcript of Shane Charter interview with Tony Hargreaves and Xavier Campbell, 7 November 2014, p. 15.
15 David Jones, John Nixon and Wayne Henwood, 'Decision of the AFL Anti-Doping Tribunal in the Matter of an Alleged Violation of the AFL Anti-Doping Code By [34 current and former Essendon players]', handed down 31 March 2015, p. 65.
16 Nima Alavi, interview with author, 18 June 2014.
17 Stephen Dank, interview with author, 16 June 2014.
18 Sonja Plompen, interview with author, 19 June 2014.
19 David Jones, John Nixon and Wayne Henwood, 'Decision of the AFL Anti-Doping Tribunal in the Matter of an Alleged Violation of the AFL Anti-Doping Code By [34 current and former Essendon players]', handed down 31 March 2015, p 103.

20 Nima Alavi, interview with author, 18 June 2014.
21 The extent of Qatar's weight problem is documented by the World Obesity Federation, formerly known as the International Association for the Study of Obesity. According to the WOF's global obesity prevalence database, Qatar ranks below only Kuwait for obesity among women and third behind Kuwait and the United States for obesity among men. Cited at www.worldobestity.org/aboutobesity/world-map-obesity/.
22 David Kenley, interview with author, 9 December 2014.
23 ibid.
24 Letter from Daniel Black, Senior Investigator, TGA Regulatory Compliance Unit, to Edward Van Spanje, 7 February 2013.
25 Shane Charter was convicted of trafficking and possessing anabolic steroids on 7 May 2015. He was fined $2500 and ordered to serve 250 hours of unpaid community service. Peta Carlyon, 'Shane Charter, Sports Scientist Linked to Supplements Scandal, Convicted of Drug Offenses' *ABC News* cited at http://www.abc.net.au/news/2015-05-07/sports-scientist-shane-charter-convicted-of-drug-offences/6453372.

Chapter 6 Get the biggest stick you can

1 John Highfield, 'Influential Trade Unionist Retires', *The World Today*, ABC Local Radio, 15 February 2000, cited at www.abc.net.au/worldtoday/stories/s100523.htm.
2 Wayne Flower, Shannon Deery and Emily Portelli, 'Stephen Milne, Former St Kilda Player Pleads Guilty to Indecent Assault as Rape Charges are Dropped', *Herald Sun*, 7 November 2014, cited at www.heraldsun.com.au/news/law-order/stephen-milne-former-st-kilda-player-pleads-guilty-to-indecent-assault-as-rape-charges-are-dropped/story-fni0fee2-1227114383288.
3 Transcript of James Hird evidence to Federal Court, VID No. 327 of 2014, 11 August 2014, p. 93.
4 Nick McKenzie, email to Tony Nolan, 10 April 2013.
5 Caroline Wilson, 'Right Thing for Hird To Do Is Step Down', *The Age*, p. 3.
6 Patrick Smith, 'Essendon Legend James Hird Has No Choice But to Walk Away', *The Australian*, 12 April 2013. http://www.theaustralian.com.au/sport/opinion/essendon-legend-james-hird-has-no-choice-but-to-walk-away/story-e6frg7uo-1226618603580
7 Andrew Demetriou, comments to reporters in Sydney, 11 April 2013, cited at www.triplem.com.au/melbourne/sport/afl/news/afl-responds-to-james-hird-allegations-made-by-stephen-dank.

8   Caro Meldrum-Hanna, 'Essendon Coach Deeply Involved In Supplement Program', ABC's *7.30*, 11 April 2013, cited at www.abc.net.au/7.30/content/2013/s3735256.htm.
9   Patrick Smith, 'Essendon Legend James Hird Has No Choice but to Walk Away', *The Australian*, 12 April 2013.
10 Andrew Demetriou, interview with Neil Mitchell, Radio 3AW, 12 April 2013.
11 James Hird, post-match press conference, 12 April 2013, cited at www.afl.com.au/news/2013-04-12/hird-postmatch-round-three.
12 Paul Little, interview with author, 19 March 2015.
13 Aurora Andruska, interview with author, 23 January 2015.
14 Bruce Reid, interview with author, 22 December 2014.
15 Jobe Watson's 24 June 2013 admission, during an interview with Fox Sports Australia's *On the Couch* program, that he believed he was injected with AOD-9604 by sports scientist Stephen Dank merely confirmed what Essendon, the AFL and ASADA already knew. Nonetheless, it breathed new vigour into a scandal that had temporarily abated. Cited at www.youtube.com/watch?v=Z6d24fng-v0.
16 'WADA Statement on Substance AOD-9604', 22 April 2013, cited at www.wada-ama.org/en/media/news/2013-04/wada-statement-on-substance-aod-9604.
17 Transcript of Paul Simonsson's comments to Essendon Football Club players and staff from a recording taken by club solicitor Tony Hargreaves on 6 May 2013.
18 Aurora Andruska, diary notes, 9 February 2013, tendered to the Federal Court on 12 August 2014, VID No. 327 of 2014.
19 Mark Thompson, interview with author, 20 January 2015.
20 Dr Ziggy Switkowski, 'Review Findings and Recommendations', 6 May 2013, cited at www.essendonfc.com.au/news/2013-05-06/dr-ziggy-switskowski-report.
21 The broad powers of the AFL Commission to deal with breaches of rule 1.6 are explained at: Peter Ryan, 'Rule-Breakers: A Short History of Conduct Unbecoming', 13 August 2013, cited at www.afl.com.au/news/2013-08-13/rulebreakers-a-short-history-of-conduct-unbecoming.
22 Steve Amendola, interview with author, 26 February 2015.
23 Caroline Wilson, 'AFL Warned Hird Against Peptides', *The Age*, 17 July 2013, cited at www.theage.com.au/afl/afl-news/afl-warned-hird-against-peptides-20130716-2q2ih.html.
24 Brett Clothier's email and files notes about the 5 August 2011 peptide meeting with James Hird were received by ASADA at 12.33 p.m.

on 17 July 2013. Clothier declined to answer questions about this in December 2013, when I first reported his belated recollections in *The Australian*, and during the writing of this book.

25   Brett Clothier declined to respond to questions about his recollections about the 5 August 2011 meeting with James Hird.
26   Early in the doping scandal, James Hird received legal advice to take notes of all conversations with Essendon and AFL senior officials. Hird adopted the practice of taking potentially sensitive calls on speaker phone so that one of his lawyers or his wife Tania could take notes. The direct quotes from this conversation between James Hird and David Evans are taken from contemporaneous notes obtained by the author of a 24 July 2013 telephone call.
27   Steve Amendola, interview with author, 26 February 2015.
28   Contemporaneous notes of James Hird's telephone conversation with David Evans, 24 July 2013, obtained by the author.
29   In David Evans' resignation statement of 27 July 2013, he describes what is happening at Essendon as a tragedy and concedes that friendship has compromised his position. 'My involvement, and indeed my family's involvement over many years at both Essendon and the AFL have given me great strength during the last 5 months, because many of the people that I deal with are close friends. This has given me great insight and assisted in making tough decisions, but those decisions now may be seen to be clouded by those relationships or be seen as a conflict, and I am not prepared to have my decisions reflect poorly on the Club either now or in future.' Cited at www.essendonfc.com.au/news/2013-07-27/david-evans-resigns.

Chapter 7   If this is all they've got, you will win

1   Josh Massoud, 'Sports Scientist Stephen Dank Forms a Link Between NRL Clubs and the Latest AFL Drug Scandal', *Daily Telegraph*, 6 February 2013, cited at www.news.com.au/sport/nrl/sport-scientist-stephen-dank-forms-a-link-between-nrl-clubs-and-the-latest-afl-drug-scandal/story-fndujljl-1226571172109.
2   Damian Irvine, interview with author, 6 March 2015.
3   Damian Irvine, email to fellow Cronulla directors, 9.09 a.m., 7 February 2013.
4   Shane Flanagan, email to Damian Irvine, 11.15 a.m., 8 February 2013.
5   Damian Irvine, interview with author, 6 March 2015.
6   Phil Rothfield, 'Cronulla Sharks Chairman Claims Players Were Injected with Horse Drugs', *Daily Telegraph*, 10 March 2013, cited at www.dailytelegraph.com.au/sport/nrl/cronulla-sharks-chairman-

claims-players-were-injected-with-horse-drugs/story-e6frexnr-1226593894057.
7 ibid.
8 Andrew Webster, 'Trent Elkin: This Is My Story. You Be the Judge', *Sydney Morning Herald*, 1 August 2014, cited at www.smh.com.au/rugby-league/league-news/trent-elkin-this-is-my-story-you-be-the-judge-20140801-zzanl.html.
9 Bruno Cullen, interview with author, 12 March 2015.
10 ibid.
11 This account of Trent Elkin's 21 March address to the Cronulla players is taken from player testimony before ASADA.
12 Chronology of 2011 supplements program contained within the Kavanagh report.
13 NSW Civil and Administrative Tribunal, Health Care Complaints Commission v Sedrak [2014] NSWCATOD 114, 15 October 2014.
14 Shane Flanagan, email to David Givney, 6 April 2011.
15 Section 229 (9) of the 2011 Australian Rugby League and NRL anti-doping policy obliges players to 'provide all reasonable assistance to WADA, ASADA and us, in the application, policing and enforcement of this ADP, including (without limitation) cooperating fully with any investigation or proceeding being conducted pursuant to this ADP in relation to any suspected ADRV.'
16 Aurora Andruska, interview with author, 23 January 2015.
17 ibid.
18 Richard Redman, interview with author, 9 January 2015.
19 ibid.
20 ibid.
21 Damian Irvine, interview with author, 6 March 2015.

Chapter 8 A very unfortunate matter
1 Steve Amendola, interview with author, 26 February 2015.
2 Australian Sports Anti-Doping Authority, 'Interim Investigation Report', Operation Cobia, Australian Football League (AFL), August 2013, p. 13.
3 ibid. p. 166.
4 Steve Amendola, interview with author, 26 February 2015.
5 Bruce Reid, interview with author, 22 December 2014.
6 Steve Amendola, interview with author, 26 February 2015.
7 Ray Horsburgh interview with author, 5 March 2015.
8 ibid.
9 Paul Little, interview with author, 19 March 2015.

10 ibid.
11 ibid.
12 ibid.
13 Chip Le Grand, 'AFL Targets Essendon Royalty', *The Weekend Australian*, 10 August 2013, p. 1.
14 Mark Thompson, interview with author, 20 January 2015.
15 Chip Le Grand, 'Bruce Reid's Angry Rebuff to Retirement Offer', *The Australian*, 16 August 2013, cited at www.theaustralian.com.au/sport/afl/bruce-reids-angry-rebuff-to-retirement-offer/story-fnca0u4y-1226698064909.
16 Andrew Garnham revealed the advice he received from ASADA about the status of AOD-9604 during an interview with journalist Gerard Whateley on Fox Footy's *AFL 360* program on 20 August 2013. The AFL released its Statement of Grounds against Essendon and its officials the following day.
17 'Paul Little Statement', published on the Essendon Football Club website, 21 August 2013, cited at www.essendonfc.com.au/news/2013-08-21/paul-little-statement.
18 'James Hird Statement', published on the Essendon Football Club website, 21 August 2013, cited at www.essendonfc.com.au/news/2013-08-21/james-hird-statement.
19 Paul Little, interview with author, 19 March 2015.
20 ibid.
21 ibid.
22 ibid.
23 The proposed terms of settlement, sent by John Wylie to Paul Little on 23 August 2013, were obtained by *The Australian* and *Herald Sun* newspapers in November 2013 as part of a six-week investigation into the drugs scandal. The source of the document remains confidential.
24 John Wylie, email to Paul Little at 7.12 p.m., 23 August 2013.
25 James Hird, post-match press conference, 24 August 2013.
26 Paul Little, text message to James Hird at 1.48 p.m., 25 August 2013.
27 Paul Little, text message to James Hird at 3.13 p.m., 25 August 2013.
28 Paul Little, interview with author, 19 March 2015.
29 Julian Burnside, interview with author, 16 April 2015.
30 Steve Amendola, interview with author, 26 February 2015.
31 Paul Little, interview with author, 19 March 2015.
32 Transcript of AFL Commission hearing contained in affidavit of David Maddocks, solicitor for Bruce Reid, sworn as part of Supreme Court proceedings SCI 2013 04575, p. 11.
33 ibid. p. 13.

34 Mark Thompson, interview with author, 20 January 2015.
35 ibid.
36 Bruce Reid, interview with author, 22 December 2014.
37 ibid.
38 James Hird, transcript of testimony to the Federal Court VID no. 327 of 2014, 11 August 2014, p. 102.
39 Steve Amendola, interview with author, 26 February 2015.

Chapter 9   A Faustian compact
1 Andrew Demetriou, interview with Mike Sheahan, 'Open Mike', Fox Footy, 18 April 2012.
2 Padraic Murphy, 'Supreme Court Judge David Beach Urges AFL to Consider Dr Reid's Plea for Independent Body', *Herald Sun*, cited at http://www.heraldsun.com.au/sport/afl/supreme-court-judge-david-beach-urges-afl-to-consider-dr-bruce-reids-plea-for-independent-body/story-fni5f22o-1226711290909.
3 'AFL Boss Sympathises with Reid', AAP, cited at www.theage.com.au/afl/afl-news/afl-boss-sympathises-with-reid-20130830-2svj5.html.
4 Chip Le Grand, 'AFL to Drop Case Against Dr Bruce Reid', *The Australian*, 13 September 2013, p. 1.
5 Andrew Demetriou, transcript of interview with Neil Mitchell, Radio 3AW, 13 September 2013.
6 Press release, 'Dr Bruce Reid – AFL Charges', issued 18 September 2013 by the Australian Football League and Perry Maddocks Trollope Lawyers.
7 Paul Little, interview with author, 19 March 2015.
8 Transcript of Andrew Demetriou interview with Gerard Whateley and Red Symons, ABC Radio 774, 20 September 2013.
9 Andrew Demetriou, interview with Mike Sheahan, 'Open Mike', Fox Footy, 18 April 2002.
10 Michael Warner and Mark Robinson, 'Secret AFL Offer', *Herald Sun*, 4 December 2013, p. 1; Chip Le Grand, 'Revealed: The Secret Offer to Hird to End the AFL's Drug Shame', *The Australian*, 4 December 2013, p. 1.
11 Transcript of Andrew Demetriou interview with Neil Mitchell, Fairfax Radio 3AW, 4 December 2013.
12 Throughout the researching and writing of this book, I took up Andrew Demetriou's invitation to 'please, if you are listening, Homer, pick up the phone' many times. He declined to take my calls and multiple requests for interviews. I was christened Homer Eugene Le Grand V, but have been known as Chip since birth, other than during the sixth grade

when I decided Homer sounded more mature. I wisely reverted back to Chip in high school, before the advent of *The Simpsons*.

13   Michael Warner, Ashley Argoon, cited at www.heraldsun.com.au/sport/afl/james-hirds-wife-tania-says-andrew-demetriou-knew-about-payments-to-suspended-coach/story-fni5f6kv-1226781015902.

14   Nima Alavi, interview with author, 13 March 2015.

15   Aaron Walker, Australian Sports Anti-Doping Authority, 'Final Investigation Report Operation Cobia', p. 92.

16   The ASADA investigator's report of 4 March 2014 sets out the case that any Essendon players who doped were also duped: 'The wilful disregard of ethical common sense and the inexplicably experimental nature of the 2012 supplement program has set a shameful and disturbing precedent in the professional sporting community. The evidence has also readily identified that players were subject of profoundly false assurances from those within positions of authority at Essendon in respect of the substances subject of the 2012 supplementation program. The deception inflicted upon the players is best exemplified by the content of the "player consent" forms purportedly signed by the player group prior to undertaking the supplement program. The assertions within the document concerning the WADC compliance of the substance "Thymosin" by way of example is simply untrue – a fact readily known to Mr Dank at the time.' A further report was completed on 9 May 2014 taking in Nima Alavi's claims that he compounded a 'second batch' of peptides from China.

17   Aurora Andruska, interview with author, 23 January 2015.

18   ibid.

19   Professor Sumantra Ghoshal regularly evoked his 'smell of the place' imagery of Fontainebleau, contrasted with the oppressive summers of his home city Calcutta, as an analogy for change management. It is included in a speech he gave to the World Economic Forum before he died in 2004 at age fifty-five. Cited at www.youtube.com/watch?v=J4lA1o8RP6E.

20   The Count De Las Cases, *Memoirs of the Life, Exile and Conversations of the Emperor Napoleon*, volume 3, p. 98.

21   Darren Mullaly, in an 8 February 2013 email to the AFL's Brett Clothier and ASADA colleagues Elen Perdikogiannis and Paul Simonsson, argues that ASADA cannot allow AFL officials to sit in on interviews with Essendon staff and players. 'We cannot have other parties, such as the AFL, present during an interview of a person of interest to whom the investigation relates.' Transcript of proceedings VID No. 327 of 2014, 12 August 2012, p. 178.

22 Essendon counsel Neil Young QC used the phrase 'Faustian compact' in his opening submission to the court when referring to ASADA's decision to provide investigative material to the AFL in breach of its strict confidentiality provisions. In this metaphor, ASADA is the scholar Faust who trades his soul to the devil for greater power and wisdom. ASADA's mistake, like Faust, is to believe it can strike such a deal without being corrupted. Transcript of proceedings, VID No. 327 of 2014, 11 August 2014, p. 9.

23 Counsel for ASADA Tom Howe QC came up with the best line of the entire trial when he described the objections to the AFL being able to use information secured through the joint investigation in its disciplinary action against Essendon as 'nonsense on stilts'. Howe argued that the relationship between the 'toxic' governance failings at Essendon and the risk of players doping was self-evident and that, in effect, ASADA and the AFL were trying to tackle the same problem by separate means. In his opening submission he told the court: 'If in fact ASADA could not disclose to sporting administration bodies such as the AFL the sort of abysmal governance and management practices on the part of one of its constituents, even in circumstances where everyone accepted the self-evident reality that those governance and management issues had contributed to the emergence of the risk of anti-doping rule violations, then that would very, very substantially compromise the fulfilment of the objectives of the scheme. And, in our submission, it would lead to an outcome which could only be described as anomalous, but wholly perverse. Indeed, Your Honour, the expression nonsense on stilts comes to mind.' VID No. 327 of 2014, 11 August 2014, p. 41.

24 Aurora Andruska, interview with author, 23 January 2015.

25 ibid.

26 Neil Young QC, transcript of Federal Court proceedings, VID No. 327 of 2014, 12 August 2014, p. 159.

27 The extent to which the Gillard Government pressured ASADA to cut short its investigation into Essendon was left as an open question during Aurora Andruska's cross-examination in the Federal Court. When Essendon counsel Neil Young QC pressed Andruska on the issue, ASADA counsel Sue McNicol QC objected on the grounds of relevance. The objection was upheld by Justice John Middleton. Transcript of VID No. 327 of 2014, 12 August 2014, pp. 162–63.

28 Aurora Andruska's most definitive evidence about the tip-off was given at the start of her testimony under cross-examination from Neil Young: 'Well, early in the meeting according to the course of your note, do you agree with me that that question was asked by Mr McLachlan, "Is it

Essendon?" and the ACC official responded by saying, "Say no more?"' Andruska: 'I agree.' Young: 'And you were careful in your note taking to record the exact words used you swear in your affidavit?' Andruska: 'I agree.' Young: 'Now, when those words were said you immediately recognised that there had been a clear identification by the ACC that one of the clubs in question was Essendon, didn't you?' Andruska: 'I agree.' Transcript of VID No. 327 of 2014, 12 August 2014, p. 147.
29 Aurora Andruska, interview with author, 23 January 2015.
30 Extracts from the Reasons of the Honorable Justice John Middleton read to the Federal Court on 19 September 2014 in VID No. 327 of 2014.
31 Xavier Campbell, interview with author, 10 April 2015.
32 Paul Little, interview with author, 19 March 2015.
33 ibid.
34 Mark Thompson, interview with author, 20 January 2015.

Chapter 10   Enthusiastic amateurs
1 Under the AFL anti-doping code, it is the AFL rather than ASADA that issues an infraction notice formally accusing a footballer or support person of an offence. Once ASADA has informed the AFL general counsel that it believes an anti-doping rule violation may have occurred, the AFL has no choice but to issue a notice. This process is explained in clause 13a of the AFL Competition Anti-Doping Code, revised 7 March 2014, p. 23.
2 Queensland Police Service, 'Technology Builds on Foundations of Investigative Technique', *Police Bulletin*, Issue No. 342, October 2009, pp. 21–24.
3 Shane Charter, text message to author, 19 November 2014.
4 Paul Marsh, partner of Marsh & Maher, email to Aaron Walker, 27 November 2014.
5 ASADA investigator Luke O'Connor's account of his dealings with Shane Charter and Nima Alavi in November 2014, including this text exchange with Donna Charter, are contained in a statement that formed part of ASADA's application to the Victorian Supreme Court to compel Nima Alavi and Shane Charter to testify at the AFL tribunal hearing. Luke O'Connor, 2 December 2014 statement tendered as part of SCI No. 06387 of 2014.
6 Shane Charter, transcript of interview with Tony Hargreaves, 9 December 2014.
7 Nima Alavi, interview with author, 13 March 2015.
8 Ron Iddles, interview with author, 9 April 2015.

9   Greg Davies' line about enthusiastic amateurs is borrowed from the stage adaptation of Noel Coward's 1967 short story *Star Quality*. Interview with author, 7 April 2015.
10 David Jones, John Nixon and Wayne Henwood, 'Decision of the AFL Anti-Doping Tribunal In The Matter Of An Alleged Violation of the AFL Anti-Doping Code By [34 current and former Essendon players]' handed down 31 March 2015, p. 50.
11 Aurora Andruska, interview with author, 23 January 2015.
12 Shane Charter, transcript of interview with Tony Hargreaves, 9 December 2014.
13 ASADA relied on a taped interview Fairfax journalist Nick McKenzie conducted with Stephen Dank in April 2013 in which Dank purportedly confirmed he administered the banned Thymosin Beta 4 to Essendon players. Dank called back the journalist and explained he had meant to say Thymomodulin, a permitted substance. The AFL tribunal found that due to Dank's lack of credibility and reliability and his refusal to attend the hearing, no weight could be placed on the interview. David Jones, John Nixon and Wayne Henwood, 'Decision of the AFL Anti-Doping Tribunal in the Matter of an Alleged Violation of the AFL Anti-Doping Code By [34 current and former Essendon players]', handed down 31 March 2015, p. 44.
14 David Jones, John Nixon and Wayne Henwood, 'Reasons for Ruling on Objections to Evidence', in ibid., p. 8.
15 The AFL anti-doping tribunal of David Jones, John Nixon and Wayne Henwood handed down its judgements in the case of Stephen Dank and the current and former AFL players in two parts. On 31 March 2015, it handed down its decision in the case of the thirty-four players and published its reasons. On 17 April, it handed down its decision against Dank and published its reasons. Although published separately, the reasons are intended to be read as a single document.
16 Shane Charter, text message to author, 7 November 2014.
17 Shane Charter, text message to author, 16 February 2015.
18 Vincent Xu, email to author, 28 October 2014.
19 Vincent Xu, email to author, 29 October 2014.
20 David Jones, John Nixon and Wayne Henwood, 'Decision of the AFL Anti-Doping Tribunal in the Matter of an Alleged Violation of the AFL Anti-Doping Code By [34 current and former Essendon players]', handed down 31 March 2015, p. 99.
21 High-performance liquid chromatography (HPLC) is a method of identifying the chemical components within a mixture. Unlike mass spectrometry, it does not confirm the chemical structure of a substance.

22 Nima Alavi, interview with author, 14 April 2015.
23 David Jones, John Nixon and Wayne Henwood, 'Decision of the AFL Anti-Doping Tribunal in the Matter of Alleged Violations of the AFL Anti-Doping Code By Stephen Dank', handed down 17 April 2015, p. 26.
24 Ben McDevitt, 'ASADA Media Statement: Decision of the AFL Anti-Doping Tribunal', 31 March 2015.
25 David Jones, John Nixon and Wayne Henwood, 'Decision of the AFL Anti-Doping Tribunal in the Matter of an Alleged Violation of the AFL Anti-Doping Code By [34 current and former Essendon players]', handed down 31 March 2015, p. 81.
26 'Final Investigation Report Operation Cobia', p. 92.
27 Purchasing contract for RD Peptide, dated 28 November 2011, produced by Shane Charter on 9 December 2014.
28 Shane Charter, transcript of interview with Tony Hargreaves, 7 November 2011, p. 37.
29 Nima Alavi, interview with author, 13 March 2015.
30 David Jones, John Nixon and Wayne Henwood, 'Decision of the AFL Anti-Doping Tribunal in the Matter of Alleged Violations of the AFL Anti-Doping Code By Stephen Dank', handed down 17 April 2015, p. 27.
31 Ben McDevitt, transcript of press conference, 1 April 2015.
32 Mark Thompson, interview with author, 20 January 2015.
33 James Hird, interview with ASADA and the AFL, 16 April 2013.
34 Paul Little, interview with author, 19 March 2015.
35 Aurora Andruska, interview with author, 23 January 2015.
36 Mark Thompson, interview with author, 20 January 2015.

INDEX

7.30 program 147

ACC see Australian Crime
    Commission
Actovegin injections 54–5, 80–1
AFL see Australian Football League
AFL Players Association 34, 151–2
Age, Hird story in 142, 145–6, 162–3
Alavi-Maghadam, Nima
  ACC examines 134
  ASADA questions 193
  Bates meets 270
  Charter works with 120–1
  Dank's relations with 110–12,
    130–1, 136–7
  Nolan interviews 228–30
  on alleged second batch of
    peptides 256–8
  refuses to sign statement 244–7,
    249–50
  sources peptides from China
    126–30, 254–5
  Willcourt works with 117–20

Amendola, Steve
  Hird advised by 159–60, 164,
    207–8, 213
  Hird urged to keep fighting by
    189–90, 216–17, 234
  reads interim ASADA report 192
amino acid injections 73
Anderson, Adrian 95–6, 162
Anderson, Robert 23
Anderson, Sue 73, 129
Andrews, Kevin 23
Andruska, Aurora
  as witness in Federal Court
    237–41
  at ASADA meeting 29–31
  at media spectacular 19–20
  background of 248
  career of 20–1
  Clothier proposes co-operation
    to 41
  denies 'deal' with AFL 152
  discusses Aperio report 29–30
  Eccles calls 47

295

Evans meets with 101
fears investigation will be shut down 231–2
final report submitted to 193
government pressure on 38–9
heads ASADA doping investigation 21–3
Hird meets with 22
invited to investigate Essendon 17
McLachlan's response to 37
meets with AFL 13, 15, 42–3
notes taken by 154–5, 236
on AFL's motives 43
on ASADA approach to hearing 252
on Dank findings 26
on drug scandal 268–9
on no-fault defence 31–4
on NRL vs AFL 179–80
on release of report to AFL 45–6
takes leave 44
Andruska, John 238
Anthony, Cedric 121–4, 254–5, 257, 260–1
ANZAC Day match against Collingwood 96–7
AOD-9604 *see also* peptides
discovery and evaluation of 89–90
legal status of 7–8, 199
may not have been used at Essendon 262–3
Melbourne players use 270
plans to test and market 131–2
proposed treatment regime 88
Reid on use of 3, 78–9, 192
Robinson uses 70
WADA consulted on 10
Watson admits to injecting 153
Zaharakis takes in cream 87
Argoon, Ashley 227
arranges ASADA–Hird meeting 25

ASADA *see* Australian Sports Anti-Doping Authority
Ashby, Noel 228
Ashton, Graham, on Aperio report 28–9
Austgrow 121–2, 254, 260
Australian Crime Commission (ACC) *see also* Project Aperio
AFP briefed by 7, 13–14
ASADA's relations with 24
denies tip-off story 15
interrogates Dank 25–6
investigates Peptide Alley 134–5
media conference by 20
notifies NRL of investigation 167
powers of 14
report by 12
Australian Federal Police (AFP)
briefed by ACC 7, 13
briefed by ASADA 13–14, 193–4
Dank speaks to 3
Australian Football League (AFL)
AFL Commission meeting 209–12
aims for ASADA meeting 29–31
allegations against Essendon 1
believes it has understanding with ASADA 151
called on to recuse itself from case 200
conflicting reports of meeting 11
cooperates in ASADA investigation 41, 179
damaged by scandal 39
decides to act against Essendon 40
Demetriou expands 42
doping tribunal held by 243–59
Eccles works with 38
Elliott takes to court 201
given ASADA interim report 41–7
Hird offered terms by 188

INDEX

information leaked by 164–5
legality of ASADA links
   questioned 233–4
media relations with 161–2
pressure placed on teams by 104–5
publishes report on Essendon
   198–9
reaction to suits against ASADA
   235
recruitment processes for staff
   53–4
response to ASADA investigation
   196
settlement package offered by
   204–5
signs up to WADC 30
Switkowski report given to 159
urged to seek arbitration with Reid
   220
Australian Government Solicitors,
   advice to ASADA 193–4
Australian Health Practitioner
   Regulation Agency 118–19
Australian Sports Anti-Doping
   Authority (ASADA)
   accepts Clothier's account of
     meeting 163
   ACC's relations with 24
   AFL 'deal' with 36, 40–1, 48
   Alavi interviewed by 228–30
   approaches Charter and Alavi
     244–5
   asserts AOD-694 not banned
     199–200
   at Supreme Court hearing 247–9
   attends AFP briefing 13
   aware of pressure from government
     38
   budget of boosted 229
   considers legal action against AFL
     47–8

critical of recruitment processes
   53–4
Cronulla investigated by 35–6,
   181, 182–4
Dank refuses to cooperate with
   125
Essendon investigated by 17, 188,
   231–2
Evans interviewed by 160
Evans makes agreement with 151
Federal Court finds for 240–1
Hird and Essendon file suit against
   235–9
Hird interviewed by 144–5, 160
Hird plans appeal against 242
implements WADC in Australia
   30
interim report by 41–7, 191–2
legality of links with AFL
   questioned 233–4
limited resources of 23–4
lists substances administered to
   Essendon players 99–101
new powers given to 193
NRL investigated by 177–80
peptides investigated by 21–2
procedural failures by 248–60,
   264–5
Sedrak investigated by 175
suspects covert clinical trial of
   AOD-964 132–3
talks to GL Biochem sales rep 256
Watson interviewed by 154
Australian Sports Commission 30,
   202–3
Australian Sports Drug Agency 23

Baker, Richard 142–3, 165
Barrett, Damian 4
Bassat, Paul 210, 219
Bates, Dan 270

Beach, David 219–20
Beauchamp, Glenys 39
Belgrave Compounding Pharmacy 175
Best Buy Supplements 125
Bloomfield, Paul 9–10
Blunden, Peter 161–2
Bock, Nathan 62, 230–1, 263
Bonds, Barry 154
Bornstein, Joe 89
Bovine Colostrum, administered to players 88
Brasher, Paul 100, 215
Burgess, Trevor 29, 40, 44–5, 248
Burnside, Julian 189–90, 211–12, 217

Calzada, Evans meets with 133
Campbell, Xavier 72, 234, 241–2
Cerebrolysin 98–9, 101, 148 *see also* peptides
Charter, Donna 246–7
Charter, Shane
  ACC examines 134
  Alavi works with 120–1
  arrested on drug charges 114–17
  attends Supreme Court hearing 247–8
  business activities of 125–7
  cut out of supply chain 130
  enters peptide business 112–14
  evidence of confirmed by Alavi 229
  in ASADA report 191
  peptides sourced from China by 121–5, 255–6, 260–1
  police investigation of 138
  refuses to sign statement 244–7, 249
CJC-1295 *see also* peptides
  alleged use on Cronulla players 174–5, 181
  Bock uses 230–1
  Dank supplies 61–2
  Robinson uses 70
Clare, Jason 19–20
Clothier, Brett
  arranges ASADA–Hird meeting 22
  ASADA meets with 29–30
  at AFL House meeting 11–12
  at AFP briefing 13–16
  concerns over report 44–6
  Evans meets with 100–1
  in ASADA report 191–2
  lodges affidavit 221–2
  proposes co-operative investigation 41
  raises possibility of no-fault defence 32
  reads ASADA report 196
  recalls Hird meeting 163–4
Coleman, Andrew 178, 183–4
Comancheros, Croad involved with 134
Commercial Arbitration Act 247
Como Compounding Pharmacy
  Alavi runs 110, 228
  Bates taken to 270
  consignments from China 126
  credit charge by 136
  MRC a customer of 131
  peptide records 256–7
Connor, Bruce 55
Corcoran, Danny
  accepts AFL terms 212–14
  after victory against Carlton 207
  ASADA meets with 22
  charges laid against 47–8
  denies being tipped off by Demetriou 15
  disciplinary action taken against 188–90, 197–8, 205
  Hird contacts 142

learns of doping allegations 2–4
leaves Essendon 49
on Dank 58–9
on Wylie intervention 204
recollections of Hird meeting 163
recruitment of 82
responds to Hird letter 85–6
Robinson and Dank meet with 58–9, 102
Robinson selected by 52–3
Robson defines responsibilities of 83
Robson talks to 12
sacking plans 155
takes over from Hamilton 107–8
wife's illness and death 84–5
Corcoran, Maxine 84–5
Cormack, Stuart 52
Corrigan, Chris 195
Craig, Neil 270
Crameri, Mandy and Bernie 87–8
Crameri, Stewart 87, 150, 259
Croad, Trent 118, 133–4
Croft, Clyde 247–8
Cronulla Football Club
  ASADA investigation of 35–6
  Dank associated with 10, 34–5
  disciplinary action against 180–2
  effect of proposed ban on 184
  linked to doping investigation 167
  player ban on back-dated 182–3
  players debate over taking ASADA deal 184–5
  players injected with TB500 171–2
  players seek out Dank privately 177
Cronulla Leagues Club meeting 176
Crow, Justin 71
Cullen, Bruno 172
Customs Department 115, 135

Dank, Stephen
  ABC interviews 73
  ACC interviews 25–6, 134
  Alavi's relations with 113, 130–1, 136–7
  ANZAC Day match plan 97–8
  AOD-9604 used by 91–3
  ASADA fails to get further testimony from 193
  association with Cronulla FC 34–5, 167–70, 172–4, 176–7
  attends Federal Court hearing 240
  author interviews 58
  Charter's dealings with 125–7
  claims medical staff approved supplement use 103
  claims WADA approved AOD-9604 use 94
  Customs Department detains 135
  Essendon sacks 108
  gives presentation to team 87
  hearing and judgement against 243, 263–4
  Hexarelin supplied to Anderson by 74
  Hird and Thompson meet with 76–7
  Hird exchanges texts with 147–8
  Hird recruits 17
  implicated in doping 25
  intentions of 262, 267
  interviewed for Essendon job 59
  interviews with reporters 143–4
  invoice for peptides given to 131
  involvement in doping 3–5
  leaves Essendon 49
  melatonin prescribed for 68
  methods used by 9
  mobile phone messages copied from 147

peptide use promoted by 109–10,
    120, 124–5
peptides administered to players
    by 98–9
players told to keep quiet about
    174–5
players' views of 86, 106–7
record-keeping inadequate 258,
    263
reported to Purana Taskforce
    137–8
Robinson recruits 55
SARMs supplied to Gervasi by
    72
subsequent career of 269–70
substances provided by 69
supplies banned substances to
    sports team staff 74–5
Switkowski on 157
takes peptides for testing 128–9
testimony regarding Cronulla 181
Thymosin administered by 95
told to stop giving Essendon
    players supplements 101–2
treatments by 55–7
unlabelled substances used on
    humans by 130
Willcourt works for 118–19
Davies, Greg 250–1
De Morton, Brendan 87–8, 98,
    103–4, 108
Deeble, John 74–5
Deloitte auditors 40, 169, 183
Demetriou, Andrew
    allegations against Essendon 2–3
    at AFL Commission meeting
        218–19
    at AFP briefing 13–14
    considers publishing report 46
    denies tip-off story 14–16
    departure from AFL 16

Evans' relations with 4, 143–5,
    156, 166
Little loses confidence in 200
media treatment of 146–7, 161–2
on AFL cooperation with ASADA
    180
on Hird case 224–6
on Reid case 220–3
on 'Statement of Grounds' 199
presents self as at arm's length 203
quizzed about payment to Hird
    227–8
response to Hird allegations 149
response to interim report 42
wants closure to investigation 197
Dessau, Linda 210, 219
Dhurringile prison 121
Di Natale, Richard 228
Dillon, Andrew
    as AFL counsel 47
    at meeting with Hird 207–8
    briefed by Haddad 40
    inquires about report 44
    on payment to Hird while
        suspended 226
Donehue, John 74, 263
Downes, Garry 231–2, 252–3
Doyle, Jim 179
Dr Ageless anti-ageing clinics 112,
    122
Dunn, Allan 85
Dutton, Peter 231, 253
Dyson, Ricky 87

Earl, Sandor 177
Eccles, Chris 38
Eccles, Richard
    at ASADA teleconference 239
    calls Andruska 47
    meets with ASADA 29–30, 42–3
    passes on AFL decision to act 40

pressure put on ASADA by 37–9
raises possibility of no-fault
    defence 32–3
Elkin, Trent 172–3, 176–7, 179–80
Elliott, John 201
Ellis, Kate, as Minister for Sport 27–8
Epigenx clinic 110, 133–4, 136
Essendon Football Club
    accepts AFL terms 212–13
    administration of 155–6
    AFL plans action against 47
    AFP briefing identifies 13–14
    ASADA invited to investigate 17
    believes it has understanding with
        ASADA 151–2
    cleared of doping allegations 265
    commitments required from 206
    competition success 39, 269
    Dank supplies staff with
        pharmaceuticals 69
    disciplinary action against 188–90,
        205–6
    doping allegations against 1–3,
        47, 49
    Federal Court finds against 240–1
    files suit against ASADA 235–8
    game against Carlton 207
    game against Fremantle 149–50
    Hird paid by while suspended 225
    layout of offices 8
    Little takes over as chair 196–9
    mistakenly billed for peptides 130
    muscle injuries in 106
    new grounds for 49
    players receive 'show cause' notices
        234–5
    players sign consent forms 87
    possibility of no-fault defence for
        32–3
    possible covert trial of AOD-9604
        on 132–3

pre-season activity 6
records kept of supplement use
    101, 105
response to charges 198–9
Robinson sends players to
    osteopath 66
'show cause' notices issued to 251
supplement rules for 77–8
weaknesses in team 51–2
winning streak by 105
Evans, David
    after game with Fremantle 150
    ASADA's relations with 29–30,
        42–3, 151, 160
    at AFL House meeting 11
    commissions review of
        administration 83
    denies being tipped off by
        Demetriou 15
    Hird consulted by 6–7
    Hird tells about Dank's messages
        148
    Hird's relations with 1–2, 16, 144,
        152–3, 158–60, 164–5
    Kelty associated with 140
    Kenley meets with 133
    leadership style 155–6
    learns of doping allegations 4
    media conference by 11–12, 17–18
    plans to revive Essendon 195
    resigns from Essendon 49, 166
    response to Hird allegations 142–3
    Robinson sidelined by 108
    seeks information about allegations
        3
    starts 2011 season 51
    statement about Hird case 146
    substance use reported to 100–1
    supports Demetriou against Hird
        165–6
    visits Reid 4–5

Evans, Ron 2, 5, 16
Evans, Sonya 166

Federal Court hearings 235–8, 243
Ferrari, Michele 262
Fitzpatrick, Mike
  agreement negotiated by 210
  as AFL Commissioner 189, 210
  called on to intervene 200
  Hird meets with 208–9, 266–7
  Kelty associated with 140
  on settlement with Reid 213–14
  refuses to refer Reid case to arbitration 219
  Wylie's relations with 202–4
Flanagan, Shane
  Cronulla stands down after investigation 170
  disciplinary action against 179–80
  on Dank's involvement with Cronulla 168
  private account kept by 172
  promises to end peptide program 176
Fontainebleau, Hird in 233
Franklin, Buddy 240
Fremantle Football Club 141–2, 149–50
Fricker, Peter 132

Gallen, Paul 172–3, 184
Garnham, Andrew 199
Gatto, Mick 114
Geelong Football Club, Wohlfahrt's involvement with 54
Gervasi, Carmelo 72
Ghoshal, Sumantra 232–3
GHRP-6 174–5, 181 *see also* peptides
Gillard, Julia 27, 30, 36
Gillard Labor government 20, 38–9, 228

Gillies, Ross 211, 213, 219
Giordani, Vania 129–30, 257
Givney, David 9–10, 170, 176
GL Biochem factory 121–3, 254–6
Gleeson, Jeff 189, 210–11, 219–20
Gleeson, Michael 4
Global Positioning System data, Dank responsible for collecting 63
Global Rhodes Scholarship Trust 206
Gold Coast Suns franchise 60, 62, 230–1
Goodwin, Simon 71–2
Gordon, Peter 16
Goyder, Richard 210
Graham, Wade 177–8, 181
Grimes, Hailey 107–8
Gumbleton, Scott 66, 106
Gunston, Ray 215, 226

Haddad, Abraham, AFL investigations by 40
Hamilton, Paul
  ASADA meets with 22
  background of 81–3
  Dank interviewed for job by 59–60
  isolated from ruling clique 156
  leaves Essendon 49, 84
  on 'injection mentality' 68
  recollections of Hird meeting 163
  Reid raises concerns with 77–81
  Robinson and Dank meet with 102
  Robson defines responsibilities of 83
  selects Robinson as performance manager 52–3
  Switkowski on 157
Handelsman, David 89, 129
Hanke, Ian 160, 191
Hanks, Peter 233–4, 243
Harcourt, Peter 64–5

Hargreaves, Tony
  advises Evans 156
  advises Little 197
  as Essendon solicitor 142
  Charter sends certificate to 261
  Essendon consults on 'show cause' notices 234–5
  Hird tells about Dank's messages 148
Harrington, Nick 159, 189–90, 216
Hasler, Des 59
HCG: 260 *see also* peptides
Heffernan, Chris, Hird called by 144
Herald Sun, coverage of doping scandal 161–2, 165
Hexarelin *see also* peptides
  Dank distributes to sporting club staff 73–4
  Dank supplies to Essendon staff 70–1
  Hird suspected of using 73, 142, 144
  source of unclear 129
Hibbert, Darren 173, 175
Hird, Allan T 2
Hird, James
  after victory against Carlton 207
  agrees to recruitment of Robinson 53
  Amendola consulted by 159–60
  as scapegoat for players 152
  as witness in Federal Court 237
  ASADA interviews 22, 41, 160
  asks about peptides 21–2
  at AFL House meeting 11–12
  ban proposed for 40
  cannot work with Robinson 108
  charges laid against 47–8
  Charter advises 113
  continues as Essendon coach 39, 50, 266–8
  Dank exchanges texts with 147–8
  Dank hired by 59–62
  denies doping allegations 6–7
  disciplinary charges against 188–90, 197–8, 205–7
  disputes interim ASADA report 191–2
  effect of on Essendon 16–17
  engages legal team 46
  Essendon pays while suspended 224–7
  Evans' relations with 1–2, 16, 143–4, 156, 158–60, 164–5
  Federal Court litigation by 219, 233–8, 240–1, 242–3
  football career 1
  Kelty meets with 139–41
  letter to Corcoran 85–6
  Little negotiates with 215–17
  media conference by 11–12, 17–18, 150
  media pursuit of 146, 163–4
  notified of doping allegations 1–3
  on Wylie intervention 203–4
  players meet with 86
  pressured to stand down 142
  puts his case to McLachlan 207–8
  reads 'Statement of Grounds' 200–1
  refuses to accept AFL agreement 211–13
  Reid consults with 8, 77–81
  Robinson and Dank meet with 94, 101–2
  Robinson claims support from 102–3
  Robinson supplies sleeping medication to 66–7
  sacking rumours 141
  starts 2011 season 50–1
  suspected of using Hexarelin 73

Switkowski on 157–8
writes supplement use policy 78
Hird, Tania
  at Federal Court hearing 236
  at Hird birthday dinner 1
  Kelty meets with 140
  on calls for Hird standing down 145
  on Hird's being paid by Essendon 227
  on holiday at Coolum 66
  on McLachlan 187–8
  reaction to judgement 190
  records AFL agreement with Hird 216
Hobson, Suki 55, 70–1, 75, 129
Holmes, Malcolm 231, 252
Hooper, Mal 97–9, 110
Horsburgh, Ray 194
Howe, Tom 239
Hurley, Michael 86
hyperbaric treatments 97–9
Hypermed treatment centre 97–9, 107, 110

Iddles, Ron 250
Ings, Richard 28
'injection mentality' 8, 68
Institute of Cellular Bioenergetics 112, 120, 130
International Court of Arbitration for Sport 265–6
Irvine, Damian
  learns of Cronulla links to doping investigation 167–8
  misled about involvement with Dank 168–9
  on Cronulla doping scandal 185–6
  resigns as NRL CEO 170–1
  Rothfield interviews by phone 171
  seeks deal for Cronulla 35–6

Jevtovic, Paul 13
Johnston, Damon 161
Jones, David 243, 252, 258, 265
Jones, Ken 229
Jordan, Ray 'Slug' 223

Karas, Tom 120
Kavanagh, Tricia 35, 170–1, 180–1
Kelty, Bill 16, 139–41, 156, 160
Kenley, David 90–1, 131–3
Kerrison, Sharon 229
Knights, Matthew 52, 82

Lalor, Benita 55
Lander & Rogers 182
Langford, Chris 210
Lau, Chris 114–15
Lawler, John
  announces Aperio complete 38
  at AFP briefing 13
  at media spectacular 19
  plans to release Aperio report 26
  reports on ACC investigation 167
Le Grand, Chip (author), Demetriou dismissive of 221, 223
Little, Paul
  accepts legal judgement 241–2
  after victory against Carlton 207
  agreement negotiated by 210–11
  approaches Thomson for head coach 242
  as Essendon chair 194–8
  ASADA meets with 100–1
  at AFL Commission meeting 212
  at Federal Court hearing 235–6
  Fitzpatrick meets with 220
  Hird pressured by 204
  Hird urged to accept deal by 208–9
  McLachlan's relations with 222
  on 'deal' with ASADA 151

INDEX

on Hird 189, 225–6, 268
on Switkowski report 158
reaction to suits against ASADA 235
Reid meets with 215
takes defensive stance 200–1
urged to seek litigation 234
Wylie consulted by 202–4
Lockett, Tony 140
Lording, David 39
Lube All Plus, administered to players 101
Lukin, Liz
at AFL House meeting 11–12
Evans advised by 156–9
Hird meets with 145–6
Hird tells about Dank's messages 148
suspected of campaigning against Hird 164
Lundy, Kate 19–20, 25–7, 37–9
Lynch, Chris 210
Lyon, Ross 141, 213

Maddock, Jack 245
Manly NRL Club, alleged use of AOD-9604 90
Marsh, Paul 246–7
Marshall, John 35–6
Massoud, Josh 167–8
Mattiske, Shane 169
Mayne, Chris 150
Mazzoni, Irene 92–4
McCartney, Brendan 53
McDevitt, Ben
defends ASADA 264
issues 'show cause' notices 251–2
on Dank 57
on Essendon scandal 258
proceeds against Essendon players 231–2

McGwire, Mark 154
McLachlan, Gillon
ASADA meets with 29, 42–3
at AFL Commission meeting 187–8
at AFP briefing 13–16
Demetriou delegates negotiations to 203, 222
desired outcome of investigation 155
Eccles works with 38
Essendon staff meet with 11–12
Evans' relations with 4, 100–1, 144–5
Haddad briefs 40
Hird puts his case to 207–8
inquires about report 44
Little's relations with 196–7, 200
on effect of scandal 42
on no-fault defence 32–3
on payment to Hird while suspended 226
response to withdrawal of letter 37
seeks to stand Hird down 140
McNamara, John 178
McNicol, Sue 239
McVeigh, Mark 67, 86
Medical Rejuvenation Clinic
Alavi told about 112
as distribution network 120
Charter and Dank involved with 126
in breach of WADA Code 264
peptides bought by 130
peptides used by 125
sales of peptides legal through 136
Melatonan II 68–9, 70, 72, 125 *see also* peptides
melatonin, injections of 67–8
Melbourne Cricket Ground Trust 202

Melbourne Football Club, Dank works for 269–70
Melbourne Rebels, Dank applies for job with 58
Meldrum-Hanna, Caro 73
Memete, Peter 107
Metabolic Pharmaceuticals 89–91, 131
methamphetamine, manufacture of 116
Middleton, John 14, 235, 237–41
Milne, Stephen 141
Mimotopes 128–9
Misson, David 270
Mitchell, Neil 220–2, 224
Mokbel, Tony 120
Mooney, Darren 34, 168, 170–1, 176
Moran, Jason 114
Moran, Lewis 114
Mostyn, Sam 210
Moufarrige, Andrew 132
Mourinho, Jose 268
Mulkearns, Peter 52
Mullaly, Darren 41, 44, 182, 248–9
Müller-Wohlfahrt, Hans-Wilhelm 54
Mullett, Paul 229
Musashi supplements 63

National Rugby League
  ACC notifies of investigation 167
  accepts ASADA deal 183
  ASADA's relations with 178–9
  Cronulla doping allegations 34
  Cronulla FC audited by 169
  peptide use in 21–2
  prepares own doping report 46
  takes action against implicated players and staff 179–80
Ng, Frank 89
Nick McKenzie 73, 142–3, 165, 253
'no disparagement' clause in Hird settlement 227
Noakes, Mark 171, 174, 181
Nolan, John
  Alavi interviewed by 228–30, 256
  draft report compiled by 45
  Evans meets with 101, 156
  Hird interviewed by 267
  list of substances administered to players 146
  starts work at ASADA 248
  supports cooperation with AFL 41
Nolan, Tony 142–3, 145, 159, 233
Norton, Kevin 56–7
NRL *see* National Rugby League

O'Connor, Luke 244–6, 252
Office of Police Integrity 228–9
O'Leary, Michael 26
Oliver, Jonah 10, 86–8, 102
Operation Cobia *see also* Australian Sports Anti-Doping Authority
  independent review of 231
  launch of 23
  procedural weaknesses in 248–9
  report on delivered to AFL 45
  results shown to ACC 25
Overland, Simon 229
Oxford University, proposed as employer for Hird 206

Palmer, Mick 24
Pavlich, Matthew 67
peptides *see also names of specific peptides*
  Age story on use of 163
  Dank acknowledges administering 57
  Dank discusses with Willcourt 119–20

Dank supplies Essendon staff with
  69–70
Dank supplies Robinsons with 61
investigation into 20–1
second batch of mentioned 256
secretagogues and 21
sourced from China 121–3, 254–5
used on Cronulla players 175, 181
value of market in 109
Perdikogiannis, Elen
  at ASADA meeting 29
  evidence prepared by 248–9
  on AFL reliability 217
  on no-fault defence 32–3
  withdraws AFL letter 36–7
  writes summary report 44
Plompen, Sonja 128
Pollard, Chris 233
Prismall, Brent 259
Project Aperio *see also* Australian
    Crime Commission
  ACC reveals plans for 24–5
  AFL briefed on 13
  information gathered by 28
  reports released 19–20, 25–6
  results of 15
pseudoephedrine, imports of 114–16
Purana Taskforce 114, 137–8

Qatar, Dank plans peptide trial in
  131–2
Quinn, John 59, 64, 113

Radev, Nik 'The Bulgarian' 114
Rawson, Craig 46–7
RD Peptides 260–1
Redman, Richard
  Cronulla Football Club consults
    34–6
  disappointed with ASADA
    approach 185
  on Graham's legal team 178
  on players' view of Dank 177
  represents Cronulla for ASADA
    investigation 182–3
Reid, Bruce
  AFL position towards
    misrepresented 218–19
  at AFL Commission meeting 211
  at Evans–Hird meeting 152–3
  author interviews 50
  cannot work with Robinson 108
  concern over AOD-9604 76–80
  concern over supplement use 84
  consent forms kept from 88–9
  contests disciplinary charges 47,
    188, 190, 197–9, 215, 220–2
  Dank consulted by 94–5, 98
  denies being tipped off by
    Demetriou 15
  denies doping allegations 4–5
  details of substances kept from 101
  disappointed over AFL failure to
    act 65
  disputes interim ASADA report
    191–3
  halts supplement use 86–7
  Hird consults over sleep
    medication side effects 66–8
  information sought from 2–3
  meetings with Dank and Robinson
    102
  on Dank and Robinson 17, 54,
    59–60, 104, 107
  on Essendon scandal 258
  on status of AOD-9604 7–8
  refuses to accept AFL agreement
    213, 215
  Robinson message fails to reach
    103–4
  sceptical about supplements 63–5
  threatens litigation 219

Reimers, Kyle 4
Robinson, Dean
  Actovegin treatments by 55
  Dank's relations with 60–3, 94, 107
  emails doctors supplement list 103–4
  Essendon employs 8–9, 49, 52–3, 107–8
  Hird and Thompson meet with 76–7
  Hird recruits 17
  Hird supplied medication by 67–8
  intentions of 267
  peptides supplied to 70
  players' attitude to 106
  players sign consent forms for 87
  recruits new staff 55
  Reid bypassed by 64–6
  Reid's evidence clashes with 191, 193
  Robson stands down 12
  Switkowski on 157–8
  told to stop administering supplements 101–3
Robinson, Mark 161–2
Robson, Ian
  as Essendon CEO 2
  ASADA meets with 29
  Dank interviewed for job by 59–60
  Evans consults 5–6
  invites ASADA to investigate 15
  isolated from ruling clique 156
  McLachlan meets with 11–12
  media conference by 11–12, 17–18
  raises possibility of no-fault defence 32
  resigns from Essendon 49, 84, 155
  reviews high-level staffing 83
  reviews injury record 106
  Robinson sidelined by 108
  silent on tip-off story 15
  Switkowski on 157
  unaware of Reid's concerns 84
Rodski, Justin 11
Roland, Paul 22, 163–4
Rooke, Max 54
Roos, Paul 72
Rothfield, Phil 170–1
Rudd, Kevin 27
Rugby League Players Association 184
Rush, Jack 197
Russell Kennedy (law firm) 35
Ryder, Paddy 150

Sales, Leigh 147
Scanlon, Peter 195
Schultz, Konrad 171, 176–7
secretagogues, investigation into 21
Sedrak, Maged 175
Selective Androgen Receptor Modulators (SARMs) 72, 260
  see also peptides
Sheedy, Kevin 50, 82
Simonsson, Paul
  at ASADA meeting 29–30
  calls McDevitt 251–2
  Essendon players addressed by 153–4
  Evans' relations with 101, 156
  raises possibility of no-fault defence 32–3, 35–6
  starts work at ASADA 248
Skinovate clinic 99–100, 192
Smallwood, John 116–17
Smith, Dave
  AFL unimpressed with 180
  concern over apparent deal 34
  contacts Gillard over alleged deal 36

contacts with Andruska 179
notified of ACC investigation 167
Smith, Karen 178
Smith, Patrick 148
snake oil salesmen 57
Spano, Paul 99–100
St George Rugby League Club, Dank associated with 55–6
Stanton, Brent 86
'Statement of Grounds' against Essendon 198–9
steroids, Charter imports 113–15
'Substance X' 98–9 see also peptides
Sullivan, Alan 36
supplements 63–4, 77–81 see also peptides
Switkowski, Ziggy 83, 154, 156–9

TB500 127, 171 see also Thymosin
Temazepan, as sleeping aid 67
testosterone, Charter uses 113–14
The Age, Hird story in 142, 145–6, 162–3
Therapeutic Goods Administration, writes letter to Van Spanje 135–6
Thompson, Mark
   accepts AFL terms 212–14
   approached for head coach 242–3
   charges laid against 47–8
   Dank interviewed for job by 59–60
   Dank ordered to stop injecting players by 69
   disciplinary action against 188–90, 198, 205
   Essendon coached by 215
   leaves Essendon 50
   on Dank 9, 104
   on effect of scandal 266
   on Essendon team 51–2, 269

on Evans 16, 156
on Hird 266
on Robinson and Hamilton 82–3
playing career of 81
Reid consults with 77
Robinson and Dank meet with 101–2
sceptical of hyperbaric treatments 97–8
supports recruitment of Robinson 53
Switkowski on 158
Thymomodulin 101, 129, 269–70
Thymosin see also peptides; Thymosin Alpha; Thymosin Beta 4
   administered to players 88, 129
   Alavi supplies 229–30
   conflicting evidence regarding 249–50, 258–9
   difficulty tracing source of 258, 260
   failure to test imports of 128–9
   hard to tell from Thymosin Beta 4 122–4, 127
   Hird aware Dank was planning to use 148
   synthesised by Gl Biochem 256
   varieties of 95–6
Thymosin Alpha 127
Thymosin Beta 4 see also TB500
   alleged second batch of 256–7
   ASADA investigation focuses on 193–4
   Dank may have possessed 230
   hard to tell from Thymosin 122–4, 127
   players suspected of taking 95–6, 101
Trengove, Jack 270
Tribulus Forte 64–5, 88, 270
Turk, Paul 55, 64, 71–2

ultrasound machine purchased 107
United Arab Emirates, obesity in 131–2

VacuMed treatments 97
Van Spanje, Edward 125–6, 128, 131, 135–6
Veniamin, Benji 114
Victorian Police 114, 137–8
vitamin injections 99–100
Vogue Shopping Plaza 109–10

Wade, Jarrod 55, 63
Walker, Aaron
  Alavi interviewed by 256–7
  ASADA recruits 229–31
  believes ASADA case established 260
  Hird interviewed by 267
  Reid and 104
Wallace, Gy 169
Wallis, Dean 105
Warner, Dave 76
Warner, Michael 161–2
Watson, Jobe
  admits to peptide injection 153–4, 199–200
  cleared of doping allegations 265
  concerned over peptide administration 86
  heads player protest over rule change 95–6
  on Dank 106–7
  reaction to admission of peptide use 262–3
Wellman, Sean 142

Whateley, Gerard 223
Willcourt, Robin
  ACC examines 134
  Alavi works with 117–20
  anti-ageing practice 109–11
  Croad works for 133–4
  Dank prescribes for 68
  suspects forgery of signature 137
Williams, Carl 121
Williams, George 121
Williams, Kim 162
Williams, Laurie 126
Wilson, Caroline 145–6, 163, 165
Winderlich, Jason 106
Windy Hill *see* Essendon Football Club
Wittert, Gary 90
Woewodin, Shane 113
World Anti-Doping Agency (WADA)
  Australia signs up to Code 30
  bans use of un-approved substances 92
  comes into force in Australia 75
  Dank in breach of Code 264
  on AOD-9604: 3, 10, 91–4, 199
  seeks rehearing of case 265–6
Wylie, John 201–4, 209–10
Wylie, TS 117

Xu, Vincent 122–3, 254–6

Young, Neil 238–9, 241
Young, Richard 153–4, 231

Zaharakis, David 86–7, 207